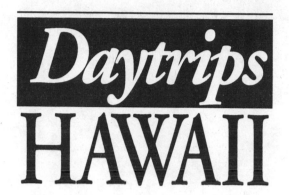

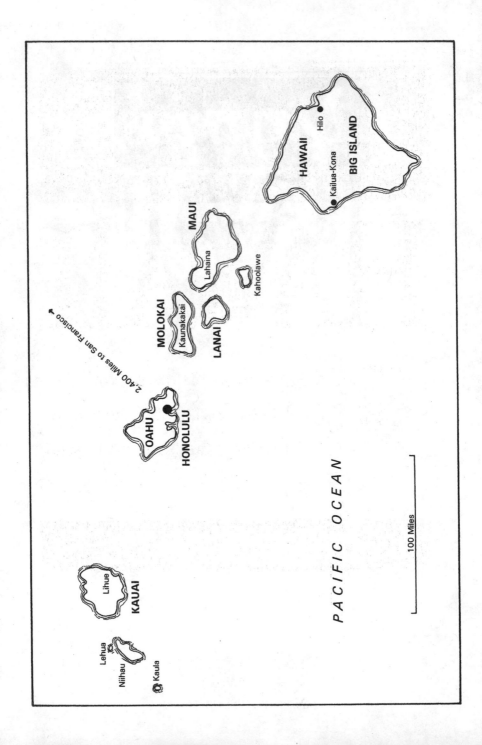

PACIFIC OCEAN

KAUAI
Lihue
Niihau
Lehua
Kaula

OAHU
HONOLULU

2,400 Miles to San Francisco

MOLOKAI
Kaunakakai

LANAI

MAUI
Lahaina

Kahoolawe

HAWAII
BIG ISLAND
Hilo
Kailua-Kona

100 Miles

Daytrips

HAWAII

50

one day adventures on six
islands by car, bus, bicycle or
walking, including 55 maps

DAVID CHEEVER

HASTINGS HOUSE
Book Publishers
Norwalk, Connecticut

Edited by Earl Steinbicker, creator of the DAYTRIPS series.

ISBN: 0-8038-9401-5

Printed in the United States

10 9 8 7 6 5 4 3 2 1

Contents

ACKNOWLEDGEMENTS

During this entire project, I can report that the Aloha Spirit is alive and well in the Aloha state. Everywhere I turned, help was proffered without boundaries. Gail Chew, George Applegate, Sue Kanoho and Charlene Kauhane of the Hawaii Visitor and Convention Bureau were champs.

Les Enderton of the Oahu Visitors Bureau is an old pal who steered me right on many occasions when it came to people, places and things on Oahu.

Darryl Kloninger of the ADWorks and Vicky Byrum of the PRWorks helped me immeasurably with accommodations and ground transportation on my many trips to the neighbor islands; it was Milton Goto of Aloha Airlines who got me to all those islands as well. Ron Wright of Continental Airlines made invaluable contributions.

Sonja Swenson of Styker Weiner Public Relations was a savior when it came to dozens of needed photos as was Linn Nishikawa at Kapalua.

I was able to lay the foundation for this book and build the structure. But the finish carpentry was done by my wife Cindy. It would not be what it is without her immense assistance.

There were indeed many more people who helped. Mahalo to you all.

Introduction

Hawaii is made for daytrips. That's because each of these wondrous islands can be either circled or taken in big chunks in a single day. That gives visitors a quick look at things. But by using the hub-and-spoke idea whereby you focus on a pieces of the pie from a central point, you can go deeper into what has often been described as "islands of breathtaking diversity."

The geography, cultural habits, foods, entertainment, and especially the people, are as diverse as anywhere on the planet.

As you make your way around the islands on various daytrips, consider that one in ten people you meet will be of Hawaiian ancestry and the same amount for Chinese/Americans; about 15 percent will be Filipino/Americans; more than a quarter will be Americans of Japanese Ancestry; and the largest minority of Hawaii's population are the Caucasians at around 30 percent.

Those numbers don't add up to 100 percent because adding to the rich mix of residents who live, work and play in Hawaii are Vietnamese, Thais, African-Americans, Samoans, Koreans, Portuguese and dozens of others.

Getting a precise handle on Hawaii's ethnic population is difficult at best because we all get along so well that there's considerable inter-marriage among the races. But that simply adds to the breathtaking diversity by producing what islanders call "cosmopolitan" children and adults of rare beauty and handsomeness.

It is understandable then, how all these ethnic groups contribute to the diversity of culture in Hawaii. As an example, you might be in a resort hotel anywhere in the islands and from one ballroom you might hear and see the incredible softness and beauty of a hula troupe performing to the gentle strumming of a ukulele while in the next ballroom you might experience a terribly exciting, noisy and scary Samoan fire dance.

Nowadays, there is a great push in Hawaii to recapture many of the authentic customs of the early Polynesians who settled Hawaii. This movement includes the Hawaiian language, but also spills over into arts, crafts, dance and even medicine. Where possible, we will try to lead you to examples of this renaissance.

Food in Hawaii is probably of greater variety than most other travel destinations. All those ethnic groups mentioned earlier have given the islands a mixture of foods that range from the relatively bland poi favored by Hawaiians to the tongue-curling spice of Kim Chee brought here by Koreans. Thai food is very popular in Hawaii, and smartly, most Thai restaurateurs offer all their menu selections prepared either mild, medium or hot.

Even snacks in Hawaii cut across ethnic lines and offer many taste treats. For instance, the Japanese brought such delicacies as dried cuttlefish, which is very chewy and salty, and the Chinese gave us Li Hing Mui, which can be a lip-puckering spicy seed. The latter is very popular with island kids.

Don't worry, however, if food adventures aren't for you. The majority of the restaurants in Hawaii serve plenty of familiar, wholesome American dishes. Among the choices of places to eat and drink, we'll sometimes offer you the unusual, but for the most part we'll lead you to restaurants that serve foods you are familiar with.

Hawaii is best known for it's incredible geography. Included in these tiny dots in the middle of the Pacific Ocean are tropical rain forests, nearly barren deserts, spewing volcanoes, white sand beaches and white snow, precipitous mountains and quiet valleys—and more. It's all here.

When it was said earlier that Hawaii is made for daytrips, that applies best to discovering and enjoying the various beauty spots throughout the islands. One day you may find yourself wandering along Honolulu's lovely shoreline enjoying sunshine, beaches and bays and the next you can choose to hike into a tropical rain forest where ginger and haleconias may be blooming in perfusion.

To top it all off, the islands offer plenty to do. There are the usual sports like golf and tennis. Water sports are, as expected, extensive. It is estimated that only 10 percent of Hawaii's visitors go in the water, primarily because most people are unfamiliar with the ocean. Here it is warm and comforting. Swimming, snorkeling, boogie boarding, sailing, surfing, kayaking and even submarine adventures are available.

Walking and hiking are very popular activities in Hawaii. Wherever appropriate, you will be offered walking tours and even hikes.

One last thought: It isn't really necessary to see everything at any given destination. Be selective. Your one-day adventures in Hawaii should be fun, not an endurance test. If they start becoming that, just find your way to the nearest beach or palm tree, stretch out and relax. There will always be another day.

Happy Daytripping!

COMMENTS? IDEAS?

We'd love to hear from you. Ideas from our readers have resulted in many improvements in the past, and will continue to do so. And, if your suggestions are used, we'll gladly send you a complimentary copy of any book in the series. Please send your thoughts to Hastings House, Book Publishers, 9 Mott Ave., Norwalk CT 06850, or fax us at (203) 838-4084, or e-mail to info@upub.com.

Section I

DAYTRIP STRATEGIES

The word "Daytrip" may not have made it into dictionaries yet, but for experienced travelers it represents the easiest, most natural and often least expensive approach to exploring many of the world's most interesting areas. This strategy, in which you base yourself in a central place (city or its suburbs or a resort) and probe the surrounding region on a series of one-day excursions, is especially effective in the case of the Hawaiian Islands.

A tactic to keep in mind is that some people come to Hawaii from a frenetic place where they live and work and aren't able to come down off that pace. They miss a large part of what Hawaii is all about—relaxation. That's why these Daytrips are of mixed length: some only take the morning, which leaves the afternoon for beaching or just plain "hanging out." Your personal mantra while in the islands should be—RELAX—RELAX—RELAX.

ADVANTAGES:

1. Freedom from a fixed itinerary. You can go wherever you feel like going whenever the mood strikes you.
2. Freedom from the burden of luggage. Your bags remain in your hotel while you run around with this guidebook and a camera.
3. Freedom from the worry of reservation foul-ups. You don't have the anxiety each day about whether that night's lodging is okay.
4. The flexibility of making last-minute changes to allow for unexpected weather, serendipitous discoveries, changing interests, newfound passions, and so on.
5. The flexibility to take breaks from sightseeing and doing things whenever you feel tired or bored, without upsetting a planned itinerary. Why not sleep late in your base resort for a change?
6. The opportunity to sample different travel experiences without committing more than a day to them.

7. The opportunity to become a "temporary resident" of your base resort. By staying there for a while you can get to know it in depth, becoming familiar with the local restaurants, shops, theaters, night life and other attractions—enjoying them as a resident would.

8. The convenience of not having to pack and unpack your bags each day. Your clothes can hang in a closet where they belong, or even be sent out for cleaning.

9. The convenience (and security) of having a fixed address in your resort base city or town where friends, relatives and business associates can reach you for fun or in an emergency.

10. The economy of staying at one hotel, perhaps on a discounted longer-term basis as a result of some kind of package plan. You can make advance reservations for your base resort without sacrificing any flexibility at all.

And, of course, for those who actually live in Hawaii, Daytrips can be the key to discovering some of the islands' fascinating places that they either didn't know about or passed over before—one day at a time.

CHOOSING A BASE RESORT

OAHU:

There are just three hotels outside of the beachside resort of Waikiki on the island of Oahu. Besides 30,000 hotel rooms within Waikiki's one square mile, there are also condominiums and apartments. Oahu only sports one motel—out in Laie on the north shore. B&B's are spotted here and there around the island, but are minuscule compared to Waikiki's many hotel rooms.

Packed into Waikiki's relatively small space is something for everyone to do. If you like shopping, this is like the Chicago's Miracle Mile and 5th Avenue in New York combined. There's food of every description—surfing lessons—portrait artists—your photo with a talking parrot—fire dances—hula performances and instruction—morning aerobics on the beach—a great white sand beach—people watching. It's all here.

NEIGHBOR ISLANDS:

On Maui there are three distinct base resorts: Kapalua and Kaanapali in the west and Wailea in the south. These three were all carefully masterplanned, generally with a few upscale hotels and a smattering of condos. Kihei in the south and the Napili/Kahana area of west Maui are for everyman with more reasonably-priced condos. All have great beaches and tons of activities to keep visitors busy.

Lanai and Molokai are separate islands unto themselves. Lanai has two upscale hotels at either end of the island and one modest hotel in the middle. Molokai has one hotel and a unique tent-a-lo experience.

Kauai has hotels and condos more spread out than other neighbor islands, with concentrations on the east side along the Coconut Coast and south in Poipu. There is a single hotel in the central town of Lihue, one on the north shore at Princeville and one in the westside town of Waimea.

On the Big Island, the eastside city of Hilo—with several good hotels—offers excellent Daytrip possibilities. It is not a resort per se. On the west side, Kailua-Kona has several hotels and condos, and then along the Kohala Coast are a string of very interesting, upscale resorts.

GETTING TO OAHU:

Honolulu is probably the only major American destination city that can only be reached by **air.** Thus it's easy to see how important the airlines are to Hawaii. People all come by air, but a majority of the cargo comes by ship.

Continental Airlines has taken an aggressive stance in travel to Hawaii, offering daily service from about 40 mainland cities with non-stops from the West Coast as well as Houston and Dallas. Continental also offers non-stop service to Tokyo and Guam from Hawaii. Within Micronesia, Continental has "Islander Hopper" service among many Pacific islands. **United** has more than a third of the Hawaii market. This airline has a dozen flights a day to Honolulu from mainland U.S. cities, many more than the other airlines. By contrast, **American** has half United's daily flights to Honolulu. Among the other majors that fly to the islands are **Delta** and **Northwest.** Quite a few foreign carriers stop in Honolulu, but usually only to refuel. Japan Airlines, on the other hand, brings millions of Japanese to the islands annually.

GETTING TO THE NEIGHBOR ISLANDS:

It is possible to fly non-stop from the U.S. mainland directly to two of the neighbor islands. United has several daily flights into Maui and a couple into Kona on the Big Island. American has one daily flight to Maui.

The largest and most reliable inter-island carrier is **Aloha Airlines.** It is the choice of residents, which tells you a lot about the airline. Call any travel agent for information and/or reservations on **Aloha's** inter-island flights or their toll-free number (800) 367-5250.

The majority of Hawaii's visitors come to Honolulu first to spend several days and then catch an **Aloha Airlines** flight to any of these neighbor island destinations: Kahului or West Maui Airport on Maui, Hilo or Kona on the Big Island, Lihue on Kauai, Lanai City on Lanai and Molokai. **Hawaiian Air** also flies inter-island, but not to as many airports as Aloha Airlines and its sister airline **Island Air.**

ACCOMMODATIONS ON OAHU:

Just about any type and price of accommodation is available in Waikiki. Variations in room rates usually go according to whether the hotel is on the beach or not. Beyond that, rates are adjusted as to whether the room is high, medium or low in the building. Such venerable hotels as the **Royal Hawaiian,** built 60 years ago originally to accommodate Matson Steamship's passengers, can be pretty steep.

Aston Hotels & Resorts is an excellent group of hotels serving all the islands. This Hawaii-based and managed company has 13 properties in Waikiki that can offer you accommodations from economy rooms off the beach to luxury condos on the beach. What makes Aston special in the whole spectrum of Hawaii hotels is that management truly has the pulse of Hawaii visitors. They know how to take care of all who come—from couples to families to business people. Call any tour operator or travel agent for reservations or call toll-free to Aston at (800) 321-2558.

Hilton, Sheraton and **Hyatt** all have behemoth hotels in Waikiki, which are fun to visit for their sheer size. Hilton has gorgeous grounds and Sheraton is a major player with four properties on Oahu and one on Maui. **Outrigger** is the largest hotelier in the Islands with over 20,000 rooms. Beyond these well-known names are endless variations on accommodations. Luxury rooms are nice, but ask yourself, "how long will I be in my room each day if I'm out daytripping?" Choose your accommodations accordingly.

ACCOMMODATIONS ON THE NEIGHBOR ISLANDS:

Aston, and others, offer a wide range of accommodations for each island, which will be covered in that island's section.

CHOOSING DESTINATIONS

With fifty trips to choose from, and several attractions for each trip, deciding which are the most enjoyable for you and yours might be problematic. You could, of course, read through the whole book and mark the most appealing spots, but there's an easier way to at least start. Just turn to the Index and scan it, looking out for the special interest categories set in **BOLD FACE** type. These will immediately lead you to choices under such heading as Museums, Historic Sites, Adventure Tours, Water Sports, Beaches and the like. The elements of one trip can often be combined with another to create a custom itinerary, using the book maps as a rough guide and a good road map for the final routing. Some of the trips, listed in the Index as **SCENIC DRIVES** are just that. They are primarily designed to observe the stunning beauty of the islands as you drive along.

GETTING AROUND

The driving directions for each trip assume that on Oahu you're leaving from Waikiki. On the neighbor islands, we will discuss the base resort for each island in its own section.

The route **maps** scattered throughout the book show you approximately where the sites are, and which main roads lead to them. In many cases, however, you'll still need a good up-to-date road map. An excellent choice for all islands are the *Drive Guides* free from all **Budget** rental car agencies. Be sure when you're at the Budget office or desk to pick up a Budget Coupon Book chock-a-block with values for food, admissions, gifts and all sorts of Hawaii stuff.

The majority of Daytrips in this book are designed to be made by **car,** which provides freedom and flexibility. Public transportation on Oahu is very good. The city **buses,** called TheBus, are usually given as an alternative to driving on several Daytrips.

There is also a private jitney service available in central Oahu called **Waikiki Trolley.** The cars are open-air and fun, almost like a San Francisco cable car. Its primary route is for shopping, however, it will take you to many well-known attractions as well.

Tour companies abound with vans and buses of varying sizes. They offer structured tours so you can spend more time looking. **Polynesian Adventure Tours** offers tours of highlights on all islands.

FOOD AND DRINK

Several choice restaurants that make sense for daytrippers are listed for each destination in this book. Most of these are long-time favorites of experienced travelers, are open for lunch, are on or near the suggested tour route, and provide some atmosphere. Many feature ethnic foods of the islands, but generally they offer standard fare too. Their approximate price range is shown as:

$ — Inexpensive.
$$ — Reasonable.
$$$ — Luxurious and expensive.
X: — Days closed.

Hawaii offers a cornucopia of foods. For example, if you like Chinese, there are about 75 establishments on Oahu alone. There are several excellent choices for Hawaiian food. There's even a soul-food restaurant on Oahu.

Most resort hotels have signature restaurants that are frequently written up in travel guides and magazines. Their prices reflect this fame, however, and you may want to only treat yourself to one of these world-class establishments.

Honolulu's restaurants have been scanned by the *Zagat Survey*, which you may want to consult if you're especially serious about food.

Just about all the fast-food restaurants have made their way to the islands. How about a picnic in Paradise at one of the island's beaches? Residents are heavy-duty picnickers, so facilities are pretty good at most of the beach parks. Picnic facilities are indicated in the practical information for those sites.

PRACTICALITIES

WEATHER:

Hawaii is all about weather—warm, sunny days and soft warm nights 12 months of the year. There are spots where it rains fairly regularly, like Manoa on Oahu and Hilo on the Big Island. But Paradise wouldn't be Paradise if it wasn't green and lush—in most places—from that rain. Rain rarely persists anywhere in the islands. You may experience a quick shower that actually feels good and dries quickly.

OPENING TIMES, FEES, AND FACILITIES:

When planning a Daytrip, be sure to note carefully the **opening times** of the various sites—these can sometimes be rather quirky. Anything unusual that you should know before starting is summarized in the "Practicalities" section of each trip.

Entrance fees listed in the text are, naturally, subject to change—and they rarely go down. For the most part, admissions are quite reasonable considering the cost of maintaining the sites. Places with free entry, especially those not maintained by governments, are usually staffed with unpaid volunteers and have a donation box to help keep the wolves from the door. Please put something in it.

Special **facilities** that a site might offer are listed in the *italicized* information for that site, along with the address and phone number. These often include restaurants or cafeterias, cafés, information counters, gift shops, tours, shows, picnic facilities, and so on. **Telephone numbers** are indicated with a ☎. The **Area code** for the entire state of Hawaii is 808.

SAFETY:

WATER. Have fun and enjoy the ocean that surrounds these islands, but follow some sensible rules: (1) don't swim alone; (2) pay attention to signs posted at most beaches telling you of water and surf conditions; (3) avoid standing, swimming or playing in the shore break; and (4) don't turn your back on the ocean when you're in it.

AUTOMOBILES. Hawaii is a safe place, but we will continually advise you during these Daytrips not to leave anything in your car. Don't make it a tempting target. State law requires seat belt usage.

SUNTANS. Everyone who comes to Hawaii wants one. Prevent burns that are detrimental to your health by always wearing strong sunscreen. Truthfully, sunscreen prevents burns, not suntans.

CONSERVATION:

MARINE LIFE CONSERVATION DISTRICTS: Frequently you will see these government protected areas. Do not disturb sea animals or coral or other protected objects.

ARCHAEOLOGICAL SITES. Hawaii's rich history and natural resources are preserved in many areas and in many ways. Always respect these areas by: (1) not climbing on or around sites so marked; (2) not removing or moving stones, foliage or any other natural element you may find; and (3) removing all refuse you brought.

HANDICAPPED TRAVELERS:

Access varies with each individual's needs and abilities, so no firm statement can be made about any site. Those that are generally accessible without much difficult are indicated with the symbol &, but when in doubt it is always best to phone ahead.

GROUP TRAVEL:

If you're planning a group outing, *always* call ahead. Most sites require advance reservations and offer special discounts for groups, often at a substantial savings over the regular admission fee. Some sites will open specially or remain open beyond their scheduled hours to accommodate groups; some have tours, demonstrations, lectures, and so on available only to groups; and some have facilities for rental to groups.

TAXES:

All prices quoted are subject to change and without tax. There is a 4 percent excise tax charged on all transactions. In addition, there is a hotel room tax of 6 percent. On rental cars, the excise tax is charged plus a $2 a day road tax and a vehicle licensing fee that can be up to 40¢ per day depending on what you rent.

SUGGESTED TOURS

Two different methods of organizing Daytrips are used in this book, depending on local circumstances. Some are based on **structured itineraries** such as walking tours and scenic drives that follow a suggested route, while others just describe the **local attractions** that you can choose from. In either case, an **area map** always shows where things are, so you're not likely to get lost. Numbers (in parentheses) in the text refer to the circled numbers on the appropriate map.

Major attractions are described in one or more paragraphs each, beginning with practical information for a visit. **Additional sites** are worked into the text, along with some practical information in italics. All are arranged in a logical geographic sequence, although you may want to make changes to suit your preferences.

Walking tours, where used, follow routes shown by heavy broken lines on the accompanying map. You can estimate the amount of time that any segment of a walking tour will take by looking at the scaled map and figuring that the average person covers about 100 yards per minute or three miles per hour.

Trying to see everything at any given destination could easily lead to an exhausting marathon. You will certainly enjoy yourself more by being selective and passing up anything that doesn't catch your fancy, and perhaps planning a repeat visit at some other time.

Practical information, such as opening times and admission fees is as accurate as was possible at the time of writing, but will certainly change. You should always check with the sites themselves if seeing a particular one is crucially important to you.

*OUTSTANDING ATTRACTIONS:

An *asterisk before any attraction, be it an entire Daytrip or just one exhibit in a museum, denotes a special treat that in the author's view should not be missed.

VISITOR INFORMATION

The addresses and phone numbers of major sights are given in the text wherever appropriate. These are usually your best source for specific information and current brochures. On a wider scale, valuable information can be supplied by each island chapter of the **Hawaii Visitor & Convention Bureau** as follows:

Oahu:
  Waikiki:
  Oahu Visitors Bureau, 1001 Bishop Street, 880 Pauahi Tower, Honolulu,
    HI 96813, ☎ (800) 624-8678.
Big Island of Hawaii:
  Hilo:
  Hawaii Visitors Bureau, 250 Keawe Street, Hilo, Hawaii 96720, ☎ (800)
    648-2441.
  Kona:
  Hawaii Visitors Bureau, 75-5719 West Alii Drive, Kona, HI 96740, ☎
    (800) 648-2441.
Kauai:
  Kauai Visitors Bureau, Lihue Plaza Building, 3016 Umi Street, Suite 207,
    Lihue, HI 96766, ☎ (800) 262-1400.
Maui:
  Maui Visitors Bureau, 1727 Wili Pa Loop, P.O. Box 580, Wailuku, HI
    96793, ☎ (800) 525-6284.
  Molokai: ☎ (800) 800-6367.
  Lanai: ☎ (800) 947-4774.

Section II

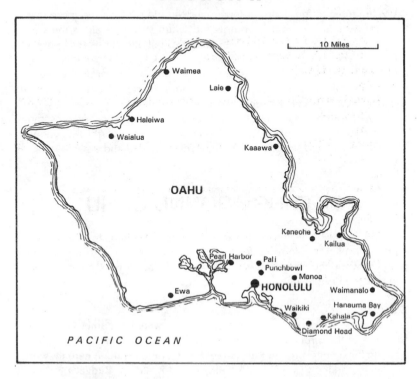

DAYTRIPS IN
WAIKIKI AND OAHU

Waikiki is the starting point for all Daytrips on Oahu. There are four sub-sections where tours are divided into "In and near Waikiki," "East from Waikiki," "Waikiki to the Middle," and "West from Waikiki." A fifth sub-section is "Circle Island."

Waikiki's fame is widespread, yet many visitors to Hawaii who stay there don't take the time to really get to know this compact area and all it has to offer. We would like to introduce you—or re-introduce you if you've been here before—to the wonders of Waikiki and Oahu. The routes have been chosen for their pure enjoyment and, of course, the scenery.

In some cases, we recommend taking a bus or other means of transportation to a site slightly outside of Waikiki, and either discovering that site and taking public transit back, or walking back to your base in Waikiki. Most walks are three to four miles in length and should take you no more than four or five hours depending on how much fun you have along the way.

Close by in downtown Honolulu are plenty of attractions to keep you busy for several trips. The distance between Waikiki and Downtown Honolulu is approximately 3.5 miles, so you can take a car or ride the bus or trolley to get there. Once you are situated in the history-laden downtown sections of Oahu, there are suggested walking routes.

And, of course, the whole island of Oahu is filled with historic sites, museums, hiking trails, beaches and shoreline spots well worth discovering. You will find a good selection of these beyond Waikiki and downtown.

GETTING AROUND OAHU

Although some of the initial tours are designed for walking, in several cases you'll still need to use some form of transportation to get to the starting points. Beyond these first few, you will almost certainly need a car. Or, you can take the bus or trolley.

BY CAR:

Budget rental cars are available by the day, week or month. They have locations at the airport and two in Waikiki: on Ala Moana Boulevard just past the Ilikai Hotel and on Kalakaua Avenue at the Hyatt. Where they are available, parking lots will be described for downtown. **Budget's** toll-free reservation number is (800) 527-0700.

BUSES:

Honolulu and the entire island of Oahu has an excellent bus system called **TheBus.** In fact, it was given a prestigious, national award for Best Bus Company in America. Adult fares are $1 and children are 50¢. It is advisable to have correct change or a dollar bill handy—or two, for the return—since drivers do not make change.

Transfers don't cost anything, but have a time limit. If you leave the bus at some destination, re-board later on, and perhaps get off again, each of those trips will cost $1. Amazingly, you can circle the entire island of Oahu for $1. If you were to stop for lunch and re-board, that would probably cost another dollar. TheBus deal for visitors is pretty good: you may purchase a four-day pass for $10 at any ABC store in Waikiki.

Disabled and senior citizens have a real deal too. If you are 65 and are willing to go to the bus office at 811 Middle Street in Kalihi, Monday through Friday from 7:30 a.m. to 3:30 p.m., you can buy a two-year bus pass for $20 or a four-year half fare discount pass for $6.

There are rules that apply to luggage and large objects like surfboards. If whatever you are carrying will fit under the seat or on your lap, it is usually okay. The driver has discretion. Moms with baby strollers are okay.

The bus fleet is 525 vehicles, almost half of which have a wheelchair lift. About one third of the fleet have bike racks. For better seating, plan to use TheBus, if possible, during non-rush hours between 9-3 and after 6 p.m.

To learn bus routes and times, call (808) 296-1818, a 24-hour attraction and general information line. Two more steps are required: enter TheBus 4-digit number which is 8287; you will be given further number options for various attractions, beaches, museums and the like. It has the daily weather too. Kinda fun.

TAXIS:

These vehicles can be used in two ways: to take you to your destination and back if you choose; or for a tour itself. If you simply want to get somewhere, Charley's is the biggest. Call (808) 955-2211. There are others in the phone book that will customize a tour for you if you like.

TROLLEY:

The Waikiki Trolley is a private jitney service that uses cars that look like San Francisco cable cars. There are plenty of them, so they offer frequent service. It is designed for an inclusive daily fee of $18 for adults and $8 for children under 11 that allows—indeed, encourages—on and off as many times as you want during a 24-hour period. It operates from 8:30 in the morning until 10:45 at night. While designed primarily for shopping, it will take you to many well-known attractions as well. Call (808) 596-2199 for more information.

SHOPPING

In truth, the number-one activity for visitors who come to Hawaii is shopping. There is every conceivable type of retailer on the island concentrated in Waikiki and **Ala Moana Shopping Center.** But it doesn't end there by any means.

Other shopping malls, visitor-attraction shopping centers and outlet malls are spread out over a 15-mile strip from Waikiki to Waikele. For details of these shopping opportunities, see Daytrip 19.

ACCOMMODATIONS

Aston Hotels and Resorts has 13 properties in Waikiki to suit every taste and purse. Eight are hotels, with the Aston Waikiki Beachside Hotel being the chain's premier property. Five are condominiums, and each of those has a fully-equipped kitchen. A special bonus (except at the Beachside Hotel) is free accommodations for kids. Aston also has properties on Maui, Kauai and the Big Island, with special rates when visitors split their seven-day (or more) stay between Aston Properties in Hawaii. For shopping, meals, rental cars and golf, this chain has worked out discounts called "Astonishing Deals." Aston's 24-hour toll-free number is (800) 922-7866.

Honolulu Shoreline Stroll

Only in the past few years has Honolulu started to pay the proper attention to its storied shoreline beyond Waikiki. Just about everyone knows about Hawaii's beaches, but the shoreline itself is made up of beaches, bays, inlets, boat harbors and breakwaters. These interesting things are what we want to discover in a stroll along the shoreline about four miles out of Waikiki.

The major changes to the waterfront—starting about 10 years ago—include turning some pretty junky areas into wonderful shoreline parks and attractions. They are there for visitors to discover. One of the major parks at the water's edge was once a total wasteland, if you can imagine that. Now it is green and beautiful.

Along the way you'll find some great shopping and a wide variety of food. One of the best urban beaches—anywhere is on the route; you can take a quick dip if you're so inclined.

GETTING THERE:

By bus: On Kuhio Avenue in Waikiki, take city bus #19 marked Airport or Airport/Hickham, or the #20 Airport.

PRACTICALITIES:

You will hear this over and over, but it needs to be repeated: before leaving your hotel, put on sunscreen. Some people have the mistaken notion that sunscreen is to be used only if you're planning to bake in the sun. Wrong. Just walking around in Hawaii's wondrous sunlight requires protection.

You will also hear conflicting advice about what level of sunscreen to apply. The consistently recommended level seems to be 35. There's only good news in using sunscreen: be assured also that you will pick up some good color using this level of sunscreen; be assured if you don't use it and get burned, it will ruin your Hawaii stay.

It goes without saying that comfortable walking shoes will enhance this shoreline stroll for you. The walk is mostly concrete which will be warm to hot, so the more cushioning the better.

Protective eye wear is also recommended since the glare off the ocean can caused tiredness in your eyes. Drink plenty of water along the way.

FOOD AND DRINK:

The Old Spaghetti Factory (1050 Ala Moana Blvd. in Ward Warehouse) This is for families. Not a huge menu selection, but tasty food at reasonable prices in an old-fashioned setting. Open for lunch and dinner Mon.–Sat., dinner on Sun. ☎ 591-2513. $

Kincaids Fish, Chop and Steak House (Ward Warehouse) Great view of the fishing and tour-boat harbor. This is called a "Celebration" restaurant. Lunch and dinner daily. Reservations, ☎ 591-2005. $$

Mocha Java (1200 Ala Moana Blvd. in Ward Centre) Try the crepes, especially for desert. Coffee drinks are tops. Open Mon.–Sat. for breakfast, lunch and dinner. Sun. lunch and dinner. ☎ 591-9023. $

Compadres Bar & Grill (Ward Centre) The best Mexican food in Hawaii served by a fun staff. Window tables overlook Ala Moana Park and Beach. Lunch and dinner daily. ☎ 591-8307. $$

Scoozee's (Ward Centre) It's hard to pigeon-hole this restaurant which serves an eclectic selection of pastas, fish and other goodies. Lunch and dinner daily. Reservations, ☎ 597-1777. $$

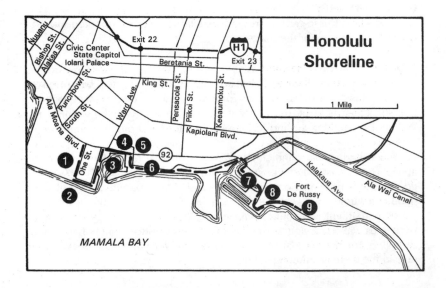

SUGGESTED TOUR:

Numbers in parentheses correspond to numbers on the map.
About 4 miles from Waikiki, get off the bus at Ohe Street just on the other side of Office Max. Tell the bus driver where you want to get off. Walk down Ohe Street toward the ocean and the:

*HAWAII CHILDREN'S DISCOVERY CENTER (1), 111 Ohe St. at the corner of Ohe and Olomehani. Honolulu, HI 96814, ☎ 592-5437. *Open all year. Closed on four major holidays. Admission starts at about $5. (Opening Fall 1998) Call for details.*
The transformation of the old Kewalo Incinerator into this stunning museum is truly amazing. If only you could have seen it before! A part of the old smokestack and shell of the building remain of the original, while an addition of 20,000 square feet of exhibit space and a theater bring the total to 37,000 square feet of fun discovery.

The Center likes to say it is for the young and young-at-heart, who can experience, explore, investigate and discover things about the world that were never before imaginable. Using the latest computer technology, children and adults are able to actively participate in discovery experiences through hands-on, interactive exhibits.

There are five galleries: **The Gathering Place,** which introduces visitors to the Center; **Fantastic You,** which is an inside look at the human body; **Your Town,** where kids can be a grown-up for a day; **Hawaiian Rainbows,** where visitors learn what makes living in Hawaii so special; and finally **Your Rainbow World,** which is an exploration of cultures, countries and celebrations from around the world.

It is the latter two galleries that make the Center very special because they are Hawaii-oriented, offering exhibits and discoveries found in no other museum of this type.

After visiting the Hawaii Children's Discovery Center, walk toward the water where you will enter **Kakaako Waterfront Park** (2). The amazing fact about this park is that not too many years ago it was a state dump. The hilliness of the park is due to the fact that the environmental engineers and planners felt it would be too difficult to remove all the waste, so instead they devised a plan to cover the years of accumulated junk with a special sealant and then topsoil, making it safe to use.

Besides the beauty of the ocean along this entire park, the hills are used by local kids for sliding on cardboard sheets. That's the closest Hawaii kids get to sledding.

After climbing the winding path to the highest point in the park, you may want to start as far to the right of the waterfront walkway as you can go. The waves sometimes crash against the breakwater here because there is no reef along this stretch of shoreline.

Five light poles from the end, there is a little path that will take you out onto Ahui Street. Here you will pass several fish processing plants, so be prepared to hold you nose. The buildings and infrastructure along this street are what the whole neighborhood looked like before the rehab started. All through this area, dramatic changes are planned to take advantage of Honolulu's wonderful shoreline.

Once on Ala Moana Boulevard again, turn right and walk toward **Kewalo Basin** (3), where many tour and fishing boats dock. Periodically you may see an Hawaii Sampan boat unloading a big tuna catch. You can board the 72-foot **Voyager Submarine** here that goes out eight times daily starting at 8 in the morning. A one-and-a-half-hour dive into Hawaii's underwater world of coral reefs with angel fish, morays and more costs under $90. *For information* ☎ *592-7850.* A three-hour daytime coastal cruise including the Arizona Memorial on the four-decker *Star of Honolulu* will cost about $25 for adults (with breakfast and lunch it's about $40). ☎ *983-7827.* If sportfishing is in your plans, try the *Maggie Joe.* This 53-foot boat has brought in the biggest fish ever caught out of Kewalo—a 1,277-pound blue marlin. A full day of fishing is just over $100. *Call* ☎ *591-8888.*

For shopping and many restaurants, you can cross Ala Moana Boulevard to **Ward Warehouse** (4). If shopping is your thing, you can keep going down Auahi Street to the next strip center, which is **Ward Centre** (5).

To continue with our shoreline stroll, re-cross Ala Moana Boulevard at Kamakee Street and enter **Ala Moana Beach Park** (6). This is largely the weekend playground for residents, but more and more visitors are discovering the beauty of this urban park. You have a choice of taking the walkway right along the seawall, or walking on the sand close to the water's edge. If you brought your swim suit, try the water. It's warm and soothing. As for a shower, these are located periodically along the beach. You can dry in the sun; no towel needed.

As Ala Moana Park Drive curves to the left, you will pass the Waikiki Yacht Club. Make your way to the right and back onto Ala Moana Boulevard. Cross the short bridge over the Ala Wai Canal and turn right on Holomoana. This curves around to the left where you will walk along the **Ala Wai Yacht Harbor** (7), where in odd-numbered years the harbor becomes a beehive of activity due to the Trans-Pacific Yacht Race from California.

As the road curves to the right, look over to the left and notice what is commonly called the **Hilton Lagoon** (8), a small body of water surrounded by sand. Make your way to the sand and circle the lagoon going counterclockwise. Once you have nearly reached the end, a concrete walkway will appear that fronts the Hilton Hawaiian Village. This is a continuation of the shoreline walkway that will take you past the recently refurbished **Fort DeRussy** (9). This whole area, which is an Army installation, was kind of scruffy before the military added to its hotel property and completely redid the landscaping.

Most of Fort DeRussy is open to the public with only a few areas restricted to the military and dependents. It is a wonderful gift from our federal government to Hawaii's residents and visitors alike.

This walk, from Kakaako Waterfront Park over the route described to the center of Waikiki is about four miles.

Trip 2

*Diamond Head from the Topside

This state monument is so well known that just about any grade-school kid can get at least one geography question right—which is to place Diamond Head in Hawaii.

In the native language Diamond Head translates into *Kaimana Hila* or Diamond Hill, which is the name given it by British sailors in the 1800s when they found calcite crystals and thought they were diamonds.

This state monument is also called Mount Leahi, meaning wreath of fire. That name comes from the ancient times when fires were kept burning around the crater rim as a guide for canoes.

According to a guidebook written by Steve Boyle, manager of the New Otani Kaimana Beach Hotel, "In ancient times five *heiau* (places of worship) were located on or around Diamond Head, but none are standing today. The heiau, *Pahu a Maui*, was located near the site of the present lighthouse and was used by fishermen."

He goes on to say, "On the peak of Diamond Head a heiau was built and dedicated to the god of the wind as protection against strong updrafts that could put out the navigational fires."

One of the better purchases made by our Federal Government was the $3,300 paid for the 729 acres that comprise Diamond Head. That was in 1904. Fortification of the landmark actually started in World War I with long-range gun emplacements. World War II saw further military use with the installation of communications rooms, barracks and mess halls.

The crater was turned over to the Territory of Hawaii in 1955 by President Eisenhower, and it was made a state monument in 1962. In 1968 it was designated as a National Natural Landmark and opened for hiking and festivals.

Thus in the 1970s, several rock concerts were promoted with upwards of 50,000 attendees streaming into the crater. These turned into huge pot-smoking, noisy orgies. What really upset the nearby residents were the thousands of cars strewn around the neighborhood. Finally the dedicated folks of the Outdoor Circle and the Save Diamond Head Association stepped forward so that today, all that nonsense has been stopped and you can thank them for being able to hike and enjoy the calm that reigns inside the crater.

GETTING THERE:

By car, take Kalakaua Avenue to the Zoo where Monsarrat Avenue bears to the left. Go up this road to the top. Part way down there is a yellow sign on the right saying "Diamond Head Crater." Turn right here and proceed up through the narrow tunnel and then onto the parking lot.

By city bus, take the # 58 or 22.

By taxi, ask to be taken inside the crater.

On foot, this is a 2.5-mile walk from the center of Waikiki. Follow the same directions as by car.

PRACTICALITIES:

The gate at the tunnel entrance is open from 6 to 6 every day of the year—otherwise you can't get inside the crater. By the same token, do not leave yourself inside the crater after it closes because you will be cited. It is recommended to get an early start if you plan to climb to the top because it can get pretty warm.

This tour follows much the same mantra: sunscreen, sunglasses, comfortable shoes and plenty of water. A fun hat is a nice addition. Some people will tell you that a flashlight is a good idea since you will go through several tunnels on your hike up to the top. If you drive, leave nothing in your car, locked or not.

FOOD AND DRINK:

There are some very interesting restaurants on the slopes of Diamond Head that not a lot of visitors know about. One includes the community college culinary dining room that serves superb food with a spectacular view.

A Cup of Joe (3116 Monsarrat Ave.) Tiny coffee spot with morning goodies and sandwiches. Features an artist of the month. Resident hangout. ☎ 737-7445. Open daily 6-10 $

Bueno Nalo and the **Juice Spot** (3045 Monsarrat Ave.) Both little spots are connected. Bueno serves terrific sizzling fajitas and fulsome chimichangas. The spot has an array of smoothies with a Hawaii flavor. Things like "Off the Lip," and "Hang Ten." Open daily for lunch & dinner. ☎ 735-8818 $

Tamarind Dining Room and **Kaikena Restaurant** (Kapiolani Community College, on the left at the top of the hill). The former serves dinner and the latter lunch when school is in session. The culinary students whip up some extravagant meals to show their stuff. The view toward Koko Crater is breathtaking. Reservations a must. ☎ 734-9488. $$

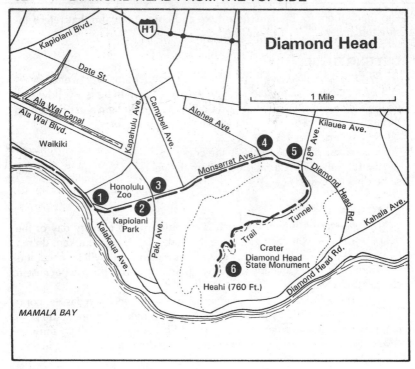

SUGGESTED TOUR:

Numbers in parentheses correspond to numbers on the map.

As you bear left on Monsarrat Avenue from Kalakaua Avenue, you will see the entrance to the **Honolulu Zoo** (1), described on Daytrip 6. On the right are two facilities in **Kapiolani Park** that offer a wide range of entertainment (check with your hotel Bell Desk for current activities): **The Band Stand** first and then **The Shell.** Also tucked back behind the Shell is the **Kodak Hula Show** (2) that has offered free shows for over 50 years. ☎ *627-3300 for times and dates.*

At the corner of Monsarrat Avenue and Paki is the **Queen Kapiolani Garden** (3). It used to feature a wide variety of roses, but the difficulty of maintaining roses in a tropical atmosphere lead the City of Honolulu Parks Department to switch to hibiscus. It's worth checking out.

As you make your way up Monsarrat Avenue, almost at the top is a street to the left named Alohea that quickly turns into Makapuu Avenue. Just up that street stands the **Diamond Head Theatre** (4) where mixed casts of professionals and amateurs produce a 12-play season of Broadway hits, and even some locally written plays. ☎ *734-0274 for shows and times.*

On top of what has now become Diamond Head Road is **Kapiolani Community College** (5), on the left. This attractive set of buildings is well worth a walk-through. Lush tropical planting and walkways that flow well draw you right through the campus. Three things to look for on campus are: a small but interesting student art gallery in the Koa Building; a large and well-stocked cactus-and-bromeliad garden on the southeast edge of the campus; and the Tamarind Dining Room sitting at the east edge of the campus.

And now for the main attraction, ***Diamond Head Crater** (6). From the comfort station just beyond the parking lot, the climb to the Diamond Head summit is .7 of a mile. Once there, you will have reached approximately 760 feet above sea level. A new trail covering makes it a comfortable climb; it also is meant to keep people on the trail since shortcuts can be dangerous and cause erosion. The trail is marked and easy to follow. It is a must to stay on it.

As you approach the first tunnel, you will not be able to see the end because it bends to the left. If you have a flashlight, fine, but if not walk with others and hold the handrail. After this tunnel you have a choice; you can go right and climb the 99-step staircase to the second tunnel or go left and take a gently switchback trail to the summit. By going left, you miss a ladder up inside two levels of bunkers and a spiral staircase in darkness. Before the trail became well used and formalized, bedding and even a PBX phone system could be seen in these bunkers, remnants of the military's use of Diamond Head in World War II.

From the summit a narrow path along the rim leads to another bunker. The continuing rim trail is off-limits since there are several radio and microwave antennae in the area. The 360-degree view from topside is like no other in the islands. Waikiki is at your feet; the ocean seems a stone's throw away; and looking back towards the mountains is pretty exhilarating. Stay a while and enjoy the fruits of your effort.

Trip 3

*Harbor/Downtown/ Chinatown

Downtown Honolulu and the harbor share a rich history together. Over many years, practically every person who came to Hawaii to trade, preach, soldier, settle, work, vacation or for whatever reason entered via the harbor. Many stayed to live and work close by, which gave rise to a busy downtown. Chinatown, for generations of immigrants moving from the sugar and pineapple plantations, has been the entry point for the journey into mainstream social and economic life in the islands. It is reported to be the first Chinatown in America.

When airplanes started to appear regularly in the early fifties, there was a subtle shift that has grown so that today no passengers come through the harbor. Now it is almost exclusively used for commerce and regular Coast Guard, with some military usage now and then. Several of the super luxury cruise ships periodically tie up at Honolulu Harbor—which can be pretty exciting if you happen to be there at the time—but they don't drop off or pick up passengers. You can take a cruise between these islands, but you must first fly here to get on the large ships.

Cheek-by-jowl with the harbor, as expected, is downtown Honolulu. Until 1968, the tallest building in the area was the landmark Aloha Tower. Today high-rises have sprouted towards the mountains and several blocks in each direction from the harbor.

More and more visitors are making their way to Downtown Honolulu to enjoy and observe the contrast between a tropical city rich in immigrant history that is also considered a totally modern business center. This walking tour will take you to areas demonstrating that contrast.

GETTING THERE:

By car, leave Waikiki via Ala Wai Boulevard. Turn left where it says to get on Ala Moana Boulevard. About 4.5 miles later, just after the Federal Building on the right, get into the left lane and follow the signs to parking for the Aloha Tower Marketplace.

By Waikiki Trolley, take the sightseeing—not the shopping—trolley directly to Pier 7. It can be boarded at any major hotel in Waikiki or the Royal Hawaiian Shopping Center. The trip will take about an hour and a half.

By bus, on Kuhio Avenue board any bus marked #19 or #20 Airport and get off at the Federal Building.

PRACTICALITIES:

This isn't such a long walk, but there's so much to see and do that you will need comfortable shoes. A hat is advisable. And sunscreen. And sunglasses. Don't leave anything in your car, locked or unlocked.

FOOD AND DRINK:

There's a big selection of restaurants in this whole area. It's more a matter of choosing which are the most interesting and tasty. Mainly, the recommendations for this Daytrip are ethnic restaurants.

Gordon Biersch Brewery Restaurant (ground floor, Aloha Tower Marketplace) Large brewpub right on the water. The garlic fries are terrific. Lunch & dinner daily. ☎ 599-4877. $$

A Little Bit of Saigon Restaurant (1160 Maunakea) Voted the best Vietnamese restaurant in Honolulu by *Honolulu Magazine.* Open daily for lunch & dinner. ☎ 528-3663. $

Indigo Eurasian Cuisine (1121 Nuuanu) Consider this meal starting with an appetizer: Thousand Loved Crab Cakes; Volcano Island Feta Cheese with Waimea Vine-ripened Tomatoes; Wokked Hot Sour Pacific Fish Pagoda; Soft Clouds in High Heaven Calamanda Coconut Cream Pie. The food and service are every bit as good as the hyperbole. Wonderful atmosphere. Open for lunch Tues.–Fri., dinner Tues.–Sat. X: Sun. & Mon. Reservations ☎ 521-2900. $$

Duc's Bistro (1188 Maunakea) Combination of Vietnamese and Continental selections in a soothing atmosphere. Lunch Mon.–Fri., dinner nightly; late night jazz Fri. & Sat. 10 a.m.–1 p.m. Reservations, ☎ 531-6325. $$

SUGGESTED TOUR:

Numbers in parentheses correspond to numbers on the map.

*HAWAII MARITIME CENTER (1), Pier 7, Honolulu, HI 96813, ☎ 536-6373. *Open daily 8:30–5. Admission to the whole Center including the four-masted* Falls of Clyde *is $7.50 for adults and $5 for people under 18. Gift shop.* ♿.

The museum touts the fact that Hawaii's story was written on the sea. The Center is compried of three attractions: A museum with 40+ exhibits;the only four-masted full-rigged ship left in the world, *The Falls of Clyde*; and a reproduction of an ancient Polynesian sailing canoe, *Hokulea*, which

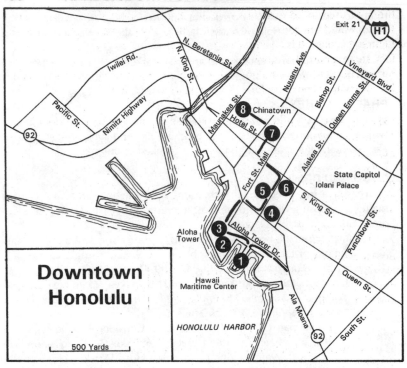

made a Voyage of Discovery in 1976 that was documented by *National Geographic.*

The Center celebrates the excitement of Honolulu's waterfront and harbor. Of particular interest is the whaling exhibit centered by a huge humpback whale skeleton. Surfing exhibits offer videos and displays of the old-time surfing greats like Duke Kahanamoku to today's hottest windsurfers.

Tied up at Pier 6 is an amazing vessel of maritime technology. Navatek I creates the smoothest ride of any cruise boat in Hawaii. Daytime, sunset and moonlight rides are offered, with whale watching from January through May. *Dinner cruises start at $75 for adults, $55 for kids 2–11,* ☎ *848-6360 for reservations.*

Also docked at Pier 7 is the *Kulamanu,* Windjammer Cruise's four-master that takes visitors out for sunset dinner cruises, moonlight sails and private charters. The newly renovated ship has three decks, each featuring an entertainment stage and bar. *The package for a cruise and an all-you-can-eat buffet is about $50 for adults and $25 for kids 4–10. It sails at 5:15 and returns about 7:30.* ☎ *537-1122.*

Right next door is **Aloha Tower Marketplace** (2) at Piers 9 & 10. This entire area used to be cheerless pier warehouses, but in the Baltimore and Boston waterfront genre, has been turned into shops, restaurants and entertainment venues. It is anchored by famed Aloha Tower. The Marketplace offers some unusual shopping experiences as well as a wide variety of restaurants. Upstairs is an open-air food court. Most stores and food establishments are open daily from about 10 a.m.–10 p.m. &.

*ALOHA TOWER OBSERVATION DECK (3), Pier 10, Honolulu, HI 96813. *Open Sun.–Wed. 9 a.m.–6 p.m. and Thurs.–Sat. 9 a.m.–10 p.m.* &. ☎ *566-2203 to check on hours. Free.*

Take the elevator up 10 floors to the Observation Deck that offers stunning views in four directions: Downtown and the mountains; toward Diamond Head and Waikiki; the harbor and ocean including Sand Island; and the Airport and west. The tower still functions as the Harbor Master's traffic control center for Honolulu Harbor.

The four-sided clock was installed in 1926 when the tower was built. Both the tower and the clock sustained damage from bullets during the Pearl Harbor attack. After that, the tower was painted camouflage for the rest of the war. The tower, which was renovated in 1994, is on both the Hawaii and National Registers of Historic Places.

As you head up Bishop Street from the Marketplace, you will pass the low-rise, arched **Dillingham Transportation Building** (4) on the right, which for many years served as the headquarters of the locally-based Dillingham empire. At one time, the corporation spread from Australia to Hawaii to California to Canada with operations in construction, cattle ranching, land development (including development of Ala Moana Shopping Center), natural gas and many others. The corporation doesn't exist today, having been broken up and sold in pieces.

In the next block on the left is the classic **Alexander & Baldwin Building** (5). That corporation is the single tenant, and is very much alive with a huge transportation division that operates Matson Lines (see Daytrip 20). A&B, as the company is fondly called in Hawaii, is the last big sugar producer in the islands. It is also active in developing and/or selling its vast Hawaiian land holdings.

*DOWNTOWN CONTEMPORARY ART MUSEUM (6), 765 Bishop St. in the First Hawaiian Tower, Honolulu, HI 96813, ☎ 526-1322. *Open Mon.–Thurs. 8:30–3, Fri. 8:30–6. Free.* &.

This new exhibit space, located in the handsome new First Hawaiian Bank Tower at the corner of Bishop and King streets, is an interesting statement on corporate support of the arts. When this $185 million edifice was being designed, the bank commissioned the architects to design the lobby to accommodate a permanent museum. It is a fascinating display of modern paintings and sculpture.

Beyond the artwork, the atrium lobby, the grand staircase to the upper floor section of the museum, and the lighting all contribute to a feeling of something far different than a normal bank lobby.

As you leave the bank, head north on King Street. Soon you will experience the contrast mentioned before between the exciting, modern world of commerce and the bustle of Honolulu's immigrant past. At Bethel Street turn right and go one block. At the corner of Bethel and Hotel streets are two giant lions that mark Chinatown Gateway.

When you cross Hotel Street, on the left is a pocket park. The next building is the historic **Hawaii Theater** (7). Built in 1922, it was a classic downtown movie house with 1,700 seats, where most islands kids had their first motion picture experience. After many years of successful operation, it started to go downhill as downtown slipped in the late 1950s and early 60s. Finally it was closed. In 1987, a developer had an option on the property and was about to tear down the theater for a high-rise condo, when a doctor and his wife and an attorney and his wife rushed forward with the money to buy out the option.

That started a ten-year restoration project (it included purchase of all the land behind the theater) that so far has cost $21 million. The front still is not restored, but don't be put off by that since the interior is splendid. The theater is open for one-hour tours on the first Monday of each month at 10 a.m. and 2 p.m. *$5. Groups can tour any time.* ☎ *528-5535.*

After the theater, the next several blocks are Chinatown, purportedly the oldest in the nation. Herb stalls, lei stands, noodle shops, tattoo parlors, tiny restaurants and more make a hubbub of activity that is fun to be a part of. The area has been preserved and buildings renovated through density and height restrictions and the advocacy of Historic Hawaii Foundation and other groups.

Two organizations sponsor walking tours of Chinatown: The Hawaii Heritage Center offers a fully narrated tour from 9:30–noon on Fridays for $4 for adults, ☎ 521-2749; the Chinese Chamber of Commerce tour starts at their offices at 42 North King Street on Tuesdays from 9:30–noon, cost is $5—☎ 533-3181 for more information.

Maunakea Marketplace (8) is tucked into a large space that partially fronts on Maunakea and Hotel streets. Off Maunakea Street, just a block north from the theater, is a courtyard that leads to a cornucopia of ethnic food and gift stalls. Chances are you will see foods you have never experienced before. Some are prepared dishes that you can eat on the spot while others are taken out for home preparation. The marketplace is a great people-watching spot. Young and old bustle around with an intensity not found at your usual mall.

*Iolani Palace/ Civic Center

Centered in this part of town is the only state residence of royalty in the United States, surrounded by historical buildings and places of great significance to Hawaii's past. This area of the city is again a combination—a blending if you will—but this time it is of Hawaiian and Western spiritual, cultural, legal, and governmental concepts.

The New England missionaries came to Hawaii in the early 1800s with ideas and ways of doing things that today seem almost totally out of place on a tropical island. Their clothing, buildings, music, art and even attitudes seemed wrong for Hawaii, yet they were embraced by the native people.

Later on, that embrace loosened considerably so that today there is some strong resentment of these early religious zealots from the east who some say "stole" hundreds of thousands of acres of land from Hawaiians. They did this along with banning the graceful hula, making Hawaiian ladies wear long dresses in the warm climate, and building houses with windows so they became stuffy and hot in the tropical temperatures. Some people today say that the most egregious act of the missionaries and their descendants was their part in the overthrow of Queen Liliuokalani in 1893. That act ended the Hawaiian monarchy and ushered in Western government.

Our walking tour will take you to and into some of the most historic places in this part of downtown Honolulu. See if you can feel the blending of the two cultures we spoke of before as you make your way on this one-mile walk.

GETTING THERE:

By car, head straight out Kalakaua Avenue—going toward the mountains—until it ends. Here it will bend left and you will be on Beretania Street. Proceed three miles to the parking garage just on the other side of Alapai. Walk down Beretania Street past the State Capitol on the left.

By bus, take any #2 bus headed downtown. Get off at Punchbowl Street and walk past the State Capitol.

By trolley, get on any sightseeing trolley in Waikiki that goes downtown. Ask the driver for the stop closest to Iolani Palace.

PRACTICALITIES:

The same mantra: sunscreen, sunglasses, a hat, comfortable shoes. Water is an excellent idea. Take a backpack, fannypack or large purse so you leave nothing in your car or trunk—locked or unlocked.

FOOD AND DRINK:

Julia Morgan Restaurant (located at the back of the YWCA at 1040 Richards.) Simple fare served Mon.–Fri. from 7–2. Try the fruit manapuas. ☎ 524-8789. $

Yong Sing Restaurant (opposite the YWCA at 1055 Alakea.) This Hong Kong-style Chinese restaurant is big and noisy since it is usually filled with politicians and business leaders from downtown. Daily from 10–9, ☎ 531-1366. $

The Ground Floor (727 Richards) Hearty food served quickly for the lunch crowd. Open for lunch Mon.–Fri. Cocktails and pupus (appetizers) 4:30–9. ☎ 538-6012. $

Columbia Inn (645 Kapiolani Blvd.) is called "Top of the Boulevard." The news crowd still hangs out here. For a filling experience, try the Loco Moco. Open Sun.–Thurs. 6–11., Fri. & Sat. 6–midnight. ☎ 596-0757. $

Yanagi Sushi (762 Kapiolani Blvd.) Considered one of the best Japanese restaurants in Honolulu where there are lots to choose from. Rolled sushi as well as combination dinners. Daily lunch and dinner. Reservations, ☎ 597-1525. $$

SUGGESTED TOUR:

Numbers in parentheses correspond to numbers on the map.

On the right side of Beretania Street, behind a high iron fence and lush foliage, is **Washington Place** (1), the Governor's official residence. It was built by ship captain John Dominis, whose son married the Hawaiian lady who became Queen Liliuokalani. She was the last queen, and after her overthrow and temporary imprisonment in Iolani Palace, she lived here until her death in 1917.

St. Andrew's Cathedral (2) is the central church for the state's 16,000 Episcopalians. The first section was built according to English plans from cut stones brought in from England. *Open 8–4 Mon.–Fri., three Sunday services.* ☎ 524-2822.

Next head down Richards St., passing the **Armed Forces YMCA** on the right. About ten years ago it was sold to a developer who restored it into

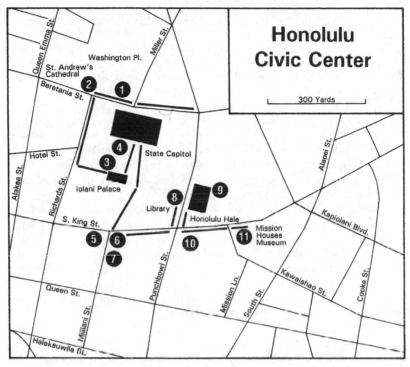

first-class offices that are now mostly occupied by State of Hawaii workers. The address is One Capitol District. In the next block, also on the right, is the **YWCA,** which along with about a dozen YW's around the country, was designed by Julia Morgan. This prolific female architect designed over 800 buildings in the 1920s and 30s in what was totally a man's world. Her best known work is Hearst's Castle, which he called San Simeon. The Honolulu YWCA is a classic. It is worth a walk through to notice the design detail in the railings, light fixtures, cornices and moldings. Nearby is the:

*IOLANI PALACE (3), 364 So. King St., Honolulu, HI 96813. *Tours every 15 minutes Tues.–Sat. 9–2:15. Reservations necessary.* ☎ *522-0832. Palace Shop sells an array of books and gifts. Adults $8, children 5–12 $3.* ♿.
   As you cross Richards you will enter the grounds of the Iolani Palace, the center of the Hawaiian Kingdom for a little more than a decade, from 1882 to 1893. As the official residence of King Kalakaua and his successor, Queen Liliuokalani, it was here that the leading men and women of the islands met and mingled with distinguished visitors from overseas. Princes, prelates, diplomats and naval officers, writers and artists, entrepreneurs and adventurers were welcomed and entertained with typical Hawaiian *aloha.*

After the end of the Hawaiian monarchy in 1893, the palace was converted into legislative halls and executive offices. The business of government continued to be conducted in the palace until the State Capitol was completed 1968 adjacent to the palace grounds. After extensive renovation by the Friends of Iolani Palace, it was re-opened to the public in 1978 as a historic house museum, once again reflecting the regal grandeur that existed there during the days of the monarchy.

Besides restoring the building, the Friends faced a daunting task in bringing back the original furnishings, most of which had been auctioned off or otherwise sold following the fall of the monarchy. What you see inside the palace today has been gathered from as far as England and as close as the Bishop Museum. Although the furnishings look complete to most of us, the acquisition of long-lost items continues.

On the main floor of the 140-by-100-foot building is the Blue Room, used for informal audiences and small receptions. Next to it is the State Dining Room. Most spectacular is the **Throne Room,** decorated in red and gold and used for royal audiences, balls and receptions. A great hall runs the entire width of the palace, dominated by a beautiful koa staircase leading to the second floor. The rooms on the downtown side of the second floor are called the King's Suite, which consisted of his bedroom and library. Rooms on the Waikiki side were devoted to the ladies.

You can reach the **State Capitol** (4) by walking from the Palace toward the mountains. As mentioned, this edifice replaced Iolani Palace as the state's seat of government in 1969. Designed by the local architects Belt, Lemmon & Lo with J. Carl Warnecke from the mainland, the idea is to show the uplifting nature of Hawaii. The two cone-shaped columns—the one towards town holds the State House and the other the State Senate—rising out of the pools are meant to be volcanoes. There is an interesting mosaic in the center of the ground floor called "Aquarius." Take one of the elevators to the top floor where the view is quite breathtaking. This floor houses the Governor's and Lieutenant Governor's offices. *Open Mon.–Fri. 7:45–4:30. Free.* &.

As you leave the State Capitol and Palace grounds heading toward the ocean, note on the right the Spanish-motif **Old Federal Building** (5). It houses some state offices and the Downtown Station Post Office.

Across from the Palace is the **Statue of Kamehameha I** (6). Talk about cross-cultural: the statue was cast in Paris from a model made by the American artist T.R. Gould, who lived in Florence, Italy. Remember, this was a Hawaiian King who fought long and hard to bring it all together and was known as the "Unifier of the Islands." What a blend! Adding to the story is the fact that the original statue was lost at sea, recovered, and now is in Kohala on the Big Island.

Another stately old building is **Aliiolani Hale** (7). The House of Heavenly Kings is also called the Judiciary Building, since it houses the State Supreme Court. It was the first major office building erected by Kamehameha V, in 1874. There are five noteworthy exhibits in this building: *The Judiciary History Center* tells a story of dramatic transition through exciting multi-media presentations, exhibits and a restored courtroom; *The Monarchy Courts Gallery* investigates the 19th-century legal and judicial processes that shaped an island kingdom; *The Center Theater* presents two multi-media programs, "Kanawai" and "Law of the Land;" *The 1913 Court Room* reflects Hawaii's territorial years; and *The Temporary Exhibit Room* has a nice little feature on Hawaii under martial law from 1941–1944. *Open Mon.–Fri. 7:45–4:30.* ☎ *586-0221. Free.* ♿.

As you head down King Street going toward Waikiki, on the left you will notice the recently-restored **Hawaii State Library** (8). When it was built in 1913, it was partially funded by Andrew Carnegie. *Open Mon., Wed., Fri. and Sat. 9–5; Tues. and Thurs. 9–8.* In the next block on the left is **Honolulu Hale** (9). It houses the offices of the Mayor, the City Council and several City departments. The open courtyard often houses exhibits and concerts. *Open Mon.–Fri. 7:45–4:30.* ☎ *523-4385. Both are* ♿. *Free.*

On the right is **Kawaihao Church** (10). The church was built with coral pieces cut from the reef off Waikiki, but is of New England style design. Inside, close your eyes for a moment and then open them and see if you don't feel like you're in a church in Boston, except perhaps for the portraits of the *Alii* or Kings and Queens of Hawaii. Buried on the grounds are King Lunalilo and many missionaries. In 1851 in a book titled "Island World of the Pacific," the Rev. Henry T. Cheever said of this church, "It shows conspicuous through the spy-glass far out to sea, and it is the first object of art the eye rests upon coming into port, and it will stand, we trust for ages, a pleasing monument to the stranger of the regard paid by this nation of emerging heathen to the institutions of the Gospel." Finish your walk at the:

*MISSION HOUSES MUSEUM (11), 553 So. King St., Honolulu, HI 96813, ☎ 531-0481. *Open Tues.–Sat. 9–4. Adults $5, seniors and military $4, kids 4–18 $1. Terrific Gift Shop.*

A rich part of Hawaii's history resides in these simple buildings, which are across a small street. The Museum is comprised of three buildings that were the hub of activities for the New England missionaries, Native Hawaiians, merchants and seaman. The 1831 Chamberlain House and the 1841 Printing Office are both of colonial design, but built of coral blocks like Kawaihao Church. The original building, the 1821 Mission Frame House, was built of wood and other materials pre-cut and shipped from Boston and is Hawaii's oldest western-style structure. Once inside any of these structures, it is hard to imagine that you are in the middle of the Pacific on a tropical island, and not in some small town in New England.

Trip 5

Ala Wai Amble

"The Ala Wai Canal is one of the great canals of the world and it hasn't changed. It's an anchor of continuity. It competes with the Grand Canal of Venice and the canals of London and Amsterdam. This canal is unique. You can stand (at one end of the canal) and look one and a half miles over water." So says Scott Hamilton in a book written by columnist Bob Krauss titled "Our Hawaii."

For terra firma, Waikiki as we know it today was created by the Ala Wai Canal. It is the *mauka* (mountain) boundary of Hawaii's most famous area. Until the 1920s, Waikiki was mostly fish and duck ponds as well as numerous rice paddies and banana patches. In fact, most of the area was about a foot below sea level except for a strand of beach and a few other higher points here and there where Hawaiian royalty and the wealthy families of Oahu—like the Castles, Hustaces and Peacocks—kept bathhouses and grand holiday cottages.

This 4.5-mile level amble is meant to take you to the other side of the tracks—or in this case—the canal. You will be close to Waikiki the whole time, but it will give you an interesting look at how Honolulu residents live, garden, dance, play games and go to school.

GETTING THERE:

On foot, start anywhere in Waikiki. Because you will only be a foot or two above sea level the whole way, this walking tour is gentle for all ages.

By bike: You can rent decent mountain bikes from Coconut Cruisers in the Royal Hawaiian Shopping Center, 2301 Kalakaua Avenue, ☎ 924-1644, 24 hours per day. The cost is nominal. Except for the start, the directions are the same as for walking. A good deal of this tour is a designated bike route.

PRACTICALITIES:

Once again, hat, sunglasses and sunscreen are recommended. Take bottled water with you from the grocery or convenience store. There are drinking fountains along the way as well, so drink often and refill your water bottle.

FOOD AND DRINK:

Hard Rock Café (1837 Kapiolani Blvd.) Pretty much the same hamburger menu as those around the world. Also the usual rock 'n roll display, but with a Hawaii-only "Surfing Wall of Fame." Dominating the place is an unusual surfing Cadillac station wagon from the Big Island. Lunch and dinner daily. ☎ 955-7383. $

Hee Hing (449 Kapahulu Ave.) Very popular Chinese restaurant serving an expansive menu of Cantonese treats. Dim sum every day at lunch. It's been going for over 34 years. Call for reservations 734-8474 $-$$

Irifune (563 Kapahulu Ave.) Small and unpretentious, but often voted among the best Japanese spots in Honolulu. It has been likened to a Japanese country inn with folk art on the walls. Lunch Tues.–Fri. Dinner Tues.–Sat. ♿: Sun. ☎ 737-1141. $

Sam Choy's Diamond Head Restaurant (449 Kapahulu Ave., upstairs) Sam is big and gained his big reputation for innovative Pacific cuisine on the Big Island. He is a one-man restaurant machine with two locations, cookbooks, cooking shows and personal appearances. Dinner daily & Sun. brunch. Reservations a must. ☎ 732-8645. $$

SUGGESTED TOUR:

Numbers in parentheses correspond to numbers on the map.

If you bike, it is advisable to take the path to the right just before the canal bridge, otherwise the directions are the same as for walking.

If you walk this tour, start on Ala Moana Boulevard near the Ala Wai Yacht Harbor. You will use all three bridges that cross the Ala Wai Canal. On the other side of the Ala Moana Boulevard bridge is a short stairway that will take you down to the Ala Wai Promenade. This tree-lined walkway is a pleasant interlude from busy Waikiki that borders what is the start of the canal.

On the left as you reach the end of the promenade is the hulking 360-million-dollar **Convention Center** (1). Many years in the making, this world-class facility accommodates groups from several hundred to many thousands. It features a 200,000-square-foot exhibit hall, 100,000 square feet of meeting space in 49 different rooms, a huge ballroom and two theaters. If the building intrigues you, you may want to walk around the front to view the unusual flying sails or palm trees that soar five stories in the air.

Cross the bridge over the canal on Kalakaua Avenue and turn left on Ala Wai Boulevard. The 250-foot-wide **Ala Wai Canal** (2) was started in 1920 and completed in 1929 at a total cost of $400,000. (Just to dredge it clean today costs millions). The concept was to divert the water running down from the mountains and drain the Waikiki area. All this water was to be sent to the ocean via the canal. The dredged material—which was mostly

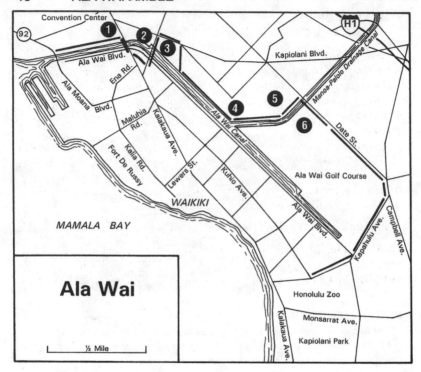

Convention Center

92

Ala Wai Blvd.

Ena Rd.

Ala Moana Blvd.

Maluhia Rd.

Kalakaua Ave.

Fort De Russy

Kalia Rd.

Lewers St.

Kuhio Ave.

WAIKIKI

MAMALA BAY

Kapiolani Blvd.

H1

Manoa-Palolo Drainage Canal

Ala Wai Canal

Date St.

Ala Wai Golf Course

Ala Wai Blvd.

Kapahulu Ave.

Campbell Ave.

Honolulu Zoo

Kalakaua Ave.

Monsarrat Ave.

Kapiolani Park

Ala Wai

½ Mile

coral—was piled up on the 687 acres that make up Waikiki as we know it today. The engineers were right; the dry land area of Waikiki represents some of the most highly-priced land on the planet.

Turn left on McCully, go across the bridge and turn right on Kapiolani Boulevard, and then right again into the **Ala Wai Recreation Center** (3). This city facility serves many purposes, with one of the main ones being large dancing events. The Hawaii Ballroom Dancing Association holds practices and events here. *Call 538-1405 for a schedule.* In addition, this is one of two very active canoe paddling venues on the canal. Outrigger canoe paddling has had a big resurgence in the last several years among all ages. On most afternoons during the season, the Ala Wai Canal is bustling with paddlers straining at their practices.

Make your way toward the canal and you will enter a paved pathway. On your left are the spacious Ala Wai Fields where residents play all manner of games. After a straight-away, the path makes a jog to the left. This is the site of the second canoe house, and just beyond that is the Ala Wai Elementary School. This is typical of public schools throughout the islands since it is a statewide school system.

Next are the **Ala Wai Community Gardens** (4), dozens of small plots provided by the city where high-rise dwellers grow fruits, vegetables and flowers. The city gives awards for the best-looking plots, and the competition is fierce.

The pathway bends to the left, and on the left is **Iolani School** (5), one of the two best-known Hawaii private schools. Iolani vies with Punahou—the other prestigious private school—for which can name more Merit Scholars, win the Math Bowl, football, soccer, volleyball and so forth. Private schools proliferate in Hawaii, claiming upwards of 25 percent of the student population.

As you turn right on Date Street, what emerges on the right is the **Ala Wai Golf Course** (6). Very popular with local golfers, it provides 190,000 rounds of golf a year and is purportedly the busiest in the world. *Call 296-2000 for computerized reservations, but do it well in advance.* Enjoy the stroll or ride along the bike path fronting the golf course.

Just before you get to Kapahulu Avenue, the bike path bends right and will take you back into Waikiki. If you cross over to Kapahulu Avenue, there is a store called Bailey's Antiques and Aloha Shirts that features tons of authentic Hawaii memorabilia including 1940's silky aloha shirts. Worth a visit. *517 Kapahulu Ave. Open Mon.–Sat. 9–8, Sun. 10–6.* ☎ *734-7628.*

Trip 6

Only in Waikiki

An intriguing anecdote is told about some newcomers to Hawaii. In 1864, Mrs. Eliza Sinclair, a rancher's widow from New Zealand, arrived with her children to create a new life in the islands. King Kamehameha IV befriended the family and offered them a strip of land running from what is now downtown Honolulu all the way to Diamond head—for $10,000.

It included all of Waikiki.

But the Sinclairs found the land inappropriate for ranching and bought the island of Niihau instead (see Daytrip 46). Did they miss the investment opportunity of a lifetime? Seems so. It's not possible, but if an acre of land in Waikiki were to become available today, the asking price would be in the range of $1,000 to $1,200 a square foot. And remember, there are 687 acres in Waikiki.

In an attempt to improve his miserable health, Robert Louis Stevenson sailed to Hawaii in the late 1880s and settled near Sans Souci Beach. His praise was pretty remarkable. "If anyone desires such old-fashioned things as lovely scenery, quiet, pure air, clear sea water, heavenly sunsets hung out before his eyes over the Pacific and the distant hills of Waianae, I recommend him to Waikiki Beach."

On this walking tour, we will explore the many beaches that make up Waikiki Beach.

GETTING THERE:
On foot, it is suggested that you start at the west end of the beach or near Fort DeRussy. As you proceed along toward Diamond Head, you will have covered approximately two miles.

PRACTICALITIES:
You will be close to the ocean most of the way and the glare can be fierce, so sunglasses are a must. So is sunscreen and a hat. If you take sandals, you can walk barefoot on the sand at times and then conveniently slip back into them when you stop for food or drink—or to explore some little-know aspect of this famous beach.

FOOD AND DRINK:

There are several hundred places to eat and drink in Waikiki. Narrowing the choices is difficult at best. The selections here are mostly a mix of historical sites on the beach. Because of that, they can be pricey, but are unique spots for a treat.

> **House Without A Key** (Halekulani Hotel, 2199 Kalia Rd.) Named after author Earl Derr Biggers' first Charlie Chan mystery. Soothing spot right next to the beach for any meal or cocktails. Hawaiian entertainment nightly 5–8:30 under the hotel's giant kiawe tree. ☎ 923-2311. $$ to $$$

> **Duke's Restaurant & Canoe Club** (Outrigger Hotel, 2335 Kalakaua Ave.) Delightful atmosphere on the beach highlighted by the history of surfing through photos and memorabilia, mostly of famed Duke Kahanamoku. Daily lunch and dinner. Reservations suggested for dinner, ☎ 922-2268. $$ to $$$

> **Banyan Veranda** (Moana Surfrider Hotel, 2365 Kalakaua Ave.) Gracious and relaxed for breakfast, afternoon tea, cocktails or dinner. Huge banyan tree is the setting for nightly free entertainment that includes harp performances, Hawaiian guitar, hula dancers. ☎ 922-3111. $$ to $$$

> **Texas Rock 'n Roll Sushi Bar** (Hyatt Regency, 2424 Kalakaua Ave.) How about a rockin' eatery featuring BBQ bourbon ribs, prime rib, Texas style pizza and sushi? Dinner and karaoke nightly on the beach. ☎ 923-7655. $$

> **Hau Tree Lanai Terrace** (New Otani Kaimana Beach Hotel, 2863 Kalakaua Ave.) At the east end of Waikiki, this smallish spot is worth the effort to get here. All three meals daily plus cocktails. Reservations for dinner, ☎ 921-7066. $$ to $$$

SUGGESTED TOUR:

Numbers in parentheses correspond to numbers on the map.

As mentioned, this walking tour will cover the collection of beaches—a nearly contiguous string—that constitute Waikiki Beach. Begin your walk at the **Kahanamoku Beach and Lagoon** (1) in front of the Hilton Hawaiian Village. The lagoon is not really for swimming and over the years there have been many proposals for its use, including a swim-through aquarium. Stay tuned. From there, continue on to **Fort DeRussy Beach** (2). The area inland from this beach is a restful 20-acre oasis owned by the Army, which recently re-landscaped the property from the sand all the way to Kalakaua Avenue. Back in the 1930s, it was the Army's parade ground with no trees and only a few cottages along the beach. Today, mostly bikinis parade the grounds.

The **U.S. Army Museum of Hawaii** (3) is housed in Battery Randolph at Fort DeRussy. It has displays and collections from the various wars, with an emphasis on the Pacific. *Open Tues.–Sun. 10–4:30. Admission by dona-*

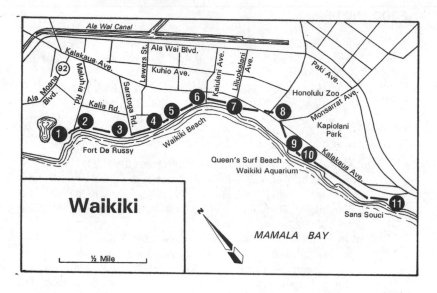

tion. ☎ *955-9552.* As you continue on the beach, you will come to the Halekulani Hotel which was completely rebuilt in 1983. The main lobby building—which now houses two five-star restaurants—is all that remains of the original. In the early days of Waikiki, it was the private residence of retired Sea Captain Brown. The beach that fronts the Halekulani is called **Gray's Beach** (4). It makes a little jog here where once a freshwater spring entered the ocean. It has a sandy channel good for swimming.

Outrigger Beach (5) is where the original Outrigger Canoe Club was located for many years. This private club has moved down the beach near Sans Souci, and in its place is the Outrigger Hotel with Duke's Restaurant. The OCC legacy of training of superb canoe paddlers lives on. Next is **Waikiki Beach Center** (6), a pretty busy place with food concessions, surfboard and canoe rentals, bathhouse, and benches and chairs for card playing. You can rent a surfboard for from $5–12. Surfing instruction is available at Aloha Beach Services where instructors guarantee "to get you up." Cost is about $25 for an hour.

Of special note near the center is a statue of a man who has been called "King of the Beach." Duke Kahanamoku was an athletic wonder, winning three Olympic Gold Medals. But more than that, he was a gracious and giving person. His talents as a waterman included swimming, surfing and canoe paddling. There he is, standing in front of a massive surf board with his arms wide open beckoning all to his beloved Waikiki Beach.

Kuhio Beach Park (7) offers a long seawall that creates calm water for novice swimmers. At the end is a wall extending from the beach into the ocean. Perfect for photographers and sunset watchers. Nearby is the:

*HONOLULU ZOO (8), 151 Kapahulu Ave., Honolulu, HI 96815, ☎ 971-7171. *Open daily 9–4:30 except Christmas and New Year's. Admission is $6 for adults, $1 for children 6–12, and kids under 5 are free.* ዽ.

Located at the entrance to Kapiolani Park, the Zoo's 42 acres are home to such animals as elephants, giraffes, ostriches, zebras, hippos, leopards; with several animals common to the islands such as the rare nene goose, Hawaiian pig, mongoose and Hawaiian wild sheep. The petting zoo is perfect for kids and is open daily 9–4. Special puppet shows and free community events are held regularly.

Back across the street and onto the sand will lead you to **Queen's Surf Beach** (9). This beach is noted for its popular surfing area called, appropriately, Queen's. All that remains of the notorious Queen's Surf Restaurant is a low stone wall by a kiawe tree, which considering the impact this venue had on Hawaiian entertainment, doesn't seem like much. Kui Lee and many other Hawaiian entertainers polished their acts here. Next is the refurbished **Kapiolani Park Beach Center.** It is the most seaward part of the 220-acre Kapiolani Park. Hawaii's last king, David Kalakaua, was a world traveler who did much for his people. Among his legacies is the park named after his wife, Queen Kapiolani. It was created from crown lands and given to the people of Hawaii in 1877.

Kapiolani Park features the zoo, bandstand, a two-mile jogging path, 13 tennis courts, Waikiki Shell and a spacious grassy area for softball, soccer, kite flying and picnicking. The Royal Hawaiian Band holds free concerts at the Bandstand every Sunday from 2–3 in the afternoon. Continue on to the:

*WAIKIKI AQUARIUM (10), 2777 Kalakaua Ave., Honolulu, HI 96815, ☎ 923-9741. *Open daily 9–5 except Christmas. Adult admission is $6; $4 for military and senior citizens; $2.50 for kids 13–17; under 12 free.* ዽ.

The beach goes away for the next several hundred yards, but it is replaced by a small gem of an aquarium. The Waikiki Aquarium, built in 1904, is the third-oldest in the United States. It has four galleries with over 40 tanks, featuring 2,000 marine animals from Hawaii and the tropical Pacific, including the famed humuhumunukunukuapuaa. You come face-to-face with two Hawaiian monk seals (an endangered species found only in Hawaiian waters) as well as mahimahi, sharks, jellyfish, living coral and much more.

The aquarium also includes a small museum that depicts how ancient Hawaiians used marine animals and ocean resources in their daily lives; an Edge of the Reef exhibit featuring the different environments that exist at each level; and a coastal garden that is reminiscent of "Old Hawaii" and contains many of Hawaii's endangered species.

The last of the many Waikiki beaches is **Sans Souci** (11). It is near here that Stevenson lived and wrote for a few years while running with what he called the "royal crowd." This beach is next to the Natatorium and the New Otani Kaimana Beach Hotel. If you had the breakfast buffet at the House Without A Key at the Halekulani Hotel in the morning on this daytrip and end it with cocktails or dinner at the Hau Tree Terrace in the New Otani, you will have bracketed the beach and experienced two of the neatest beachside restaurants in the islands. You're probably tired too.

Lotsa Kahala

This entire area was farmland at one time except for a strip of modest cottages along Kahala Beach. In the early 1960s one of Honolulu's developers saw the potential for an upper middle-class residential neighborhood in an area stretching back from the beach all the way to the mountains. He was hugely successful in his housing endeavor, but his crown jewel was a Hilton International hotel built at the very end of Kahala Avenue in 1964. Because the Kahala Hilton was situated in such isolation from Waikiki, many in the visitor industry thought it would fail. It was a struggle at first, but the hotel turned out to be a money machine that attracted business moguls, international politicians, Hollywood types, and the rich in general. It still does.

On this tour, we will explore the beach, the Kahala and Kaimuki neighborhoods, and the now-famous hotel.

GETTING THERE:

By car, head out of Waikiki on Kalakaua Avenue. It will take you around Diamond Head and then on to Kahala Avenue.

By bicycle, follow the same route.

PRACTICALITIES:

We've already introduced you to the idea of only taking what can be carried in a fannypack or small purse. We want to reinforce the message. Do not leave anything in your car, locked or unlocked, including in the trunk. Take it with you, even if you only leave your car for a few moments.

Here comes the threesome again: sunglasses, sunscreen, hat.

FOOD AND DRINK:

Plumeria Beach Café (Kahala Mandarin Oriental Hotel, 5000 Kahala Ave.) Superb setting as though you are on a private beach. Sumptuous buffets daily for breakfast, lunch and dinner. Reservations, ☎ 739-8760. $$$

Kahala Moon (4614 Kilauea Ave.) The chef/owner describes his creations as "contemporary island." Many unique dishes. Lunch Tues.– Fri. Dinner nightly. X: Mon. Reservations, ☎ 732-7777. $ to $$

California Pizza Kitchen (4211 Waialae Ave. in Kahala Mall) Part of a chain, but out-of-the ordinary pizzas, pastas and salads. Crowded and fun. Daily lunch and dinner. Reservations, ☎ 737-9446. $ to $$

Verbano Italian Ristorante (3571 Waialae Ave.) Unfancy setting, but good variety of tasty Italian foods. Great bread. Lunch Mon.–Sat., dinner daily. Reservations suggested, ☎ 735-1777. $-$$

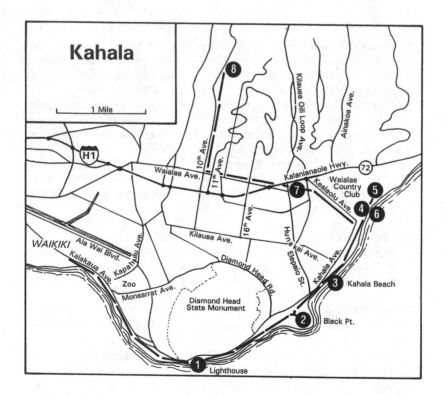

SUGGESTED TOUR:

Numbers in parentheses correspond to numbers on the map.

Most of this tour will concentrate in the Kahala area, but we'll also take a little side trip to an adjoining neighborhood called Kaimuki. Our first stop will be the **Diamond Head Lighthouse** (1) about a mile out of Waikiki. This beacon, almost as famous as the geography behind it, was built in 1899 on the exterior, southwest corner of the volcano. It has been guiding ships from east and west ever since. In odd years, it serves as the finish line for the famed

TransPac Yacht Race from Southern California. The building on the right side of the lighthouse is the official residence of the Coast Guard 14th District Commander who carefully guards our shores.

As you proceed on past the crater, turn right on Papu Circle opposite what locals call "Triangle Park." This is the Black Point area where many of the rich and famous—like Doris Duke, heiress to the American Tobacco fortune, and actors Jim Nabors and Tom Selleck have resided. The reason for this little side trip is to take you past maybe the second or third most expensive single family residence in Hawaii. When you reach the top of Papu, turn right and go down Kaikoo and around the circle almost to its end. Stretching along the sea side at 4375 Kaikoo Place is the former **House of Chris Hemmeter** (2). This is the person who developed and built numerous mega-resorts in Hawaii including the Hyatt Regency on Oahu, the Hyatt and Westin on Maui, the Westin Kauai, and the Hilton Waikoloa Village on the Big Island. The latter hotel is complete with monorail, gondolas and swim-with-the dolphins program (see Daytrip 29). What's interesting is that when Hemmeter decided to sell his Kaikoo Place abode for $65 million, no one had ever occupied it including him. Hemmeter wanted to charge realtors $500 just to show prospective buyers through, but he had no takers.

Retrace your route and turn right on Kahala Avenue. About a mile farther there is a street to the left called Hunakai. Park near there on the beach side of Kahala Avenue. Just to the right of a red tile-topped wall is a right-of-way to **Kahala Beach** (3). We suggest a walk along this stretch of sand to eyeball the sometimes humongous, sometimes garish homes mostly built in the late 1980s during the Japanese money invasion of Hawaii. Both sides of Kahala Avenue went through an astonishing transformation during this period; from comfortable, shingled beach homes of long-time residents to the multi-gabled, copper-crusted, glass block-infused mansions of part-time foreign owners. It still is a shock to lots of Honoluluans.

This beach is still nice though. Wander until you've had enough and either turn around on the beach or take another right-of-way out to Kahala Avenue and walk back to your car.

Keep heading out Kahala Avenue. Don't turn. As the residences end, on either side is the private **Waialae Country Club** (4), for many years home of the PGA's annual first-of-the-tour event called the Hawaiian Open. As you continue past the clubhouse, you will come to the circular drive for the **Kahala Mandarin Oriental Hotel** (5), formerly the Kahala Hilton. Over the years, this gem on the beach has attracted a veritable who's who of the silver screen, with the likes of John Wayne, Frank Sinatra, Lucille Ball, Eva Gabor, and Julie Andrews languishing by the pool. Notables such as Jack Lemmon, Jerry Lewis, Johnny Carson, Tony Bennett, Goldie Hawn and Carol Burnett signed their names to the register along with Burt Reynolds, Bob Newhart, Bette Midler (a Hawaii high school product) and Liza Minelli. The Kahala also became the hotel for royalty, heads of state and legends of sports, musical and literary worlds. Queen Elizabeth and Prince Philip stationed themselves at the Kahala when coming through the islands, as did Emperor Hirohito, Prince Rainier and Princess Grace, Juan Carlos and the Queen of Spain, Indira Ghandi and the Dalai Lama.

Prince Charles and Princess Diana once booked 100 rooms for their party's stopover. And every president since Nixon has trod the Kahala's special red carpet on the way to the Presidential Suite.

The grounds are worth a tour in themselves, especially the pool and lagoon area where dolphins perform a short program at 11, 2 and 4 o'clock. Note the colorful fish and the turtles in the wandering pools.

If all of that is a little overwhelming, including the food prices in the Plumeria Café, may we suggest a stop at **Kahala Beach Park** (6). There are two sections connected by a foot bridge. Either side is an ideal spot for a picnic. If you are so inclined, head for the **Kahala Mall** (7) where you can either make your own from the local supermarket or buy prepared sandwiches from the deli. The mall has numerous shops and restaurants as well that you may want to check out, including Island Treasures and Vue. Both sell mostly made-in-Hawaii products.

On the *mauka* (mountain) side of the mall is Waialae Avenue. Get on that road and head back as though you were going to Waikiki. Keep right, which will keep you from the freeway and on Waialae Avenue. At the top of the hill is Kaimuki, a quaint town with cozy shops and a smattering of good and affordable restaurants. **The Temari Center for Asian and Pacific Arts** is a small art center tucked away at 1329A 10th Avenue. ☎ *735-1860.* It offers classes in basketry, book binding, flower pressing, lei making, origami paper and painting on silk. **Kwilts 'n Koa** at 1126 12th Avenue, Suite 101, is a small shop offering the fabled Hawaiian quilts and selected items made of the most beautiful of all woods—koa. *Open weekdays 10–6, Sat. 10–4.* ☎ *735-2300.*

To reach **Kawamoto Orchid Nursery** (8) continue on Waialae Avenue to 10th Avenue. Turn right and then right again on Waiomao Road. This 3.5-acre nursery offers a fascinating variety of orchids. You may want to take plants with you or have them sent. *Open 8 to 3:30 Mon.–Sat.* ☎ *732-5808.*

East Coastline/ Hanauma Bay

The eastern shore of Oahu is packed with fun things to do and see. Much of the area is best known for its water activities, although there are a couple of interesting parks as well. About 12 miles from Waikiki you enter the domain of the fabled Henry J. Kaiser—thus the name Hawaii Kai. He signed a massive master lease with the Bishop Estate in the late 1950s for all of the land area to the left reaching into the valley and up the ridges. He dredged the area to make a sizable marina, and through his own efforts and those of other developers built about 4,000 homes. Mr. Kaiser also was heavily involved in building the Hilton Hawaiian Village in Waikiki.

GETTING THERE:

By car, which is the only practical way to stop frequently and explore, take Kalakaua Avenue out of Waikiki. That street turns into Diamond Head Road, and then Kahala Avenue. At the end of Kahala Avenue, there is a flashing light; turn left on Kealaolu and follow that until it bears right. This will take you onto Route 72 (Kalanianaole Highway).

By bus, take a #22 Beach Bus or the #58 Hawaii Kai/Sea Life Park. The problem here is that you have to get off after the bus turns on Lunalilo Home Road and walk back on Kalanianaole Highway about a mile to the top of the hill and entry to Hanauma Bay.

PRACTICALITIES:

Sunglasses, sunscreen, hat and a swim suit if you want to partake of some of the plentiful water activities available on this part of the island. Don't leave anything in your car, locked or unlocked.

FOOD AND DRINK:

Philip Paolo's (333 Keahole) Good value in Italian food plus subs, pizza and steak. Caters to children with a special menu. Lunch and dinner daily. Reservations suggested for Fri. and Sat., ☎ 395-5502. $ to $$

Marina Grill (7192 Kalanianaole Hwy.) American cuisine with an Hawaii flavor. Blackened ahi is their specialty. Lunch and dinner daily. Live entertainment Fri. and Sat. ☎ 396-2228. $ to $$

Roy's Restaurant (6600 Kalanianaole Hwy.) Roy has set the standard in new Pacific cuisine with restaurants popping up all over. The taste equals the presentation, which is superb. A real treat. Dinner daily. Reservations, ☎ 396-7697. $$$

The Shack Hawaii Kai (377 Keahole) Casual, serve-yourself plate lunches and hamburgers. Sports atmosphere. Lunch and dinner daily. ☎ 396-1919. $

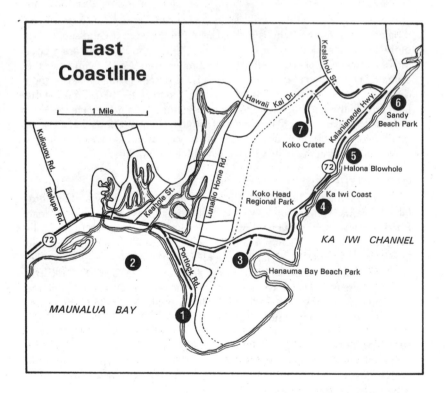

SUGGESTED TOUR:

Numbers in parentheses correspond to numbers on the map.

Let's start this tour by cruising past one of the most expensive residences in Hawaii. Just after crossing over the marina bridge in Hawaii Kai, look for a street to the right called Portlock Road. Follow this tree-shaded road to the end, which is a cul-de-sac. On the right on a slight rise behind a fence is the **Kaiser Estate** (1), built by none other than Henry J. himself. It has three residences, a boat house, two tennis courts, two pools, dog kennels and on and on. Spectacular views back toward Diamond Head from the 7.2 acres. It's been told that Jacqueline Kennedy, Caroline and John, Jr. stayed in the boat house during the summer of 1966. Also, when Lyndon Johnson was a guest at the estate, he liked the mattress he slept on there so much that he got permission to take it back to the White House with him. The estate is currently on the market for $22.5 million, fee simple.

As you drive back over Portlock Road to the highway, you are following a body of water on the left called **Maunalua Bay** (2). This relatively calm bay is the scene of many water sports activities. Turn right on the highway and left into the Koko Marina Shopping Center, where you will find all manner of water activities offered. The best known is Aloha Dive Shop, a full service retail, rental and repair dive center.

What makes this shop unusual is that it has been owned for over a quarter of a century by Jackie James, "The First Lady of Diving in Hawaii." Jackie has certified over 5,000 divers, blazing a trail in a sport dominated by men. Going way back, she presented the underwater world of scuba to physically challenged and handicapped students before it was in vogue or at best feasible. *Koko Marina Shopping Center.* ☎ *395-5922.*

If water skiing is your thing—or you want to try a wake board—try Suyderhoud Water Ski Center in the same shopping center. ☎ *395-3773.* If you're feeling a bit more intrepid and would like to jetski or shoot up into the air on a parachute behind a speeding boat (called parasailing), check out Sea Breeze at Watersports, Ltd. In Koko Marina. ☎ *396-0100.* Continue on to:

*HANAUMA BAY BEACH PARK (3). *Fees: parking $1, adults $1, free under 13. Open 6–7 daily, closed Wed. mornings until noon. Snack shop and snorkel rental at beachside.*

This park is without a doubt one of the most popular visitor attractions on Oahu. The reason lies in the fact that it is an extinct seaside volcano where a portion of the crater has been eaten away by the ocean waves for over thousands of years, thus letting in clear seawater to a protected cove. That has led to a sizable reef fish population of amazing variety and color that can easily be viewed with a snorkel. The white sand beach adds to the uniqueness of this Oahu-only attraction.

As you leave Hanauma Bay, turn right which will take you to the **Ka Iwi Coast** (4) made up of everything from steep, wave-carved cliffs, to shooting sea spouts to a white sand beach famed for body surfing. The major difference in this coastline from everything you have passed so far coming out of Waikiki is the lack of an off-shore reef. As you pull into the

Scenic Viewpoint parking lot, note the worn rocks caused by endless waves crashing against them. Signs warn you from hiking down to the water's edge because of the unpredictability of the waves. It is good advice. In the distance on most days you can see three of Hawaii's neighbor islands: on the right is the small island of Lanai; closest is the low lying Molokai, and behind it rising to the summit of Haleakala is the island of Maui (see Daytrip 32).

As you continue on Route 72, you will come around a corner to the **Halona Blowhole** (5) which is sometimes called Bambo Ridge. The Blowhole is created by the power of the waves crashing against the rocks at this point and finding a small hole that causes a spouting effect. Just beyond is **Sandy Beach Park** (6). Again, because of no reef on this side of the island, the water here can be treacherous. Most of the body and board surfers you see have been at it a long time. But the beach can be enjoyed for sunning.

In the grassy area on the *mauka* side of the park road you will usually see expert kite flyers. The winds at this point on Oahu make for perfect kite flying conditions. Often times in the afternoon, there are instructors of world-class caliber willing to teach anyone interested how to professionally fly a kite. Try it.

When you leave the park turn right. At the stop light turn left on Kealahou, which after half a mile will take you to a left turn where a sign says Koko Crater Stables. Up this rather rough road is **Koko Crater Botanical Garden** (7). This large nature park inside the crater offers many varieties of African plants, cacti, succulents, plumerias and bougainvillea. A loop trail leads you to these and a native wiliwili grove. *Free.* ☎ *522-7060.*

Sea Life Park/Waimanalo

On this part of the island, you'll get the feel of country more than along the east and south shores. Granted there are housing tracts and smallish towns on this side, but the horses and farms and fields—and of course, great stretches of white sand beach—dominate. The immediate impression as you round Makapuu Point is the awesomeness of the mountains. Here the *pali* (mountains) are a sheer backdrop to the relaxed people and places. The reason the *pali* are so precipitous—as opposed to the more gently sloping backdrop to Honolulu—is that the winds are almost always offshore, or windward. Over the millions of years, the winds have buffeted these *pali* more severely than the other side. Most visitors are engaged by the allure of the ocean here, but enjoy a few moments taking in the silent strength of these windward mountains.

GETTING THERE:

By car, leave Waikiki on Kalakaua Avenue and head out toward Route 72. You will see signs that say, "Hanauma Bay." Keep going all the way along the coast to Makapuu Point.

By bus, get on the #58 Hawaii Kai/Sea Life Park bus. Remember that each time you get off, if you exceed the time on your transfer, there is another $1 charge.

PRACTICALITIES:

This is a trip to enjoy the scenery along the water, but there are interesting things to do as well—highlighted by the world-renowned Sea Life Park. Sunglasses, sunscreen, hat. Clear all your possessions out of your car, locked or not.

FOOD AND DRINK:

Keneke's (41-857 Kalanianaole Hwy.) Plate lunches don't get much better than this. Be prepared to eat a lot for a little. Kalua pig and cabbage, and teriyaki chicken are favorites. Try the strawberry and coconut shave ice. Breakfast and lunch daily 9–5. ☎ 259-5266. $

Bueno Nalo (20 Kainehe in Kailua.) Longtime stop for good Mexican food. Casual, busy place for families and large groups. Lunch and dinner daily. ☎ 263-1999. $

Sea Lion Café (41-202 Kalanianaole Hwy.) Cafeteria-style breakfast and lunch, serving plate lunches, burgers, pizza and *bentos* (boxed lunches) daily. ☎ 259-9911. $

Olomana Golf Links and Restaurant (41-1801 Kalanianaole Hwy.) Solid sandwich and entree menu, open to all. Neat view of the golf course from the dining room. Breakfast and lunch served daily. ☎ 259-7926. $

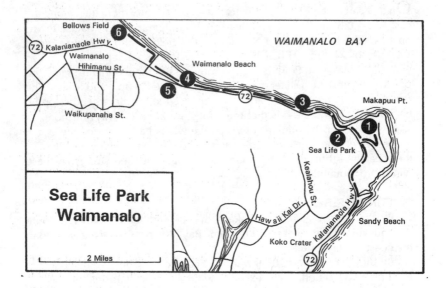

SUGGESTED TOUR:

Numbers in parentheses correspond to numbers on the map.

As you drive along the Ka Iwi Coast beyond Sandy Beach, the road curves to the right and just as it starts up the hill there is a turnoff to the right with a heavy metal gate. This is the entry to **Makapuu Point State Wayside** (1). If you are inclined to take a one-mile walk up to the point, at times along a steep cliff, find a place to park your car along the highway. Your reward will be spectacular scenery toward Molokai as you round the point. The old road will take you to a lookout close to the lighthouse. In the late 1800s, ship owners lobbied King Kalakaua to build a lighthouse on this point. Not much happened until the luxury liner *Manchuria,* with almost 300 passengers, smashed into the rocks at Makapuu in 1906. It was built shortly thereafter on this 400-foot headland. This lighthouse, one of 21 in Hawaii and over 400 in America, has the largest lens of them all.

Back on the highway, at the top is another lookout toward Rabbit Island, Makapuu Beach and on toward the Windward Coast. The water colors at this spot—as you look along the coastline—are very striking. You will see the full range of blue hues changing to turquoise and pale green. Makapuu Beach below is one of the best known body-surfing beaches anywhere. Nearby is the:

*SEA LIFE PARK (2), 41-202 Kalanianaole Hwy., ☎ 259-7933. *Open daily 9:30–5. Closed Thanksgiving, Christmas and New Year's. Adults $19.95, children 4–12 $9.95, under 4 free. Seven theme shops. Restaurant.* ♿.

This 62-acre marine park features the delightful antics of dolphins, penguins, sea lions and a variety of colorful marine life during five shows that also feature scuba divers, an Hawaiian princess and more. Enjoy the 300,000-gallon Hawaiian Reef Tank with over 4,000 colorful fish from Hawaii's waters. You can feed sea lions and green sea turtles. See the world's only "wholphin," Kekaimalu, the offspring of a bottlenose dolphin and false killer whale.

A new feature is Splash U! It's a fun hour where "students" learn from professional trainers how to work with dolphins. After the training, students can touch the animals, give them commands and see how the dolphins behave. If they do as the students tell them to, the animals are rewarded with fresh fish and the students get a degree in Dolphinology. Students can go behind the scenes to see how young animals are trained. Class sizes are limited, so call for reservations. The cost is less than $50.

Just beyond Sea Life Park is the **Makai Research Pier** (3). The larger building is run by the State's High Technology Research Corporation, but in the smaller building on the end of the pier are the offices for a worldwide undersea cable company. The view from this part of the pier back toward the Makapuu Lighthouse is worth the short trek out onto the pier. This may be one of your best chances for shore fishing as well.

Next you will pass through a portion of Waimanalo Town. On the right past the McDonald's is the **Waimanalo Bay State Recreation Area** (4). Down this short road is a restful area with trees and picnic benches fronting a lovely white sand beach. *Open from 6 in the morning until 7:45 in the evening.* Practically across the highway is the **Waimanalo Polo Field** (5) at 41-1062 Kalanianaole Highway. The Honolulu Polo Club presents matches on Sundays at 2 in the afternoon, usually from May through November. *Call* ☎ *396-7656 to confirm days and times.* Polo has a long tradition in Hawaii because of the English influence during the 1880s. The present-day matches can be exciting and fun to watch—and on any Sunday there may be a visiting team from England or Argentina playing a sporting game against some of the better local amateurs.

Bellows Field Beach Park (6). While the airfield at Bellows is no longer active, nonetheless other types of training exercises are conducted by the Air Force during the week. That means that this treasure of a beach park is only open from noon on Fridays through Sunday afternoon. But if you can make it anytime during those hours, do it—if you like sand like white sugar, relatively calm swimming water and a tree-lined coastline. It is usually a good idea to get here in the morning since the wind tends to come up in the late afternoon. Perfect for picnicking.

Windward Explorer

This side of Oahu is a celebration of beaches, bays and mountains. Some of the best beaches in the nation are on the windward side. We will get a close look at Kaneohe Bay, and we'll get near to the mountains too. On the windward side the mountains are precipitous—so much so that they can't be climbed or hiked quite like those at the back of Honolulu. These mountains provide a dramatic backdrop for the beaches, bays and inlets along the coastline.

Kaneohe Bay has many faces; for recreation, for military activities and for commerce. The bay, mountains and winds are such that it's wetter on the windward side, which accounts for the heavy foliage throughout the area. It isn't unusual for people who live on the windward side, but work in Honolulu, to tell you they wouldn't think of driving back over the *pali* even on weekends once they're home. It's only 10 miles distance in most cases, but for windward-ites, the two areas are worlds apart.

GETTING THERE:

By car, get on Ala Wai Boulevard and turn right on McCully. Cross over the freeway and make an immediate left turn. Follow this for a short distance. At the stop sign, turn left again and then right, which will lead you to the freeway. Go on H-1 until you see the Pali Turnoff (Exit 21B). Go over the mountain to Kailua town and straight to Kalaheo Avenue. Turn right and follow this road until you reach a stop sign. Turn left at the stop sign and this road will lead you to Aalapapa.

PRACTICALITIES:

Any day of the week is a good time to wander along the windward shore from Lanikai to Kailua to Kaneohe. Sometimes rainshowers pop up, but they are usually in the late afternoon or evening.

Bring sunglasses, sunscreen, hat, and sandals for beach walking; and a swim suit if you're so inclined. A simple beach mat might come in handy. Don't leave anything in your car, locked or unlocked.

FOOD AND DRINK:

The food on the windward side is eclectic at best. Our suggestions are a contrast that range from plate lunches to fine dining with a view.

Buzz's Original Steak House (413 Kawailoa Rd. just over the bridge) Casual dining in an idyllic South Seas atmosphere near the beach. Steaks, seafood and a great all-you-can-eat salad bar. No credit cards. Lunch and dinner daily. ☎ 261-4661. $$

Koolau Ranch House (46-077 Kamehameha Hwy. in Kaneohe) Complete menu from burgers to Super Sandwiches, fish and a selected Japanese Menu. Try the Hawaiian-style chop steak. Breakfast, lunch and dinner daily. ☎ 247-3900. $

The Deli (46-499 Kamehameha Hwy. at the end of Heeia Pier) The fishermen and other local types enjoy the plate lunches that rotate with such selections as luau beef stew and mochi chicken. Sit outside to eat. Breakfast & lunch daily. ☎ 235-2192. $

Chart House at Haiku Garden (46-336 Haiku Rd.) Set in a tropical rain forest; enjoy steaks, fresh seafood daily. Overlooks lovely Haiku Gardens, site of many weddings. Dinner daily. Reservations ☎ 247-6671. $$ to $$$

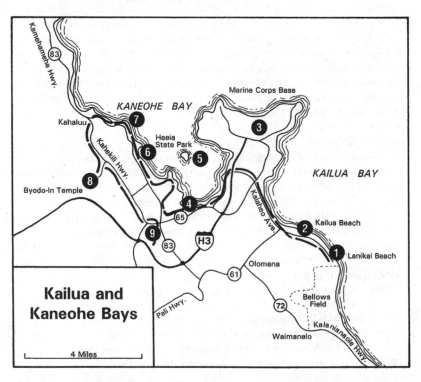

Kailua and Kaneohe Bays

4 Miles

SUGGESTED TOUR:
Numbers in parentheses correspond to numbers on the map.
When you reach Aalapapa in Lanikai, follow it around to the end when the road turns into Mokulua. This is a very friendly, comfortable neighborhood of mostly modest beach-type homes. There are some monster houses along Mokulua that front the beach. The road is one-way with a bike lane usually fairly busy with joggers and bikers. Find Haokea Drive, park and take the right-of-way to the beach. In 1996, **Lanikai Beach** (1) was voted the best beach in the nation by University of Maryland coastal geologist Stephen Leatherman, know as "Dr. Beach." We will hear more about Stephen as we proceed. For strolling, this beach is tops. For swimming, the water is almost always calm and comforting. Few people besides residents find their way here, so it is never crowded. Take the time and sit or stretch out on your beach mat to enjoy the sun, sand and water. After all, you're doing it on the best beach in America! The two smallish islands on the right are the Mokulua Islands. As you look left, you will see a rather large land mass jutting out into the water. This is actually a peninsula that houses an active military facility.

Drive back the way you came to **Kailua Beach Park** (2). You can either park across from Buzz's, or follow along the road and turn at the next beach park sign. Now, we even have competition among beaches in Hawaii for national ranking. We just visited Lanikai as #1. Kailua Beach, on the other hand, was voted #2 by Stephen Leatherman. In this case, being #2 is good for this reason: #1 gets dropped off the list for 10 years, so Lanikai is gone from the rankings. Kailua has been #2 for several years and is very content with that ranking because it stays on the list. By the way, Stephen lists six of the top 20 beaches in the nation in Hawaii. Whatever. At the very beginning of Kailua Beach you will often see dozens of colorful windsurfers darting out to the surf and then screaming back into the beach taking full advantage of the constant, offshore breezes on this part of Oahu. If you feel intrepid enough to try it, sometimes there are rental companies on this part of the beach. They give lessons, too, in the fine art of balancing on an elongated surfboard while sailing.

A walk along the beach is another treat. Note the beach-type homes as you make your way down the sand. There seem to be more people on Kailua beach than Lanikai, but it's still far from crowded. Each year in February, the architecture students from the University of Hawaii enter a sand-castle building contest on Kailua Beach. Some of the designs are intricate beyond belief.

When you leave the beach park, turn right on Kalaheo Avenue. Follow this road as it winds through homes set back from the beach. At the stop light, the cross street is Mokapu Boulevard, which leads to the entrance of the 2,951-acre **Marine Corps Base Hawaii** (3). What a spot for the 9,000 active-duty military and approximately 1,600 civilians who work here! It's not always possible because of schedules, but if you have an interest in visiting the base, call ahead to Community Relations at ☎ 257-5744. They sometimes can arrange a tour.

When you go straight ahead, you are now on Kaneohe Bay Drive, which for the next two miles twists and turns along the bay shoreline until you come to the continuation of Mokapu Boulevard. Turn right. Periodically, you can catch a good glimpse of the bay as you drive. A suggested stop is the **Bay View Golf Links** (4), 45-285 Kaneohe Bay Drive, simply because of the view of the bay. There's also innovative miniature golf, and a regular 18-hole golf course. ☎ *247-0451 for starting times.*

At the next major intersection, bear right onto Kamehameha Highway. About half a mile into town, turn right on William Henry Road. Turn left at Wailele Road and then right on Lilipuna Road. Now we are taking you up close and personal with Kaneohe Bay. This narrow, windy road exposes the bay in all its splendor.

At a slight rise, on the right is the fabled **Coconut Island** (5), now used mostly by the University of Hawaii for marine research. It's past, however, it quite interesting, and it served as the opening scene for *Gilligan's Island.* In the 1930s, Fleischman Yeast heir Christian Holmes acquired the island and added about 12 acres for a total of 25. According to a report in the Honolulu *Advertiser,* "Holmes is said to have spent much of his time at numerous wet bars that dotted the island. He also built fishponds to provide him with a constant supply of fresh fish."

California industrialist Edwin Pauley bought the island in 1946 and helped establish what is now called the University of Hawaii Institute of Marine Biology. In the Japanese investment invasion of the 1980s, billionaire Katsuhiro Kawaguchi purchased the island for his own use. But he had a criminal record that he didn't report, so he was deported, forcing him to sell the island. To complete the circle, in 1995 the Pauley Foundation gave the University of Hawaii Foundation a grant to buy the island and make improvements to its research labs.

At the stop light, turn right onto Kamehameha Highway. The next stop is **Heeia State Park** (6). ☎ *247-3156, open from 7–6:45 during the school year and an hour later during the summer.* The park is actually a spit of land extending into Kaneohe Bay that is the water end of the traditional land division called *ahupuaa.* This means a piece of land that extends from the mountains to the sea, generally in a wedge shape. In ancient Hawaii the king gave *alii* or royalty *ahupuaa* throughout the islands. Later, some nonnatives acquired or were given *ahupuaa.* The park features a rich garden of indigenous plants and trees, an ancient fishpond and live coral reefs. The facilities include a visitor center used for workshops, lectures and classes; an exhibit hall with displays of marine life, coral, native flora, ethnobotany and ecology; and a gift shop usually open during the weekdays. No admission fee.

Almost next door is the **Heeia Kea Boat Harbor** (7). Besides working and recreational fishing boats, other water activities are available on the pier. Kaneohe Bay Cruises offers glass-bottom boat rides four times a day Mondays through Saturdays for under $10. They also offer snorkeling and swimming tours. *Call 235-2888.* Captain Bob's has a bay cruise from 10:30 to 2:30 Mondays through Saturdays that includes snorkeling, a BBQ picnic, swimming, barefoot sailing, glass-bottom viewing and Hawaiian-style water volleyball. All this for under $70. The pier is also good for people watching, including the card game that goes on all day long outside The Deli plate lunch restaurant.

At the next stop sign, turn left onto Kahekili Highway. At Valley of the Temples Memorial Park, turn right and head toward the back of the park to the:

*BYODO-IN TEMPLE (8), 47-200 Kahekili Hwy., Kaneohe, HI 96744, ☎ 239-8811. *Open daily 8:30–5. Adults $2, seniors and kids 12–18 $1.* &.

Nested at the foot of misty mountains is the Byodo-In Temple, finished in the summer of 1968 and a replica of a wooden temple built in Japan in the shape of a Phoenix. This is a mystical bird representing life and spiritual hope. The gardens exude calm. They are the largest of their kind outside of Japan, and are designed to reflect traditional grace and serenity. The reflecting ponds surrounding the temple are home to more than 10,000 carp. Inside the temple is the largest wooden Buddha carved in 900 years.

Continue on Kahekili Highway and follow the signs to Kailua. You will loop around and find yourself heading back toward Kaneohe. Turn right on Kamehameha Highway. Look for Luluku Road and turn right. This will take you to the **Hoomaluhia Botanical Garden** (9). The name means "a place of peace and tranquillity." This 400-acre park includes a lake, campground, walking trails and picnic areas. The Visitor Center has an exhibition hall used by local artists, a workshop and botanical library and the largest collection of tropical plants in the United States. You will see many varieties of palms, aroids, heliconias and tropical trees. Guided nature hikes are offered at 10 a.m. on Saturdays and 1 p.m. on Sundays. *Call 233-7323 for more information and to register.*

Surrounding this peaceful park is the most expensive highway built in America. It is called H-3 and it has been not only costly, but very controversial. Since it travels through Moanalua Valley on the other side of the *pali,* some Hawaiian groups have protested for years that the highway has destroyed ancient burial grounds and *heiaus* (outdoor temples). If you want to return to Honolulu on this freeway, go back to Kamehameha Highway and follow signs to H-3.

Trip 11

Manoa Adventure

There are lots of valleys within urban Honolulu, but none quite like Manoa. History, culture, recreation, and the arts are all packed into this wonderful piece of real estate. The valley is anchored by the University of Hawaii. This state school has two others campuses—in Hilo on the Big Island and West Oahu—but the Manoa campus is the mothership with about 25,000 students. As might be expected, the UH (as locals call it) has gained a wide reputation for ocean sciences and astronomy, the latter because of the many telescopes and astronomical facilities atop Mauna Kea on the Big Island (see Daytrip 25). It also has an Hawaiian Studies program, with its own handsome set of buildings, lead by a controversial lady of Hawaiian ancestry. Besides the educational component of the valley, it has long had attraction for many of Hawaii's business and government leaders and thus you will see quite a few gracious homes. A very large stone mansion on Manoa Road is still owned by descendants of the Cooke family of Castle & Cooke and Dole Pineapple fame. Perhaps the frequent rain showers that keep the valley cool and very green is one reason the wealthy have settled in Manoa. Manoa is also a microcosm of the many ethnic groups that have long existed in Hawaii. They have left their mark in temples and cemeteries and other public buildings.

GETTING THERE:

By car, get on Ala Wai Boulevard and turn right on McCully. It turns into Metcalf. Go to the end, which will be University Avenue, turn right and then left at the next light on Dole Street. You are now on the campus of the University of Hawaii. The next turn will be at East-West Road, where you will turn left. The parking is controlled on the campus from 6:30–4 Monday through Friday, so at the parking booth you will have to pay $3 for the day. Parking on campus is free on weekends and holidays. Visitor parking is a left turn around the booth which takes you right behind Kennedy Theatre.

PRACTICALITIES:

There's always more going on during the school year and on weekdays, but it is a nice place to visit any time. If school is out, you might miss some art shows, plays and the like, but can still enjoy the buildings and grounds.

Bring sunglasses, sunscreen, hat and comfortable shoes. As you go deeper into the valley, mosquito repellent is a good idea. Don't leave anything in your car, locked or unlocked.

FOOD AND DRINK:

Paesano Ristorante Italiano (2752 Woodlawn in the Manoa Marketplace) It's a puzzle how a Vietnamese family can turn out such superb Italian food, but they do. Lunch Mon.–Sat. Dinner daily. Reservations, ☎ 988-5923. $$

Shipley's Ale House & Grill (Manoa Marketplace) Good Northwestern cuisine in a woody atmosphere with the largest selection of beers and ales in Hawaii including bitter, pale, brown, Belgian and Hawaiian. Lunch & dinner daily. ☎ 988-5555. $$

Beau Soleil (2970 E. Manoa Rd.) A small place that serves up inventive breakfast and lunch daily. Sunday brunch. Specials each day. ☎ 988-1336. $-$$

Waloli Tea Room (2950 Manoa Rd.) Lovely setting in huge trees. Like Old Hawaii where Robert Louis Stevenson used to come for lunch. Serves sandwiches, soups, salads. Bakery. Gift Shop. Open 8–6 daily. ☎ 988-5800. $

SUGGESTED TOUR:

Numbers in parentheses correspond to numbers on map.

Since you have already parked behind the **Kennedy Theatre** (1), walk around to the front to see what is playing. If it's during the school year, there are frequent plays and dance productions put on by students and faculty. Some are original dramas written and produced by the students. *Box Office* ☎ *956-7655.*

Across the street at 1777 East-West Road is Jefferson Hall or the Hawaii Imin International Conference Center. This is the main building of the **East-West Center** (2) on the University of Hawaii Manoa Campus. The Center was established by Congress over 20 years ago to build bridges with Asia. The idea is that America has been focused on Europe for most of its history, yet growth and ideas are booming throughout Asia, and our interests will be well served by studying this important part of the world. A small number of students come from Asian countries to study at the Center each year. There are seminars and conferences among Asian and American leaders as well. The decision to place it in Hawaii was made primarily because of the state's position in the middle of the Pacific and because of the strong Asian population in the state.

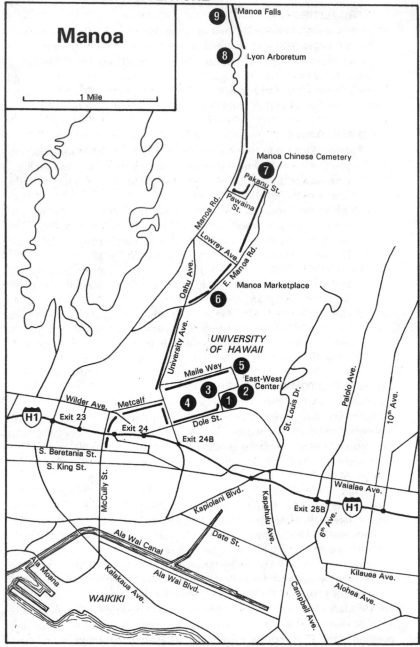

Manoa

1 Mile

Manoa Falls

Lyon Arboretum

Manoa Chinese Cemetery

Pakanu St.

Pawaina St.

Manoa Rd.

Lowrey Ave.

Oahu Ave.

E. Manoa Rd.

Manoa Marketplace

University Ave.

UNIVERSITY OF HAWAII

Maile Way

East-West Center

St. Louis Dr.

Palolo Ave.

10th Ave.

Wilder Ave.   Metcalf

H1   Exit 23

Dole St.

Exit 24

Exit 24B

S. Beretania St.

S. King St.

McCully St.

Waialae Ave.

Kapiolani Blvd.

Kapahulu Ave.

Exit 25B   H1

6th Ave.

Ala Wai Canal

Date St.

Kilauea Ave.

Ala Moana

Kalakaua Ave.

Ala Wai Blvd.

Campbell Ave.

Alohea Ave.

WAIKIKI

Visit Jefferson Hall and be sure to see the **Japanese Gardens** behind it. Interestingly, Japanese visitors frequently hold weddings in the gardens, so from a social point of view at least, the Center is accomplishing its mission. The timelessness of all the East-West Center buildings was created by world-renowned architect I.M. Pei.

Cross over East-West Road, and just before Henke Hall take the pathway. This will lead you through the main campus quadrangle. Just as you get to the end of this pathway, on the left, is the **Art Building** (3). The building alone makes a statement about the commitment of the University to the visual arts. If school is in session, you will see all manner of painting, sculpture and drawing underway. Be sure to visit the Student Art gallery in Building 144. *Open during the school year Mon.–Fri., 10–4 and Sunday from noon to 3. Closed Saturdays and holidays.* ☎ *956-2212 to find out about special showings.*

As you bend around to the left, soon you will see the **Campus Center** (4). There is another Art gallery in Room 313, and the bookstore in the lower level. If you are in need of books, one advantage of buying them here is you do not pay the 4 percent state sales tax.

From the Campus Center, walk out Farrington Road and turn right on Maile Way. This short walk will bring you back to East-West Road; straight ahead is the elaborate **Center for Korean Studies** (5). If you've never seen a Korean temple before, take time to study the exterior including the intricacy of the decorations—especially on the roof supports and soffits. All the colors and designs are meant to ward off evil spirits. It can't be entered.

Go back down East-West Road, and after you get to your car, you can leave the campus by going out Maile Way. At the stop light, turn right on University Avenue. Follow this road until you come to the next stop light and turn right at East Manoa Road. About a half mile on the right is the **Manoa Valley Theater** (6) at 2833 East Manoa Road. As you walk back to the newish theater building, you will be passing through an old Hawaiian cemetery. At one time, the Manoa annex of fabled Kawaihao Church in downtown stood where the theater is now. Purportedly, this was where the country Hawaiians worshiped as opposed to the city Hawaiians in downtown at Kawaihao. The church still owns the land and the theater pays it rent. This small theater produces six shows a year from September to June. All are Hawaii premieres since they are mostly off-Broadway productions. *Box Office* ☎ *988-6131.*

Continue on East Manoa Road until you see the **Manoa Chinese Cemetery** (7) straight ahead. This cemetery was established in the 1880s on a hilltop in Manoa to honor the early Chinese immigrants. If you walk up to the small observation pavilion at the top, there is a stunning view of the whole valley down to Waikiki.

Turn right on Pakanu Street and then right again on Pawaina Street. This will take you to Manoa Road where you will turn right again. The road narrows as you approach what used to be a large bird park. Big trees and heavy foliage characterize this part of Manoa due to the heavier rainfall. Keep going until the road narrows to a single car width and this will take you to the **Harold L. Lyon Arboretum** (8) 3860 Manoa Road. Mr. Lyon was a university professor who specialized in botany and the school established (and now runs) this pleasant facility to demonstrate its capability in plant species work. *Open Mon.–Sat. 9 to 3.* ☎ *988-7378 for special events.*

If you still have the energy, there is a three-quarters of a mile hike up to **Manoa Falls** (9). Continue on up the trail past the arboretum. You will follow Manoa Stream most of the way passing under huge trees that seem like a tropical jungle. The hiking is only rugged when you cross a couple of patches of deep roots. The vertical climb is mild, and the falls give off a nice cooling mist. Depending on how full the falls are, some people take a dip in the pool at the base. Do not hike beyond the falls.

*Punchbowl/Tantalus/ Roundtop

The area right above downtown Honolulu holds some fascinating tour opportunities. One of the best known is the cemetery in an extinct volcano usually called "Punchbowl." It is the final resting place for veterans of three wars. The hills behind downtown are readily accessible via a road that winds through tall trees and foliage very much like a rainforest. The whole area is laced with hiking trails that go through yellow and white ginger and a thick bamboo forest. Koa and ohia trees, and many other varieties known only in Hawaii, are evident almost around every turn.

At the end of this daytrip, we'll see contemporary art displayed in a lovely old mansion built by one of Honolulu's first families. The circuitous Tantalus/Roundtop drive is only ten miles long, but if straightened out it would span a mere two miles. Meanwhile, no matter where you are in this whole tour, the views are stunning.

GETTING THERE:

By car, get on Ala Wai Boulevard and turn right on McCully. Cross over the freeway and make an immediate left turn. Follow this street to the stop sign and turn left again and then right. This will lead you to the freeway. Continue on H-1 for about a mile and a half and get off at Exit 22/Vineyard Boulevard. At the second stop light, turn right on Queen Emma Street, which becomes Lusitana Street after crossing over the freeway. Watch for relatively small green signs that say, "Veterans Administration, National Memorial Cemetery of the Pacific."

PRACTICALITIES:

As mentioned before, it is a good idea to take only what you can carry in your pockets, a fanny pack or a small purse. Leaving things in the car— even in the trunk—is not a good idea. Even if you don't plan to take pictures, but have your camera in the car, take it with you when you get out.

Bring sunglasses, sunscreen, a hat and shoes suitable for gentle hiking should you plan to take a jaunt down one of the many trails in this area.

FOOD AND DRINK:

The Contemporary Café (2411 Makiki Heights Dr.) A tree-shaded garden setting offers a wide selection of salads, sandwiches, chef's specials and homemade desserts. Open Tues.–Sun. for lunch. Closed Mon. ☎ 523-3362. $ to $$

Pacific Chop Suey (1997 Pauoa Rd.) Low-key eatery serving a wide selection of Cantonese food. Their soups—when available—are among the best in town. Open daily for lunch and dinner. ☎ 536-4202. $

The Hungry Lion Coffee Shop (1613 Nuuanu) Built around a giant banyan tree, this coffee shop-type restaurant is open 24 hours, seven days a week. Good value. ☎ 536-1188. $

SUGGESTED TOUR:

Numbers in parentheses correspond to numbers on the map.

After you leave the freeway and head toward the hills, Punchbowl will loom on your right.

*NATIONAL MEMORIAL CEMETERY OF THE PACIFIC and the HONOLULU MEMORIAL (1), 2177 Puowaina Dr., Honolulu, HI 96813, ☎ 546-3190. *Open Mar.–Sept. 8–6:30; Sept.–Mar. 8–5:30. Free. Parking at designated lots within the Memorial.* ♿.

The memorial is located in Puowaina Crater, which means Consecrated Hill or Hill of Sacrifice. It got that name because it was the site of many secret *Alii* (Hawaiian Royalty) burials. Offenders of certain *kapu* were sacrificed here, and in the early 1800s, the crater was an important stronghold for those Hawaiians who fought against Kamehameha's invasion of Oahu.

It became a permanent cemetery site when major objections were made to the temporary WWII burial sites in the central and south Pacific areas. It is one of two hallowed resting places in the vast Pacific, with the other being in the Philippines.

As you enter Punchbowl, a tree-shaded road leads straight ahead to the Honolulu Memorial. On the left is the Overlook Area and to the right is the Committal Court and Columbarium. The first internments in the 116-acre Punchbowl were in January, 1949. As of mid-year 1997, there were nearly 40,000 service men and women buried at Punchbowl with another 29,000 memorialized.

The Honolulu Memorial was built in 1964 to honor the sacrifices and achievements of American Armed Forces in the Pacific during World War II and in the Korean War. In 1980, it was enlarged to encompass the Missing of the Vietnam War. It consists of a nonsectarian chapel, two map galleries, a monumental stairway leading from the crater floor to the Court of Honor; ten Courts of the Missing, five flanking each side of the stairway and a Ded-

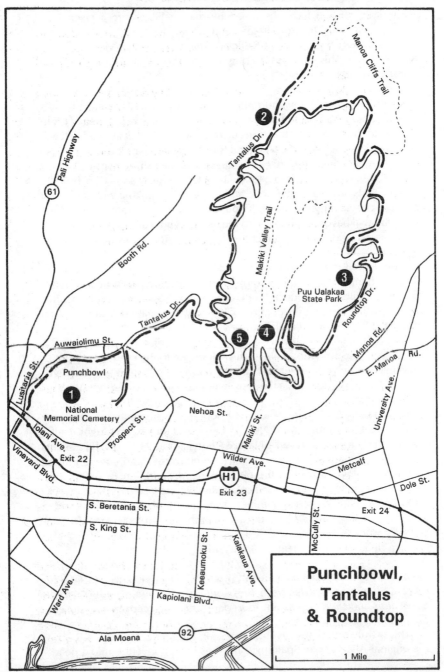

Punchbowl, Tantalus & Roundtop

1 Mile

icatory Stone. If you have the time, the map galleries are a fascinating depiction of the WWII battles in the Pacific.

The reward of a visit to the Overlook Area is a sweeping view of downtown Honolulu. This area was the original site of Puowaina Crater's sacrificial rock.

As you leave Punchbowl, turn right on Tantalus Drive. There are houses for another three-quarters of a mile, but soon you will be in a heavily foliated area as the road twists and turns up to about 1,000 feet above sea level. There are frequent overlook areas and it is suggested that you stop at these as they give different views of Honolulu. As the road straightens for a short distance after about three miles, look on the left for the **Manoa Cliff Trail** (2). This trail starts down a gentle slope and you will be walking with an almost complete tree canopy overhead. If you follow it the whole way, about 3.5 miles, you will have to walk back on the road to your car or retrace the trail. Better to go in about a mile and enjoy the foliage and views, and then hike back out.

Another half-mile up and you reach about 1,500 feet above sea level as the road changes name to Roundtop Drive. Continue down Roundtop for about three miles until you see **Puu Ualakaa State Park** (3) on the right. This lovely opening in the forested area offers another great view of Honolulu and Waikiki. Walk out onto the grassy area to fully enjoy the scene.

Turn right when you leave the park; at a short distance on the left is a wide-open view of Manoa Valley. This wide spot in the road is very popular with Japanese visitors—it has almost become a "must" among Asian visitors—who stream up here in the early evening in long white limos. Perhaps you will agree.

As you near the lower portions of Roundtop, a grassy area will appear on your right. Look for Makiki Heights Drive and turn sharply right. Half a mile up the road is the **Hawaii Nature Center** (4) at 2121 Makiki Heights Drive. The primary aim of the Center is to educate island children about their unique environment in the out-of-doors. In addition to school programs that includes 30 hands-on displays, the Nature Center provides weekend nature education for families and adults that includes guided interpretive hikes, nature adventures, and earth-care projects. *Free.* ☎ *955-0100 for weekend hikes.*

Turn right on Makiki Heights Drive and go up about one mile to:

*THE CONTEMPORARY MUSEUM (5), 2411 Makiki Heights Dr., ☎ 526-0232. *Galleries and garden open Tues.–Sat. 10–4, Sunday noon–4. Adults $5, Seniors and children 12+ $3. Tours daily at 1:30 (except Mon.). Museum Shop.*

This is truly one of the loveliest places in Honolulu. Built on 3.5 acres, the original Alice Cooke Spalding estate has been converted into a peaceful—and at the same time stimulating—experience as the Contemporary Museum. The gardens alone are worth the price of admission. They were created between 1928 and 1941 by the Rev. K.H. Inagaki, a Japanese Christian minister and landscape gardener living in Hawaii. Transforming a barren ravine below the sloping lawns into a secluded valley garden, Rev. Inagaki's intention was to create a retreat in which to meditate and experience the beauty and harmony of nature. In the late 1970s, the gardens were revamped and restored. With the subsequent addition of selected pieces of sculpture from the permanent collection, the gardens provide both a natural setting for works of art and—now more than ever—a quiet place for contemplation and renewal.

The museum consists of five galleries in the main building, as well as the Cades Pavilion. The museum's principal activity is the presentation of temporary exhibitions of works in all media by artists of local, national and international reputation.

Trip 13

Haleiwa/Waimea

Now we're going to get serious about discovering the North Shore. Once there, our range will only be about four miles from Haleiwa to Waimea Bay and Valley. But there's lots to see and do in that short distance.

Today, the North Shore is really about surfing. Years ago it was agriculture, but most of that is gone now. During the winter months when the surf reaches 30 feet at Waimea Bay and points beyond, young men and women from around the world are drawn in droves to this part of the island. When the surf gets unusually high, Hawaii residents come out from town too—just to look—and the traffic can back up for miles on weekends. It may sound a little strange to drive out to the North Shore just to gawk at some waves, but the show can be dramatic and powerful. That makes the trip understandable. And when you see the surfers actually ride those monsters, that can be thrilling.

If surfing isn't your thing, there's plenty of other activities like biking and sport fishing to keep you amused. The city and state have done an excellent job of building parks all along this route. That means good beaching and picnicking too.

GETTING THERE:
By car, get on Ala Wai Boulevard and turn right on McCully. Cross over the freeway and make an immediate left turn. Follow this street to the stop sign and turn left again and then right. This will lead you to the freeway. Continue on H-1 for about 12 miles and begin to look for signs to H-2 and Wahiawa. Get off at Exit 8A. As the freeway ends, do not get off at Wahiawa, but follow signs to Schofield Barracks and Route 99. About a mile and half after the end of the freeway, turn right on Kamananui Road. At the stop sign turn left on Kamehameha Highway and follow the signs into Haleiwa Town.

PRACTICALITIES:
To the mantra of sunglasses, sunscreen, and hat you might add a swim suit and beach mat so you always have the option of sitting on a beach and/or taking a swim if the mood strikes. No need to take picnic stuff since

you can get it all right there. Take everything with you when you leave your car, locked or unlocked.

FOOD AND DRINK:

Aloha Joe's (66-011 Kamehameha Hwy.) Tasty steaks and seafood in neat setting overlooking the boat harbor. Relaxing atmosphere. Lunch and dinner daily. Reservations suggested for dinner, ☎ 637-8005. $$

Jameson's by the Sea (62-540 Kamehameha Hwy.) This is a three-in-one with delicious burger-type pub lunches daily, fine dining upstairs Wed.–Sun., and a fun gallery, gift shop and fudge works. Dinner reservations, ☎ 637-4336. $$ to $$$

Portofino (66-258 Kamehameha Hwy.) Casual Italian cuisine. Many entrees baked in wood-burning oven to create healthful dishes including roasted veggies. Breakfast, lunch and dinner daily. ☎ 637-7678. $ to $$

Kua Aina (66-214 Kamehameha Hwy.) World-renowned burgers made with special sauce (it's Vermouth based) in a wide variety to satisfy every taste. Usually long lines. Lunch and dinner daily. ☎ 637-6067. $

LOCAL ATTRACTIONS:

Numbers in parentheses correspond to numbers on the map.

Haleiwa is a fun spot for wandering, shopping and eating. The first suggested stop is at the **North Shore Marketplace** (1), 62-250 Kamehameha Highway, where you will find the **North Shore Surf and Cultural Museum.** The name sounds a little pretentious for this smallish facility that "preserves the legacy of the North Shore—from surfing and fishing to sugar growing and Hawaiian culture," according to a recent newspaper article. Curator Lynn Oakley says about the surfing side of the museum, "that a lot of the old-timers are looking at their role in surfing and seeing now that as they get older, they want to preserve and cherish and dignify and respect their history here on the North Shore." Well worth a visit. *The museum is open 10–6 daily. Donations appreciated.* ☎ *637-3334.*

In the same shopping complex is **Raging Isle Sports,** which is a combination surf and bicycle shop. These guys have it figured out since some of the best surfing and biking in Hawaii is on this part of Oahu. You can cruise the shore or go into the mountains with a rental from Raging Isle. A full-suspension mountain bike with helmet, lock and tools rents for around $35 a day. They throw in a waterbottle for you to keep. It's a good idea to make a reservation for a bike at ☎ 637-7700.

A visit to Haleiwa without eating a shave ice from the **M. Matsumoto Grocery Store & Shave Ice** is sinful. Be prepared to stand in line for a cup of ice with flavoring that is out of this world. Others can only compare them

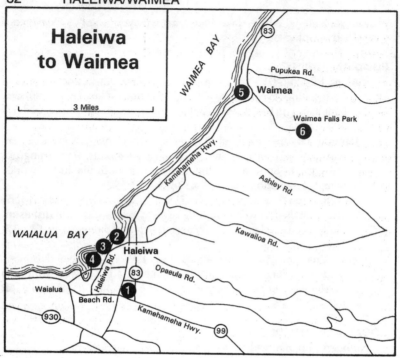

Haleiwa
to Waimea

3 Miles

WAIMEA BAY

83

Pupukea Rd.

5 Waimea

Waimea Falls Park
6

Kamehameha Hwy.

Ashley Rd.

Kawailoa Rd.

WAIALUA BAY

2
3
Haleiwa
4
Haleiwa Rd.
Opaeula Rd.
83

Waialua
Beach Rd.
1
930
Kamehameha Hwy.
99

selves to Matsumoto. The place has been there forever, and yes, one of the founders still works in the store most days of the week. You can get your picnic stuff there too if that is in your plans. *66-087 Kamehameha Hwy.* ☎ *637-4827. Open daily 8:30–6.*

There are many fun shops in Haleiwa, but another intriguing small one is **Ralston Antiques and Collectibles** at 66-030 Kamehameha Highway. This shop, in an old bank branch, is owned by Rick Ralston, who is the founder of Crazy Shirts. For many years he has been an antique collector, and as his collection grew too big for its storage area, he decided to open a shop and share some of his treasures with others. The antique Hawaiiana is especially interesting, including the lamp with a hula girl who moves her hips when the light is on. *Open Wed.–Sun. 10:30–6.* ☎ *637-8837.*

As you turn left on Haleiwa Road, you will see the **Haleiwa Boat Harbor** (2) on your right. This small marina holds some goodies for those who like to venture out onto the water. **Chupu Charters** takes out small groups in their 40' boat for sportfishing and turtle, dolphin and whale watching (the latter during the season, which is usually from mid-December through April). *They go out most days, but it's a good idea to call them for reservations at 637-3474. Rates are: full day from 7–6 around $100, half-day from 7–1; inquire.* If they're full by any chance, **Kuuloa Kai Sportfishing** offers about the same services. Their rates are a minimum of $300 up to three people. *Reservations can be made at* ☎ *637-5783.* If you're looking for speed, then perhaps a jetski rented by **Connection Watercraft** is for you. They take you out of the harbor on a boat-like platform, and once out in calm waters, the jetskis are launched from there. You can zoom around out in the ocean for a half hour for about $35, or a hour for $60. *Call 637-8006.* For those who want a calmer water experience, **Northstar Catamaran Sail** offers a slew of ocean activities such as snorkeling, whale watching, picnics and sunset sails. The nice thing about their 40' boat is the stability provided by the two pontoons that make it a catamaran. *A four-hour snorkel/picnic from 10:20–2:30 is $54. A sunset sail for two hours is about $30. Times vary depending on the time of year, so call 638-8279 for times and a reservation.*

When you come out of the boat harbor, turn right on Haleiwa Road. First you will come to **Haleiwa Alii Beach Park** (3). This grassy area leads to a pretty good surfing beach. Lots of activity here on the weekends since this is a favorite with residents. *Open 6 a.m.–10 p.m.* Just half a mile down the road to the right is **Kaiaka Beach Park** (4). You can usually have this spacious area all to yourself, except perhaps for some campers now and then (camping at state beach parks in Hawaii requires a permit which you can get by calling (808) 587-0300, but call early because popular parks on popular holidays fill up very quickly). The white sand beach here is lined with ironwoods, and off to the left is a wonderful little bay. The old Waialua Sugar Mill can be seen in the distance. What makes this park so special is that the wide reef creates a series of small waves that roll in continuously in that soothing ocean sound; combined with the gentle rustle of the ironwoods, this is a place for relaxation. The water is not for swimming because of the reef, which is all the more reason to sit on your beach mat to vegetate and enjoy.

Go back out Haleiwa Road and turn left on Kamehameha Highway. About three miles down the road on the left—just over a slight rise—is Waimea Bay. The water and waves are usually pretty manageable during the summer months, but during the winter the big ones can reach an awesome 30 feet. **Waimea Beach Park** (5) is a favorite for swimmers, surfers and sunbathers. *Open 7 a.m.–7:45 p.m.* Nearby is:

*WAIMEA FALLS PARK (6), 59-864 Kamehameha Hwy., ☎ 638-8511. *Open daily from 10–5:30. Cliff diving show starts at 11:15 and is held about every hour until 5. Adults $19.95, children 6–12 $9.95. &.*

This whole area was a special place for the early Hawaiians for many reasons. Foremost was the beauty created by the lush foliage. It was a sacred place too, because around 1470 the Hawaiians built a *heiau* (or open-air temple) dedicated to the god Lono. Today, this 1,800-acre park offers a fascinating scope of activities. You can walk or take a free tram throughout the park so you can enjoy the exotic plants and flowers and see the actual site of an ancient Hawaiian village and temple. As you visit the restored Hawaiian living site, you can listen to native storytellers, learn Hawaiian crafts and test your skills with the games of Hawaiian warriors. At the top of the tour, Waimea Falls makes a magnificent backdrop for fearless divers who leap from a cliff above and somersault down 62 feet into the lagoon below.

There's an active side to the park as well. It offers All Terrain Vehicle rides called "Land Surfing," for rates between $20 and $75 depending on the time and whether park admission is included. Downhill mountain bike adventures in remote areas of the park are available at $35 for a two-hour tour, and kayaking in the Waimea River runs $15 per person. Most of these activities require an additional charge for admittance.

Schofield/Waialua/ Mokuleia

This trip will provide you with some low, medium and high adventures. We will go through the middle of the island with its expanse of agriculture, and dip down to touch the north shore. Sugar and pineapple used to rule on this part of Oahu, but sugar is gone and you might say pineapple is an endangered species—at least here. The land has become too valuable for commodity crops that can be grown elsewhere for half the cost of those raised in Hawaii.

Because of that fact, Castle & Cooke, the owner of Dole Pineapple and its huge fields in central Oahu, decided about 20 years ago that it would create a whole new town called Mililani. It did so out of pineapple lands at the highest point on the saddle between the Koolau and Waianae mountains. Some other large Hawaii landowners chose to do the same with their former ag lands, but it most cases they created resorts. Mililani Town is now home to nearly 4,000 Oahu families.

More and more, activities and attractions for visitors are popping up all over the place in this part of Oahu—from riding a horse along a gorgeous north shore beach to strolling through a man-made tropical rainforest. This is good for visitors who can pick and choose on this daytrip.

GETTING THERE:

By car, get on Ala Wai Boulevard and turn right on McCully. Cross over the freeway and make an immediate left turn. Follow this street to the stop sign and turn left again and then right. This will lead you to the freeway. Continue on H-I for about 12 miles and begin to look for signs to H-2 and Wahiawa.

PRACTICALITIES:

Sunscreen, sunglasses, hat and water. Don't be tempted to leave anything in your car, locked or unlocked.

FOOD AND DRINK:

Rex's Steak & Seafood (95-221 Kipapa Dr. in Mililani Shopping Center) Nice variety of meals to choose from. Their specialty is prime rib slow-roasted daily with a special spice blend. Open for lunch and dinner daily. ☎ 623-2544. $ to $$

Maile Seafood Chinese Restaurant (95-221 Kipapa Dr. in Mililani Shopping Center) With almost 150 Chinese dishes to choose from, you won't go hungry. Combination plates and lunch specials. Open for lunch and dinner daily. ☎ 623-2221. $ to $$

Sugar Bar & Pizza Garden (67-069 Kealohanui in Waialua) This noisy joint is just down a bumpy road from the now-closed sugar mill. Narrow, tall building once was a branch of the Bank of Hawaii. Pizzas and calzones. Lunch and dinner daily. ☎ 637-6989. $

Dot's in Wahiawa (130 Mango) American and Japanese fare served in an atmosphere reminiscent of the early days when sugar and pineapple were king. Lunch and dinner daily. ☎ 622-4115. $

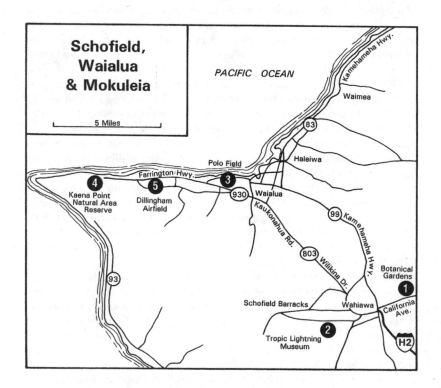

Schofield, Waialua & Mokuleia

SUGGESTED TOUR:

Numbers in parentheses correspond to numbers on the map.

Go into Wahiawa, which is a town of contrasts because it straddles two very different cultures: agriculture and the military with Schofield Barracks next door. It can get chilly in the evening on the heights above the town because of the altitude, and it rains 80–100 inches a year. Sitting in the middle of town is Lake Wilson, created long ago by the sugar plantation to feed water to the voracious cane growing below.

Turn right on California Avenue and go up about half a mile. On the left is **Wahiawa Botanical Garden** (1). This 27-acre garden—sitting on the edge of a deep ravine—was originally a nursery and experimental station started in the 1920s by the sugar planters. What they wanted to do was find tropical plants and trees that would stop erosion along the many gulches found on their sugar lands on this part of the island. Being always thrifty, they thought it might make a good nursery at the same time. Their legacy is a man-made rainforest with an interesting collection of tropical trees and plants requiring a cooler environment. The garden was given to the City of Honolulu in 1950. *1396 California Ave. Open 9–4 daily. Free.* ☎ *621-7321.*

Leave Wahiawa the way you came, but follow the signs to **Schofield Barracks** (2). Since Schofield is now an "Open Post," (unlike most other military facilities where guards will stop you), you can freely enter the McComb Gate. Head straight for the **Tropic Lightning Museum.** It is located in Carter Hall on Waianae Avenue. There are exhibits on the Barracks and the 25th Infantry in World War II, Korea and Vietnam. What is especially interesting is the exhibit that shows the damage the Japanese did to Schofield during the Pearl Harbor raid. The Japanese Zeros flew straight down the center of Oahu with their main mission being the navy ships, but they also wanted to inflict damage on the Army's facility so they couldn't retaliate as fast. *Open 10–4 Tues.–Sat. Free.* ☎ *655-0438.*

When you leave Schofield, turn left on Wilikina. That will turn into Kaukonahua and eventually Farrington Highway. Enjoy the scenery as you go through ag lands and so start dropping down through ironwood trees to the junction of Waialua. Go toward Mokuleia. This is all former sugar lands. Periodically, you will see truck farms that grow fruits and vegetables for sale at supermarkets in Honolulu.

About two miles from the Waialua junction you will see on the right the **Hawaii International Polo Club** (3). The polo grounds were started by some of Honolulu's wealthier gentlemen over 30 years ago as a way to enjoy their favorite sport, but also to draw people out to this part of the island to sell them land. The Dillinghams and other elite families from town owned large tracts of land where they had ranches and beach cottages. Today, the polo season runs from March to September with matches every Sunday at 2 in the afternoon. It is quite a sight to sit watching an exciting polo match with the beautiful blue ocean as a backdrop. *Admission is $5.* ☎ *941-7656.*

You can enjoy going near that beach on a horse too. Go Noguchi is a polo instructor who takes groups for one-hour horseback rides above the shoreline at Mokuleia almost every day. If horses interest you at all, this is a special treat. Imagine yourself astride a polo pony (known for their agility and easy response to commands) making your way along a white sand beach with endless small waves creating that calming ocean sound. In the ironwood trees along the shoreline, the gentle breeze makes a rustling sound heard no where else. *Call him at either 941-7656 or 227-8399 to make a reservation.* The cost depends on the length of the ride, which can vary if a group has specified a longer ride, and is between $50–100.

As you leave the polo grounds, turn right. Pretty soon on your left will appear an airfield built originally by one of the scions of a prominent Honolulu family—both for his own use and to encourage others to fly out to this remote portion of the island. If you want to explore the coastline, go past the entrance gate and to the end of the road. At this point you are stopped by a gate to the **Kaena Point Natural Area Reserve** (4). For many years, the westernmost point of Oahu was desecrated by four-wheelers, motorcycles and others in just plain ordinary vehicles who tore up the fragile ecosystem. Several years ago the State of Hawaii put a stop to that by erecting strong gates. Now the whole area is a reserve with the plants and animals making a good comeback. You can take a walk along the trail/road. The wind and sea are more turbulent here. Enjoy the very remoteness that the state is trying hard to preserve.

Now things can get pretty exciting. On you way back, you will see an entrance gate to **Dillingham Field** (5). Today, this airfield is best known for attracting visitors for glider rides, aerobatic rides, flight instruction and sky diving. Soar Hawaii Sailplanes offers scenic glider rides along Oahu's famous north shore. You can experience the thrill and serenity of soaring, silently flying with only the whispering sound of the wind outside the cockpit. Along the way, you can see the lush Waianae Mountains, rugged cliffs, coral reefs and breaking surf. Depending on the length of the ride and weather conditions, you may see most of the island of Oahu including Pearl Harbor, Diamond Head and Honolulu.

For the especially intrepid, this company also offers aerobatic rides. This is the ultimate for the truly adventurous. You strap on a parachute and climb into the cockpit along with an experienced aerobatic pilot. The glider used for this type of flying is built stronger than most World War II fighter planes. Take a look at the world from a whole new perspective—upside down! Feel up to four Gs pushing you into your seat. You decide how many aerobatic maneuvers and what kind, mild or wild, you want. You call the shots. *All rides, one or two passenger, scenic or aerobatic, run between $120 and $160, depending on the time, which can be from 20 to 50 minutes. Open every day, weather permitting. Call 637-3147 for information and reservations.*

Foster Gardens/ Pali Lookout

The Nuuanu area spans about five miles of geography and about fifty years of fascinating royal history. A splendid display of tropical plants and trees anchors Nuuanu Valley where kings fought wars, a queen spent her summers in the cooler temperatures of the valley, and nowadays foreign consulates and churches proliferate. Tucked back into the valley are sizable homes of business titans, educators, a former governor, doctors and lawyers. It also provides the main artery between downtown and the windward side. When you are on one of the high ridges above the valley today, the noise of the Pali Highway is a constant hum, whereas when you take a side street away from this busy roadway, the silence and the canopy of trees and dense foliage can be very restful.

Nuuanu is also known for the elaborate water system the early Hawaiians established throughout the valley. Because the mountains at the pass are almost constantly in the clouds, rain falls nearly every day creating long, narrow waterfalls that can be seen on the right going toward Kailua. The early Hawaiians took advantage of all that moisture by building a system of collection ponds and ditches to bring the water under control and create a constant flow of water to their taro patches throughout Nuuanu valley. Evidence of this early engineering feat can still be seen today.

GETTING THERE:

By car, get on Ala Wai Boulevard and turn right on McCully. Cross over the freeway after three stop lights and make an immediate left turn. Follow this street to the stop sign and turn left again and then right. This will lead you to the freeway. Continue on H-1 for about a mile and a half and get off at Exit 22, Vineyard Boulevard. Go through three stop lights, and on the right will be Foster Gardens.

PRACTICALITIES:

Any day of the week is a good time to visit this part of Honolulu. Sometimes during the week, school children can be seen studying Hawaii's history at some of the attractions in Nuuanu valley, but these classes won't interfere with your enjoyment.

Sunglasses, sunscreen, a hat and comfortable shoes are always advised. Leave your car empty whether you lock it or not.

FOOD AND DRINK:

Zippy's Vineyard (59 Vineyard Blvd.) This is a four-for-one that can take care of most food and drink needs; an open air patio with fast food, a bakery, Charlie's Bar, and a pleasant coffee shop with a good selection. Open 24 hours daily. ☎ 532-4211. $

Liliha Bakery and Coffee Shop (515 N. Kuakini) A must for residents when they crave special guava cake. Try palm leaf brownies and a wonderful assortment of breads. Good coffee shop too. Open 24 hours from Tues. at 6–Sun. midnight. ☎ 531-1651. $

City Chop Suey (1632 Liliha St.) Very tasty Hong Kong-style Chinese food in a very plain atmosphere. Try egg flower soup and pot roast chicken. Open for lunch and dinner 10–9 daily. ☎ 537-3210. $

No Ka Oi Hawaiian Food (1425 Liliha St.) Feast on some of the best Hawaiian food in Honolulu including lau lau, kalua pig with cabbage and their specialty, chicken luau. Open for lunch and dinner daily 10–8. ☎ 524-3077. $

SUGGESTED TOUR:

Numbers in parentheses correspond to numbers on the map.

As you approach **Foster Botanical Gardens** (1) on the right side of Vineyard Boulevard, past Nuuanu Avenue, you know this is a different place because no buildings are visible among the sizable trees and bushes. Turn right at the sign, but after you park your car, walk back to the small **Kwan Yin Temple** adjacent to the gardens. The temple is dedicated to the Chinese goddess of mercy. The aroma of incense is evident almost any time of day as worshipers pray to the goddess.

The garden was begun by Dr. William Hillebrand in 1853 on royal land purchased from Queen Kalama. This 14-acre oasis in the midst of busy downtown Honolulu offers visitors a refreshing change from the chaotic city. Lush tropical plantings include many rare and exceptional trees. There is a free self-guided tour brochure available and guided tours at 1 p.m. Mondays through Fridays. The first director of the garden was Harry Lyon, also the father of Lyon Arboretum in Manoa Valley, who started the exciting orchid collection called appropriately the Lyon Orchid Display. There is also an extensive collection of palms. Included on the grounds are the Foster Garden

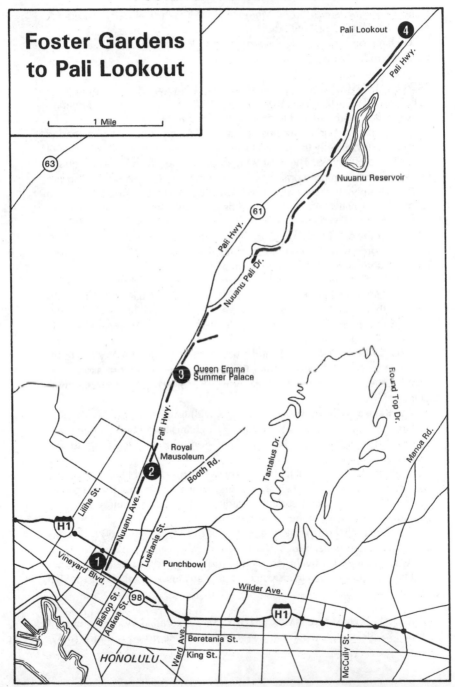

Foster Gardens to Pali Lookout

1 Mile

Gallery and Bookstore. *50 N. Vineyard Blvd. Open 9–4 daily. Adults $5; kids 6–12 $1.* ☎ *522-7066.* ♿.

Go back on Vineyard Boulevard and turn left on Nuuanu Avenue a little over a mile. On the right is the:

*ROYAL MAUSOLEUM OF HAWAII (2), 2261 Nuuanu Ave., Honolulu, HI 96817, ☎ 536-7602. *Open Mon.–Fri. 8–4:30 and two Hawaiian Holidays —Kuhio Day (Mar. 26) and Kamehameha Day (June 11). Free.*

These solemn burial grounds are called *Mauna 'Ala.* The tree-shaded area contains basically three burial sites, in the center of which is a chapel in the shape of a cross. The west wing of the chapel, which was originally the **Mausoleum** built of coral block, was started by Queen Emma and her husband Kamehameha IV after their son died in 1862, and there was no room in the royal crypt on the grounds of Iolani Palace. Because Kamehameha IV died shortly thereafter, the wing wasn't completed until 1864. In 1865, after the other three wings of the building were completed, there was a solemn torchlight procession that carried 18 caskets of high chiefs from the royal crypt at Iolani Palace to Mauna 'Ala.

In 1887, after the death of Princess Bernice Pauahi Bishop (she was the last royal descendant of Kamehameha I), her husband Charles Reed Bishop decided that open storage of the caskets in the mausoleum was inadequate. So he had an underground vault constructed for the Kamehameha family where the caskets of 21 of the line are entombed in the **Kamehameha Vault.** In 1904 a second underground vault, the **Wyllie Tomb** was built to house nine of Queen Emma's relatives and close associates. Robert C. Wyllie, a Scot, served the monarchy for 20 years as foreign minister.

The **Kalakaua Crypt** was built in 1907 with funds from the Hawaii legislature. On the evening of June 25, 1910 chants and choral singing accompanied the carrying of 20 caskets from the old building to the underground crypts.

The true significance of this area to Hawaii's history is best illustrated by the fact that only two of the eight Hawaiian monarchs are not buried within Mauna 'Ala. The resident curator is traditionally a descendant of the chief Ho'olulu who hid the bones of Kamehameha I. The current curator is the sixth in the family line to hold the post. *Call Bill Maioho at 536-7602 a day ahead for a personalized tour. There is no cost.*

As you leave the Royal Mausoleum, turn right and just before the stoplight take a right turn that leads you over the Pali Highway following the sign to Kailua and:

*THE QUEEN EMMA SUMMER PALACE (3), 2913 Pali Hwy., Honolulu, HI 96817, ☎ 595-3167. *Open daily 9–4. Adults $5, seniors $4, under 18 $1.*

Self-directed tours with docents in each room for more information. Gift shop.

The long Hawaiian name for the Queen Emma Summer Palace is Hana-iakamalama. The house was actually built by a man named Lewis in 1848, but was sold at auction in 1850 to John Young II, Queen Emma's uncle. He willed it to her in 1857, when it became her summer home.

According to the Lewis family history, the house frame was pre-cut in Boston and shipped out to Hawaii. Some say it is a perfect blend of New England and early Hawaii architecture. The delightful house is a large, one-story structure with six main rooms and a wide front lanai with a roof supported by six Doric columns. Symmetrically placed doors and windows insure good ventilation from the gentle trade winds blowing down the valley.

The grounds are not extensive, but originally were planted in rose bushes and other shrubbery. Maile grew in the trees and quantities of wild spider lilies grew all over the grounds. In front of the house there was a pond filled with pink water lilies where Queen Emma sometimes served tea.

The furnishings in the house are among the most beautiful of any place in Hawaii. The Queen's bedroom has exquisite koa furniture. Her bed is flanked by two *kahilis* made from the wing and tail feathers of kaiwa and koae birds. In the Edinburgh Room (living room) is an impressive cabinet with convex and concave glass panels that was made in Germany for Queen Emma and Kamehameha IV from koa wood sent from Hawaii. A one-of-a-kind baby grand piano—also made of native koa—has elaborate designs and intricate carvings.

When you leave the Summer Palace, turn right on Pali Highway. Less than half a mile on the right is Dowsett Avenue, where you turn right. Stately homes line this loop road, which will take you back to the Pali. Take note of the small, open stream that fronts several of the homes, since this is what remains of the extensive **Auwai**—or water system—mentioned before. The significance of the *Auwai* is that at one time Nuuanu was considered the "breadbasket of Honolulu" because of the many taro fields or ponds that cascaded down the valley. Queen Emma established her own taro plantation adjacent to her summer home.

Once back on the Pali Highway, go to the stoplight and turn right on Nuuanu Pali Drive. This was the original winding road through the valley. The Nuuanu stream is visible most of the way. At an opening about a mile up there is a small white pump house at the back of a pond. This pond is, again, an example of the Auwai preserved by the Honolulu Board of Water Supply.

At the end of the road, you will come again to the Pali Highway. Turn right and go about half a mile and turn off at the **Pali Lookout** (4). It can be windy and cloudy here at times, but when it is clear the expansive view of the windward side is spectacular. It was here in 1795 that Kamehameha the Great defeated the warriors of Oahu's ruling chiefs in a bloody battle, thus adding the island to his realm. Thousands of defeated warriors were forced over the precipice to meet death on the jagged rocks below.

Plantation Village/Ewa

This tour will be mostly about sugar, however we won't see much in the field since none is produced commercially on Oahu any longer. But it was the production of sugar that brought hundreds of thousands of immigrants to Hawaii's shores starting in the 1800s. All this sugar activity had to be organized and the result was the "plantation system." For good or evil, this system left a deep imprint on Hawaii that lasts to this day.

What we will see up close is how the sugar plantation workers lived. We can inspect examples of their housing, their religious buildings, commercial activities and even their health care. Many artifacts from the beginning of the 20th century used by the sugar workers have been preserved and are on display.

Unlike other preserved villages in America that focus on our European heritage,—like Sturbridge in Massachusetts or Williamsburg in Virginia—this one is all about Pacific Rim cultures. For example, in one of the re-created cooking houses, the utensils and cookery are for making tofu. The Chinese Society Building includes a religious shrine upstairs; and the community *furo* bath is of Japanese design.

GETTING THERE:

By car, get on H-1 Freeway going west. Travel about 14 miles and look for Exit 7, Waikele/Waipahu. Follow signs to Waipahu. Turn right on Waipahu Street and follow signs to Hawaii's Plantation Village.

PRACTICALITIES:

Sunglasses, sunscreen, hat and comfortable shoes.

FOOD AND DRINK:

At the Ewa Beach Shopping Center there are three fast-food, ethnic-type restaurants right in a row. You can eat there, or get take-outs for a picnic at a park described later on. For a change of pace from the just mentioned hurry-up places, there is a fourth choice in a lovely setting with great lunches.

Shiro's Saimin Haven & Hula Hula Drive-In (91-919 Fort Weaver Rd. in the Ewa Beach Shopping center about two miles from Renton Rd.)

For plate lunch, you must try the Hula Hula Chicken or the Supa Dupa Hula Burga. Breakfast, lunch and dinner daily. ☎ 689-0999. $

Ewa Beach Korean Barbeque (same shopping center) The Kal Bi short ribs and soups and noodles are the finest. Seafood combination plates too. Lunch and dinner daily. ☎ 689-4821. $

Loco Moco Drive Inn #3 (same shopping center) The garlic shrimp is a specialty. Local people love loco moco (2 hamburgers, 2 eggs, 2 scoops of rice, macaroni salad and gravy.) Lunch and dinner daily. ☎ 689-8321. $

Bird of Paradise Restaurant (91-1200 Fort Weaver Rd. at the Prince Golf Course) This restaurant serves excellent lunches 365 days a year in a stunning setting at the edge of the golf course. American and Japanese menus. ☎ 689-2270. $–$$

LOCAL ATTRACTIONS:

Numbers in parentheses correspond to numbers on the map.

*HAWAII'S PLANTATION VILLAGE (1), 94-695 Waipahu St., Waipahu, HI 96797, ☎ 677-0110. *Open Mon.–Fri. 9–3, Sat. 10–3, closed Sun. Adults $5, seniors over 62 $4, kids 5 and above $3. Small gift shop. Guided tours on the hour.* ♿.

This restored plantation village is the best-known segment of the larger **Waipahu Cultural Garden Park.** The entrance to the village is actually through the Okada Education Center where you will find a limited gift shop, a large community room where local people can be seen making leis and other crafts and an intriguing exhibit area. The latter contains dozens of artifacts from the halcyon days of sugar in this part of Oahu. A pleasant picnic area is also available on the grounds.

But the collection of buildings that make up the Village is where you will perhaps best be able to experience the lifestyles, struggles and contributions of Hawaii's sugar plantation workers. Starting in 1823 with the first Chinese imported laborers through about 1910 with the Filipinos, Hawaii's sugar plantations in the intervening years also brought in thousands upon thousands of workers from Portugal, Puerto Rico, Japan, Okinawa and Korea.

Since wages were about $9 a month in the early 1880s, these people had to be housed and their food, religious, health and social needs had to be taken care of as well. The twenty structures in the Village—both those restored and replicas—are arranged basically as workers were brought into Hawaii. The first building is a handsome Chinese Society Building from 1909. On the ground floor is a meeting and social room and on the second floor is a Confucian Shrine or Spirit Room. Most remarkable as you move

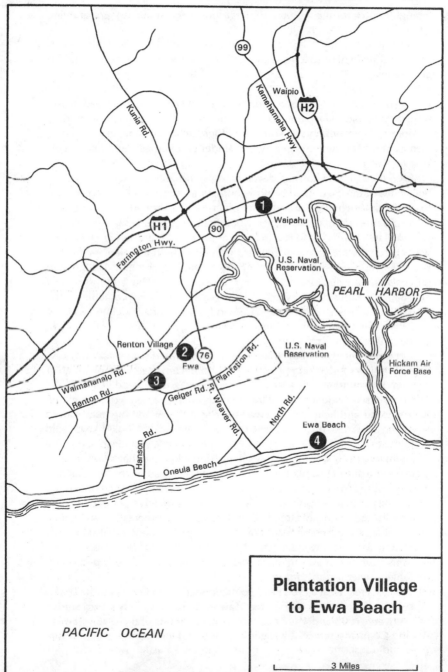

**Plantation Village
to Ewa Beach**

3 Miles

through houses for the various ethnic groups is the small amount of living space.

Also on the grounds is a structure known as an Hawaiian Hale, which you might recognize as a grass shack. These were not generally found on plantations.

As you leave the Cultural Garden, go straight on Waipahu Road. It will wind through old sugar plantation areas for a little bit and then through some of today's rather ordinary housing developments. Turn left on Leoku and then right on Farrington Highway. Just under an overpass, turn left on Fort Weaver Road.

Even though new housing developments and golf courses are thick on both sides of the road, you are now journeying through former sugar cane lands. It was originally dry and dusty plains until a shrewd Irishman by the name of James Campbell bought 41,000 acres and drilled the first artesian well in Hawaii. This led to the creation of the **Ewa Plantation** in 1890. Ewa was a very tough area in which to grow anything, and the plantation experienced some very rocky years financially in the beginning. In 1898, it had 35 wells and produced a record 20,000 tons of sugar, but still lost money and had a sizable debt. By contrast, it became hugely profitable in the 1920s. Many respected business names in Hawaii were associated with the Ewa Plantation (eventually it became Oahu Sugar Company)—Campbell, Castle, Dillingham, Renton and Bond.

But times change. Labor strikes over the years sent wages way up, government sugar support dropped and the land became too valuable to grow a commodity product like sugar. Oahu Sugar closed for good in 1996.

We will see evidence of that tremendous change when we turn right on Renton Road and head for the **Ewa Sugar Mill** (2). As the big trees start to shade the road, note on the left the grand white house that looks like it could be in Boston. The is the former plantation manager's residence. Compare that with what you saw the workers living in back at the Plantation Village. Note too the distinctive plantation office buildings, also on the left, that previously housed various bosses but now hold a number of churches and other community activities. On the right you will see a massive project taken on by the City and County of Honolulu. It is the redevelopment of existing plantation villages via a combination of new construction and rehab of former plantation workers' dwellings into 1,500 housing units. Because Hawaii's housing costs are so astronomical, the City is shooting for sixty percent affordable—whatever that means.

Next is a real treat as you keep going down Renton Road past the bridge and onto a fairly rough road to the **Hawaii Railway Society's Ewa Station** (3). Between 1890 and 1947 the narrow-gauge trains of the Oahu Railway & Land Company served the sugar mills, carried vital equipment and supplies and transported passengers from Honolulu to as far away as Kahuku.

The trains primarily carried raw sugar and molasses from the various mills to the docks in Honolulu Harbor for export.

During World War II the O.R. & L. was pressed into service 24 hours a day. Heavier weight rails had to be laid to haul ammunition, troops and military supplies from Pearl Harbor to other military sites on the island.

The Society has restored a Whitcomb diesel locomotive and you can choose to ride in either an open gondola or a covered car. Sunday departure times are 12:30 and 2:30 for a one-and-a-half-hour ride that takes you through some fascinating territory. Points of interest along the way are Barbers Point Naval Air Station (which will revert to the community by the year 2000), the circa 1930s Fort Barette, Barbers Point Harbor, the ghost town sites of Gilbert and Sisal, and past the majestic Makaha mountain range and the historic fields of Ewa Plantation. If school groups use the train, 45-minute weekday rides sometimes are available. *Sunday fares are $8 for adults, $5 for kids 2–12 and seniors over 62. Because it's a shorter ride, weekday rates are $4 for adults, kids and seniors $3.* ☎ *681-5461.*

Go back out Renton Road and turn right on Fort Weaver Road. This will take you to the town of Ewa Beach. Continue on Fort Weaver Road as it bends left. After about four miles, stop at the small **Ewa Beach Park** (4) on the right side of the road.

The shoreline here is unprotected since there is no reef, but the beach is white and wide and the view back to Honolulu and Diamond Head is spectacular. This is a wonderful beach park for picnicking, so if you got food along the way, enjoy it here.

Trip 17
*Bishop Heritage/Damon

If you truly love Hawaii and all it stands for, this daytrip will enrich your appreciation of the state and its heritage. Most of it is about the legacy of the Bishops: Charles Reed Bishop and his wife Princess Bernice Pauahi Bishop. He was a businessman who came to Hawaii for a short visit and stayed. She was the last direct descendant of the royal line of Kamehameha.

Their impact on Hawaii today and into the future is inestimable. Think of the fact that she left 400,000 acres of Hawaii land—and the income from it—in trust to Kamehameha Schools. This school for K–12 is the sole beneficiary of her will. Among the many treasures he left is a museum that attracts over 300,000 visits annually. He built it in 1889 as a memorial to his wife. They were the original power couple—with lots of Aloha.

We'll also make a visit—outside the influence of the Bishops—to another special place, a natural place, that is the legacy of Henry Damon. The Damon Estate, while considerably smaller than the Bishop Estate, still has land and other assets estimated to be close to $1 billion. But in the true nature of one of Hawaii's early titans, Damon left some of his lands for the enjoyment of all.

GETTING THERE:

By car, get on H-1 Freeway and take Exit 20B, Houghtailing Street, and follow signs to the Bishop Museum.

By bus, from Kuhio Avenue in Waikiki, take the #2 bus to School Street and walk two blocks to the museum.

By trolley, from the Royal Hawaiian Shopping Center in Waikiki, take the trolley to Bishop Museum which is stop #10.

PRACTICALITIES:

Any time is a good time to visit the Bishop Museum, except on major holidays. Moanalua Gardens can be visited anytime too. But the school exhibits are tightly restricted, so you will have to inquire.

Sunglasses, sunscreen, hat and comfortable shoes.

100

Another reminder to take only what you can carry out of your car is in order—even though it is repetitious.

FOOD AND DRINK:

The restaurants in this daytrip all have character, but don't expect anything fancy. Each will give you a taste of what Honolulu residents enjoy for food.

Mama's Mexican Kitchen (376 N. School St.) No glitz here, but a good selection of Mexican dishes. Chimichangas top the list. Lunch and dinner daily. ☎ 537-3200. $

Silver Dragon Chop Suey (1620 N. School St. in Kamehameha Shopping Center) A feature is the daily ox-tail soup, which has put this spot on the map. Lunch and dinner daily. ☎ 847-5222. $

Uptown Saimin (522 N. School St.) It's been here a long time, so don't let the lack of new paint put you off. Their saimin and other noodle soups are famous. Breakfast, lunch and dinner Mon.–Fri.; lunch and dinner Sat. and Sun. ☎ 537-1881. $

Kenny's Burger House (Kamehameha Shopping Center) Teri Burger is their most popular item, with reasonably priced salads too. Sun.–Thurs. 6–1; one hour later on Fri. & Sat. ☎ 841-4782. $

LOCAL ATTRACTIONS:

Numbers in parentheses correspond to numbers on the map.

*BISHOP MUSEUM (1), 1525 Bernice St., Honolulu, HI 96817-0916, ☎ 847-3511. *Open 9–5 daily except Christmas. Adults $14.95, kids 6–17 and seniors $11.95, under 6 free. Museum shop and food.*

This wonderful resource likes to call itself "A Living Adventure." Even a brief tour of the museum will give added meaning to your experiences in Hawaii. That's because it has become recognized over the past 100 years as the premier guardian, chronicler and exhibitor of Hawaii's rich natural and cultural heritage.

It is a living adventure because of the "please touch" exhibits in the Hall of Discovery, where you'll see such involving displays as "Life in a Lava Tube." You'll also discover how volcanoes shaped these islands and how life developed here. There are royal cloaks, crowns, masks and weapons. Of particular interest to many visitors is seeing folk artists at work on traditional island crafts, and experiencing the engaging music and dance of Hawaii.

Also on the museum's 12-acre campus is the Planetarium. Daily shows use state-of-the-art audio, video and computer-controlled automation. The presentation "Journey by Starlight" lets visitors explore the voyaging techniques of early Polynesian navigators. Remember, the first discoverers of Hawaii came without any navigational instruments. This will tell you how they did it.

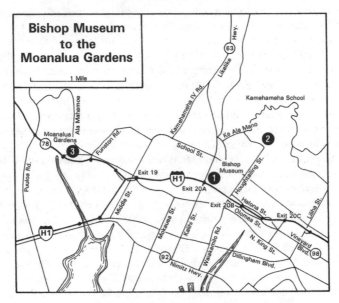

Besides the six museum galleries, there is also the Hall of Discovery with changing exhibits. A recent exhibit called "Ocean Planet" took visitors deep underwater where they could operate a robotic arm to collect specimens from the ocean floor. Among many activities, they could also touch real seaweed, make fish prints and generate a wave in a special tank.

Each day of the week features a different craft demonstration. Coconut weaving and *wili lei* making are very popular as is stone and bone carving.

High on a hill above the Museum is the **Kamehameha School** (2), established in 1887 by the will of Bernice Pauahi Bishop to educate children of Hawaiian ancestry. More than 4,000 children are served in preschool-through-grade-12 programs statewide, making Kamehameha the largest independent school in the United States.

While the school has occupied several different campuses over the years, today the Kapalama Heights campus covers 600 acres. Over 3,000 students attend classes on this site, which features 70 major buildings. Two of the most interesting are the **Memorial Chapel** and the **Heritage Center.** The latter was built in 1988 to preserve and display some of the furniture and other personal belongings of the Kamehameha School's founder, Bernice Pauahi Bishop, and her husband, Charles Reed Bishop.

When you cross the Center's threshold, you step back into another time: Honolulu during the last half of the 19th century and the "greatest center of hospitality in Honolulu." Members of the Kamehameha Royal family greet you from framed portraits hanging on the reception area's walls. The next room is decorated as a bedroom and features Princess Ruth's four-poster bed. The main room has a collection of outstanding treasures that belonged to Bernice. Two beautiful koa rocking chairs, a handsome German Steinweg piano and a koa wave bench are just a few of her possessions on display.

The chapel was also built in 1988. The lava rock foundation is reminiscent of ancient Hawaiians' first place of worship, the *heiau*. And the chapel itself resembles the *halau* or long houses of old Hawaii. It is a grand structure with an interior inspired by the simplicity of historic Hawaiian churches. Besides the beautiful koa pews, a 3,000-pipe organ and a cross at the altar made of rare, solid sandalwood are featured. The eight Hawaiian islands are each represented by a pair of distinctive *kahili* made of feathers and materials found on that particular island.

Open weekdays during the school year, the Heritage Center is a private museum usually restricted to Kamehameha School students, alumni, parents and faculty. *The Center and Chapel can be visited by others, but by invitation only. Call 842-8635.* If there are no other activities, and they can squeeze you in, you may get an invitation. To get there take Maukuahine right off North School Street. Turn right again on Makua, which becomes Ke Ala Mano. The guard at the gate with give you directions on campus.

A visit to **Moanalua Gardens** (3) is next. When you leave the Bishop Museum and/or Kamehameha School, get on North School Street, follow that until it becomes Middle Street, and turn right on the Moanalua Freeway. Take the next exit and look for signs for the gardens.

This area is such a wondrous sanctuary among the hustle and bustle of the freeway that can be seen across the broad expanse of the park. Most noticeable among the many spectacular trees are the giant monkeypods and ficuses. Also scattered throughout the landscape are Polynesian-introduced varieties such as milo, kamani, kukui as well as native Hawaiian loulu, wiliwili, hala and koa.

At the entrance to the gardens on the left is the Prince Lot Cottage. This was a place of relaxation for the man who would become Kamehameha V. The Prince entertained local and foreign visitors at the cottage, and encouraged and promoted the celebration of hula in this peaceful setting. Samuel Mills Damon bought the cottage and property in 1884.

At the back of the gardens is the Chinese Hall, with attractive *koi* ponds in front. This building was shipped in pieces from China in 1904. Originally, it was located near the old Oahu Railway and Land station and was used by the Damon family for entertainment. The Latin cross-shaped interior of Chinese Hall has walls decorated with intricately carved three-dimension sandalwood and camphorwood panels. You'll have to take our word about the interior since both these buildings are closed to the public.

Relax, spread out your beach mat and enjoy the peacefulness of this privately-owned garden that is open to the public every day of the year from sunup to sundown.

Trip 18

*Pearl Harbor and Beyond

Long before the United States eyeballed Pearl Harbor as a good spot in the middle of the Pacific to house warships, native Hawaiians really did paddle outrigger canoes into the five fingers (or lochs) of the harbor and dive for crabs and oysters. They called it *"Wai Momi,"* meaning "Water of Pearl." It was a pretty idyllic site according to early depictions.

As with so many things in Hawaii, all that changed dramatically around the turn of the century when the first US Naval facilities were built and ships were stationed in the protection of Pearl Harbor. Most of us know how terribly tragic the area became on December 7, 1941, when the Japanese launched a sneak attack that sank 21 vessels and destroyed innumerable planes and shoreside facilities. The attack killed 2,388 men, women and children. Included in that number are 48 civilians killed from Waikiki to Pearl City, often by exploding anti-aircraft munitions. The youngest civilian killed was 7 months old.

Today, Pearl Harbor still hums with ship and submarine repair, training exercises of all sorts and the hundreds of other activities associated with war readiness. It is the headquarters of the US Pacific Fleet operations called CINCPAC, which is the base for 20 surface ships and 42 submarines. Stationed at Pearl Harbor today are approximately 25,000 men and women in the armed services. Civilians supporting the Navy's efforts number about 10,000 as well.

At the peak in WWII, over 130,000 active military were stationed at Pearl Harbor. There are three significant attractions at Pearl Harbor that we'll visit today. The first is the Arizona Memorial which signifies the start of the war in the Pacific; in between is the submarine Bowfin which was a highly decorated underwater fighter in the Pacific; and finally the USS Missouri where the Japanese surrendered, signifying the end of the Pacific war.

GETTING THERE:
   By car, get on H-1 Freeway and after about ten miles, turn off at the USS Arizona Memorial Exit. Follow the green and white signs to the Memorial. The Bowfin and Missouri are accessed from this location.

By bus, take a #20 Pearl Harbor bus from Waikiki right to the Memorial.

Shuttle buses leave from various points in Waikiki, some offering free service and others charging a modest fee. Check with your concierge.

By tour boat, usually from Kewalo Basin. Star of Honolulu (☎ 983-STAR) and Dream Cruises (☎ 592-5200) are two that will take you into the harbor, but the disadvantage is you do not land on the Memorial or the Missouri. The advantage is no waiting in line and you see more of the harbor and other ships.

PRACTICALITIES:

Because the Memorial is such a huge draw, it is better to get started early in the morning. On school holidays and during summer vacation, the Visitor Center can get very crowded. There are times when the wait is from one to three hours.

Sunglasses, sunscreen, hat and comfortable shoes. Take everything with you from your car.

FOOD AND DRINK:

Marina Restaurant (just beyond the Memorial and submarine museum) What a view of Pearl Harbor from this second-floor restaurant! The Navy brass' yachts are at your feet. Buffet and good, reasonably priced food. Open Mon.–Sat. for lunch and dinner. ☎ 477-2451. $

Eastern Garden Chinese Seafood Restaurant (98-150 Kaonohi) Marvelous dim sum (small delicacies like pan fried taro cake) served from roaming carts, mid-morning until 2 p.m. daily. Regular menu for dinner. ☎ 486-8882. $ to $$

Anna Miller's (98-115 Kaonohi) Very popular family restaurant. Great burgers and hot sandwiches. 21 varieties of pies. Open daily for breakfast, lunch and dinner. ☎ 487-2421. $

Bravo Restaurant and Bar (in same building as Anna Miller's) Serves basically Italian food. Plenty of pasta dishes and tasty pizzas. Open daily for lunch and dinner. ☎ 487-5544. $$

LOCAL ATTRACTIONS:

*USS ARIZONA MEMORIAL (1), 1 Arizona Memorial Dr., Honolulu, HI 96818-3145, ☎ 422-0561. *Open daily 7:30–5 except Thanksgiving, Christmas and New Years. One-hour-and-15-minute tours start at 8 and end at 3. National Park Service Rangers begin each tour with an historical film, and then a shuttle to the Memorial. Gift shop and exhibit area. All individuals must pick up their own ticket. Tours are free. ♿.*

Pearl Harbor and the Memorial are the most visited sites in Hawaii.

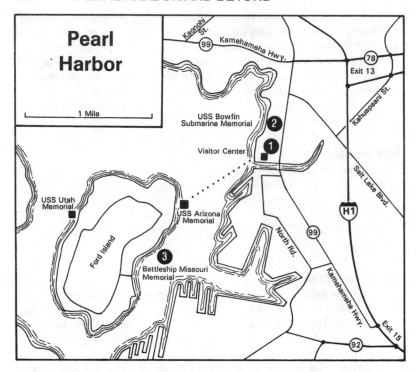

About 1.5 million people explore its waters annually, either on Navy or commercial tour boats. Only Navy boats may land at the actual Memorial; tour boats only cruise past. The Visitor Center and Memorial are a joint effort of the Navy and National Park Service. You will see upwards of 20 volunteers who are WWII Pearl Harbor Survivors helping to direct visitors.

There is little doubt that everyone who visits the Memorial is moved in one way or another. Initial recognition came in 1950 when Admiral Arthur Radford ordered a flagpole erected over the sunken battleship USS *Arizona*. The present Memorial was dedicated in 1962. It spans the midsection of the Arizona and consists of three sections: the entry and assembly rooms; a central area designed for ceremonies and general observation; and the shrine room where the 1,177 names of those who lost their lives on the battleship are engraved on the marble walls.

*USS BOWFIN SUBMARINE MUSEUM & PARK (2), 11 Arizona Memorial Dr., Honolulu, HI 96818, ☎ 423-1341. *Open daily 8–5 except Thanksgiving, Christmas and New Years. Adult admission to the submarine and museum $8, kids 4–12 $3. The museum only for adults is $4 and $3 for kids. Gift shop.* ♿.

Most of us have never been on a real submarine. All the stories, movies and television exposure we've had can now be a reality, such as how extremely cramped they are inside. Some other impressions you may walk away with are: the bunks over the torpedoes look very spooky; the commanding officer had the smallest desk imaginable, almost like a child's; and there was a lot of spit and polish.

The USS *Bowfin* was launched on the East Coast appropriately on Dec. 7, 1942. Since it was a year after the Pearl Harbor attack, she was nicknamed the "Pearl Harbor Avenger." She completed nine successful war patrols and earned the Presidential Unit Citation and the Navy Unit Commendation.

BATTLESHIP MISSOURI MEMORIAL (3) P.O. Box 6339, Honolulu, HI 96818, ☎ 423-2263. *Open daily 8–5 except Thanksgiving, Christmas and New Years. Adult admission $10, kids 4–12 $6. Guided tours add $4. Transportation to the ship leaves from the Bowfin Park frequently. The main deck is* &.

Through a great deal of hard work, a volunteer group in Hawaii was able to bring the famed battleship to Pearl Harbor to signify the end of World War II since this is the ship where Douglas McArthur accepted the surrender of the Japanese government on Sept. 7 1945.

It has been said that the Missouri is the other bookend to the War in the Pacific: the Arizona Memorial sanctifies the start and the Missouri signals the end.

The Missouri docents have lots of interesting tales of the exploits of the ship—even up to its service in Desert Storm—as they guide you from the main deck to the Surrender Deck to the Ward Room and the bridge.

After all this drama and history, you may be ready for a relaxing walk. Turn left coming out of the Bowfin Museum and continue on what now becomes a road/bike path. You will see some military storage buildings and then the Marina Restaurant on the left. This is a place for lunch, or take-out for a picnic just a bit farther on.

As you enter the bike path and turn suddenly left, there is a Quonset hut-type building labeled the CINCPAC Fleet Boat House. This small facility among the shoreline trees holds what are called the "Admiral's Barges." Actually, they are large, spit-and-polish motor launches that take VIPs out to the Memorial. It is off-limits to you and me, but if you walk to the left of the building you can catch a glimpse of these luxury yachts.

Continue on the bike path through the trees. After about a quarter of a mile there is a jog in the path, and on your left appears a wonderful small park. It is right at the water's edge and affords a spectacular straight-ahead view of the Arizona Memorial, the Bowfin and the USS Missouri. A picnic here under some of the giant trees is a great way to go slightly beyond Pearl Harbor and reflect on what it all means.

Trip 19

Shop, Shop, Shop

This trip is a challenge—to see if you can cover the ten shopping areas we talk about here. Starting just outside Waikiki, these centers are stretched out in a row covering 15 miles. Except for two near the Pearl City area, all are open-air. All have free parking except two close to downtown: one has a small charge with validation and the other is free with validation. The huge swap meet has a tiny admission. Restaurants abound in each center, so we'll only highlight one or two. You can discover others for yourself.

Hawaii is a shopping mecca, especially for our Asian visitors. Taking presents home for friends, relatives and co-workers is a way of life for the Japanese. It's called *omiyage*. Visitors from the mainland US, Canada and other foreign lands are also present-takers. And don't forget yourselves. Some nifty little blouse, shirt, hat or other goodie that says HAWAII is always popular at home. Island fashions have gone mainstream, so colors, styles and patterns usually work most places.

GETTING THERE:

By car, get on Ala Moana Boulevard. Go out of Waikiki half a mile and turn right into Ala Moana Center. Since most of the centers are on this route, follow it unless other directions are given for a particular center.

By bus, you can get to anywhere along Ala Moana Boulevard (which becomes Nimitz) on either the #19 or 20.

By Waikiki Trolley, there are eight pickup points in Waikiki. It generally runs every 15 minutes from 8:30-11.

Other types of transportation for each center will be given in that section.

PRACTICALITIES:

All major credit cards are accepted at most stores. Out-of-state personal checks are generally not accepted. Most centers have automatic teller machines that take Plus, Cirrus and the other major ATM networks. You shouldn't have any trouble spending money at any of these centers.

Same mantra: sunglasses, sunscreen, hat and definitely comfortable shoes. Don't leave anything in your car, locked or unlocked.

FOOD AND DRINK:

Some restaurants in these centers have already been listed, but at least one other will be covered within each center.

SHOPPING ATTRACTIONS:

Numbers in parentheses correspond to numbers on the map.

ALA MOANA SHOPPING CENTER (1), 1459 Ala Moana Blvd., ☎ 946-2811. *The center's own shuttle picks up passengers from eight points in Waikiki and takes them directly to the center. It runs every 15 minutes from 10–10. Fare $2. Open Mon.–Sat. 9:30–9 and Sunday from 10–6.*

Without doubt, this is Hawaii's best-known shopping center. It is reportedly the largest open-air center in the world with 187 stores. Neiman Marcus is the latest addition to do battle with Hawaii's homegrown department store, Liberty House. Lots of upscale stores like Cartier, Tiffany, and Gucci can be found here, and then there are the standards like Sears and J.C. Penney. The little, fun shops are here too.

There is a large Food Court.

WARD CENTRE (2), 1200 Ala Moana Blvd., ☎ 591-8411. *Open Mon.–Sat. 10–9 and Sun. 10–5.*

This center is weighted more toward eating than shopping. The Borders Bookstore at the end, however offers great book shopping—and it has a marvelous outdoor café upstairs overlooking Ala Moana Beach Park. Look for Island Provisions at Vagabond House which features many island-type gifts and decorator items. R. Field Wine is a yummy place for food gifts and picnic stuff.

A good eating experience is in store for you at **Ryan's Grill**. Lively atmosphere and food. *Open daily for lunch and dinner.* ☎ *591-9132. $$.*

WARD WAREHOUSE (3), 1050 Ala Moana Blvd., ☎ 591-8411. *You can get there the same way as for Ward Centre since they are side-by-side. Open the same hours.*

Unlike strip malls that offer lots of national chain stores, this one has almost entirely Hawaii or local retailers. Take a comfortable stroll on either side of a covered walkway. A must here is Nohea Gallery. Superb art from local artists including jewelry and furniture of Hawaii materials.

Overlooking Kewalo Basin is **Stuart Anderson's Cattle Company Restaurant,** which features excellent beef selections—and more. *Open for lunch and dinner daily,* ☎ *591-9292. $ to $$.*

RESTAURANT ROW (4), 500 Ala Moana Blvd., ☎ 538-1441. *You can get here the same way as the other centers. Hours vary by store and restaurant, but generally 10–10.*

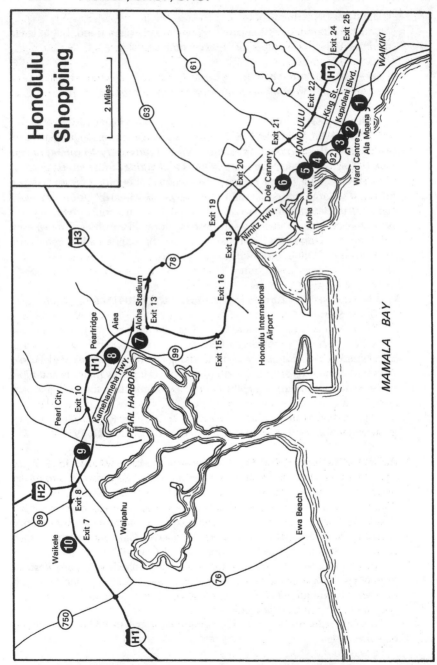

Honolulu Shopping

Eating is the main event at this center as the name suggests. A neat little shop is the Honolulu Chocolate Company. It's no secret what Opal Fields carries along with other types of jewelry. Wallace Theaters shows the latest flicks on nine screens.

A fine food establishment is the **Sunset Grill**. You can count on great taste and presentation in nouvelle cuisine. *Open for lunch and dinner daily,* ☎ *521-4409. $$.*

ALOHA TOWER MARKETPLACE (5), I Aloha Tower Dr., just off Ala Moana Blvd., by the Aloha Tower, ☎ 528-5700. *Just past Restaurant Row, by car look for signs to the left for the Marketplace. Parking is $2 with validation. The Marketplace has its own trolley that runs every 20 minutes from 10 stops in Waikiki, 9:15 a.m.–9:40 p.m. Open Mon.–Sat. 9–9, Sun. 9–6, although some restaurants are open later.*

This festival marketplace was designed by the same people who developed those in Boston and Baltimore. Located right on the harbor and surrounding Aloha Tower, it is a true outdoor market bazaar featuring specialty retail shops, many good restaurants, and an air-conditioned food lanai. Check out Martin & McArthur for Koa wood gifts

A unique decor greets you at the **Big Island Steak House.** Yes, steaks, but good seafood too. *Open daily for lunch and dinner.* ☎ *537-4446. $$.*

DOLE CANNERY (6), 650 Iwilei Rd., ☎ 531-2886. *After leaving Aloha Tower Marketplace, go left. Ala Moana Blvd. has become Nimitz.*

This place used to hum with hundreds of workers cutting and canning fresh pineapple at the heavy harvest time. But the cannery is closed and now it is a collection of shops. The Dole logo shop has many crisp items that are great for take-home. Lots of parking. There is a food court.

ALOHA STADIUM SWAP MEET (7), Aloha Stadium, ☎ 486-1529. *Turn right on Nimitz and follow signs to the Airport, then look for signs to Aloha Stadium. It is about five miles. Bus #47 takes about an hour and a half. There is a shuttle from Waikiki that runs three times each morning 7:30, 9 and 10:30 from the Ilikai with other points. $6 round-trip includes admission. Call 955-4050. Admission is 50¢. Open Wed., Sat., and Sun. from 6–3.*

This is the ultimate bazaar, with over 300 merchants selling everything from alligator belts to Hawaiian print muumuus in the huge parking lot of the stadium. It's quite a walk around the whole thing, so take your time. If you can't find it here, it probably doesn't exist.

Food vendors are in good supply offering mostly quick foods like hot dogs and chips.

PEARLRIDGE CENTER (8), 98-1005 Moanalua Rd., ☎ 488-0981. *Get on Kamehameha Hwy. and look for signs to the shopping center. Open Mon.– Sat. 10–9, Sun. 10–6.*

This is Hawaii's only two-phased mall connected by a monorail system. Worth the 25¢. What separates the two sides is an old, old watercress farm. The farmers sold the land for the center except what remains. Big chain stores, little boutiques and everything in between.

The **Monterey Bay Canners Fresh Seafood Restaurant** is everything its name says and more. The watercress farm is in full view. *Lunch and dinner daily,* ☎ *483-3555. $ to $$.*

PEARL HIGHLANDS CENTER (9), 1000 Kamehameha Hwy., ☎ 453-2800. *Turn right on the highway and go about three miles. Hours depend on the various merchants.*

This "Power Center" is dominated by Sam's Club for members only. You'll also find Old Navy, Ross Dress for Less and many other stores typical of this mainland genre. Food court and movie theaters.

WAIKELE OUTLET CENTER (10), 94-790 Lumi Aina, ☎ 676-5656. *On leaving Pearl Highlands, turn right on Kamehameha Hwy. Take the Makakilo/Waianae on-ramp and get off at the next exit, which is #7. You will see the center on the right. This will cover about 15 miles from Waikiki.*

The outlet portion includes many stores you may have seen before like Oshkosh For Kids, Bass, Converse and Corning/Revereware. One of the highlights of this very successful center is Off 5th which is Saks Fifth Avenue's outlet store. Rocky Mountain Chocolate factory is always a hit.

The lower portion—connected by a custom trolley—is called the Value Center and it includes Borders Books and Music, Sports Authority and many others.

Food is plentiful, but you might try **Jurison's Inn,** which serves a mix of ethnic plate lunches. The Hawaiian food plates are ono. *Lunch and dinner daily,* ☎ *676-1171. $*

That about winds up the shopping challenge. Congratulations if you made it to all ten shopping centers. You should get a prize.

Drive to Another Island

Who says you can't visit another island by car from Honolulu? Well you can—and it has good beaches too. Furthermore, if you have a strong arm, you might be able to throw a small stone across to downtown Honolulu; it's that close. We're talking about Sand Island.

Getting there takes you through some industrial areas, but that's the price for this special visit to a neighbor island in your own auto. In the waters surrounding Sand Island are some great water activities, and tucked away down a dusty road is one of the restaurant treasures of Honolulu. There's even a tiny fishing village island offshore.

We'll also take a look at present-day shipping to the islands when we pass the massive container yard on Sand Island. The sheets you slept in last night, the car you're driving in now and your breakfast cereal all came in through this single, vital facility.

GETTING THERE:

By car, get on Ala Moana Boulevard in Waikiki and head toward the airport. After about eight miles, look for signs to the left for the Sand Island Access Road.

PRACTICALITIES:

Sunscreen, sunglasses, water and hat. Consider taking swimgear if you are moved to get in the water. Leave nothing in your car when you stop.

FOOD AND DRINK:

> **Pita King** (111 Sand Island Access Rd.) A neat little place with a combination of Middle East and Greek foods. Tuna melt in a pita is excellent. Open for lunch Sun.–Fri. ☎ 841-7482. $

> **Kawakami Delicatessen** (237 Kalihi St.) This is not your usual deli. It's mostly plate lunches and other local foods served buffet style. Delicious. Open from 5:30–1:30 in the afternoon. ☎ 845-8102. $

> **La Mariana Sailing Club & Restaurant** (50 Sand Island Access Rd.) This is a real sailing club with 400 members. It's also a real marina, but best of all is the South Seas atmosphere in the restaurant. Heavy fo-

liage and a collection of authentic artifacts give a strong Polynesian feel. Tasty food and fun. Open daily for lunch and dinner. Fri. & Sat. 'til midnight for the sing-along. Reservations, ☎ 841-2173. $$

Sam Choy' Breakfast, Lunch and Crab (580 N. Nimitz Hwy.) Be prepared for wonderful food in a fishmarket atmosphere. There's a whole sampan fishing boat inside. They brew their own beer. Can be hectic, so make reservations, ☎ 545-7979. $, $$, $$$

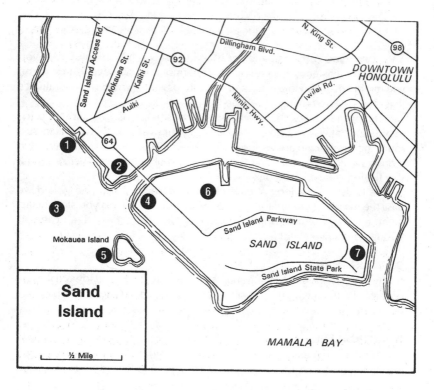

LOCAL ATTRACTIONS:

Numbers in parentheses correspond to numbers on the map.

This daytrip is off the beaten track, but it offers some sights and experiences usually enjoyed only by residents.

As you travel down Sand Island Access Road, it will bend to the left. Look carefully on the right for a sign that says, "HB." Turn right and just ahead is **La Mariana Sailing Club** (1) on Keehi Lagoon. The restaurant is mentioned above, but the story behind it is worth a brief telling. Now 83, Annette LaMariana Nahinu came to Hawaii with her husband in 1955. They decided to start a "poor man's yacht club" in what was a junkyard on the Lagoon.

Through sheer will and very hard work they eventually transformed a run-down area into 100 boat slips and the restaurant. At that location for 22 years, the state—which owns the land—suddenly made them move. Annette did it without her husband since he threw in the towel over the whole situation. She and a crew went ahead and moved the clubhouse, 20 docks, 30 boats, 83 palm trees, a monkeypod tree and countless other plants and shrubs just several yards from the original location. It has prospered in the new location ever since. The place exhibits that kind of spirit, and you'll enjoy the easy-going, Polynesian feel.

Turn right on Sand Island Road and look for a sign **KMC Ocean Sports** (2) at 24 Sand Island Access Road. Here you will find all manner of ocean activities. **N&N Tours** offers Jet Skis, parasailing, scuba diving, powerboat rides and a short helicopter tour. Each can be purchased separately, or you can choose any three for a package price of under $100. *They are open daylight hours every day except Thanksgiving, Christmas and New Years. Call 847-6299 for reservations.* **Alii Divers** offers daily dive tours from 9–1 in the afternoon for around $70. They have lessons, and you don't have to be certified. *Call 843-2882 for reservations.*

At the same location is a brand-new attraction called **Hawaii Ocean Thrills** (3), which is a floating adventure island out in the lagoon. Their feature attraction is a one-seater race boats where six people compete. They also offer water bumper boats, a water maze and lots of other unique water activities. A shore boat takes you to the catamaran out in the lagoon. Snack shop and showers. *Open daily. Adult full admission is $89; non-race admission is $69; kids 6–11 $19. Call 539 9400, reservations 1-888-472-GRAY.*

At this point, you are still on the island of Oahu. But, when you turn right and go over the short drawbridge, you are now on **Sand Island.** See, you can get to another island by car. The state gave the drawbridge a $15 million makeover in 1990, but it never worked right. It would get stuck in an up position so container trucks from either side would be backed up in the hundreds. After that, they put it down permanently. Now the state is talking about a quarter-of-a-billion-dollar tunnel instead of a bridge. You'll still be able to drive to another island even with the tunnel.

Just after you cross the drawbridge, look for a sign on the right saying **Marine Education and Training Center** (4), a part of Honolulu Community College. The building is a state facility to train students in boat maintenance and repair. This $8.7 million facility was originally conceived in the late 1980s when the state was courting the America's Cup Challenge. The big parking lot gives a fine view of Keehi Lagoon—and is a good spot for a picnic.

From the parking lot looking out over the lagoon, you will see three tiny islands. The first is **Mokauea Island** (5), which is the only inhabited one of the three. In fact, Mokauea is home to four families that total 18 villagers.

The island ranges in size from about nine acres to 14 acres depending on the tide. Regardless of size, residents mostly fish in what is considered an old-style fishing village, but some grow vegetables and bananas. Mokauea has no roads, no phone lines, no electricity, no vehicles, no mail delivery and no stores or businesses. Dean Uchida administers the island for the State's Department of Land and Natural Resources, which holds the lease for the island, and says of the residents, "You have to be a very special character to live out there. They have an interesting lifestyle. Very laid back. Things get done whenever they get around to it."

Looming on the left as you go farther along Sand Island Road are the huge container yards and the 200'+-high cranes of **SeaLand and Matson** (6). This area is vital to everything Hawaii does. It is literally the entire state's lifeline. For example, Matson handles about 200,000 containers annually bringing in everything imaginable, except perhaps petroleum products which go directly to the refineries at Campbell Industrial Park. Matson, which has 75 percent of the ocean shipping to Hawaii, alone brings in about 85,000 cars a year. Some other goods certainly come in by air, but that is a pittance compared to ocean shipping.

Matson isn't new at this game since it started bringing goods to Hawaii by sailing ship in the late 1880s. Nowadays, the company uses 750' container ships that arrive four times a week bringing food, clothing, housing materials, computers, light bulbs and all sorts of stuff in between. They used to go back almost full of pineapple and sugar, but now they go back 70 percent empty.

Farther down the road you will see the entrance to **Sand Island State Park** (7). For years this was a forgotten part of Hawaii's world until the state came along about ten years ago and built a 300-acre park. Now it is open from 7 in the morning until 7:45 in the evening for camping, shoreline fishing, picnicking, beach walking and the like. The shoreline just inside the park affords a different view of downtown Honolulu. This is the view passengers on cruise liners see when they enter the harbor. There is a concrete lookout left over from the war that is fun to climb.

Circle Island

There's a wonderful sense of completion when you circle Oahu all in a day. It's as though you can throw your arms around her and give her a gentle embrace. That's the good part. The not-so-good part is that none of us can even begin to do and see all that stretches along the 112 miles around Oahu. The island has been circled in just about every means imaginable, including those intrepid souls who have done it on foot. They got to see it at the right pace, but few of us have the 9–10 days it takes to do it at a walking speed. Columnist Bob Krauss in his book "Our Hawaii," quotes Harmony Bentosino who is circling Oahu's shoreline on foot, intermittently over several years, "This trip has made me appreciate Oahu. To me a circle symbolizes wholeness and unity, completeness. I feel that if I circle the island, it will become part of me."

Most of us get in a car, bus or van and pick and choose from the abundant activities and scenic delights along the way. You can do it ad hoc or with a complete plan—either way will fill a pleasurable day.

Recently, Honolulu-based travel writer John McDermott made his annual drive around Oahu, and in an article exclaimed that he sounded like a visitor to his own island. "Look at the colors in the ocean. See the fantastic shapes in the cloud formations behind the mountains. How many shades of green are there in those cliffs?" he exalted. He concluded his piece with the declaration, "We do live in such a pretty place."

GETTING THERE:

By car, leave Waikiki as though you were headed for Hanauma Bay. Stay on Kalanianaole Highway the whole way until you get to Kailua. Once there, if you turn right, Kailua Road will take you to the shore road as explained in Trip 10, Windward Explorer. If you go left it is the Pali Highway. At the third stoplight turn right at Kamehameha Highway, which will eventually connect you with the Trip 10 route. At the other end of the circle—at Dole Pineapple Pavilion near Wahiawa—follow signs to Honolulu and then Waikiki to make the entire circle.

By bus, it's better to get started in the morning. From Waikiki take the #19 Airport, #19 Airport/Hickam, #20 Airport or #8 Ala Moana Center. Because you will change buses at the center, ask for a transfer. You can choose to go clockwise by getting on bus #52 Wahiawa/Circle Island or counter-clockwise by taking #55 Kaneohe/Circle Island. Both go completely around the island, but they must say "Circle Island."

By bicycle, follow the same route as by car. If you stop a good number of times for sightseeing and refreshments—and you are in modestly good condition—the ride will take you eight to ten hours.

PRACTICALITIES:

Any day is good day to take this circle island tour. Weekdays you will find slightly less traffic because residents are not headed for the many beaches and parks along the route.

If you want to pick up delicious food grown along the way for a North Shore picnic, buy one of those styrofoam coolers at a drug or convenience store.

Sunglasses, sunscreen, hat, swimgear, perhaps snorkel and fins (which can be rented), beach mat and plenty of time. Leave nothing in your car, locked or unlocked.

FOOD AND DRINK:

Many food and drink spots are listed in the daytrips at the beginning and end of this Circle Island Tour. Refer to Trips 7-10 and 13, 14. These additional restaurants are for your consideration:

> **Crouching Lion Inn** (just before Kahana Bay at 51-666 Kamehameha Hwy.) Built as a residence in 1927, it seems like you're in a Tudor mansion with high wood beams and a giant fireplace. Try the chicken macadamia nut. Open daily for lunch and dinner. Art gallery and gift shop. ☎ 237-8511. $$

> **Ahi's Restaurant** (53-146 Kamehameha Hwy.) Good list of shrimp specials. Fresh ahi or mahimahi daily. Laid back atmosphere. Lunch and dinner Mon.–Sat., closed Sunday. ☎ 293-5650. $ to $$

> **Palm Terrace** (in the Turtle Bay Hilton Hotel, 57-091 Kamehameha Hwy.) Pleasant room with a splendid dinner buffet to satisfy everyone. Breakfast, lunch and dinner daily. Good view of the bay, so you can watch for turtles. ☎ 293-8811. $$

SUGGESTED TOUR:

Numbers in parentheses correspond to numbers on the map.

The beginning of this trip has been reviewed in Trips 7-10 starting in Kahala and proceeding through the windward side. Most of the important Local Attractions and Food and Drink are in those sections—for the beginning of the Circle Island anyway. At the other end, tours for Waimea, Haleiwa, Wailua and Schofield are covered in Trips 13 and 14.

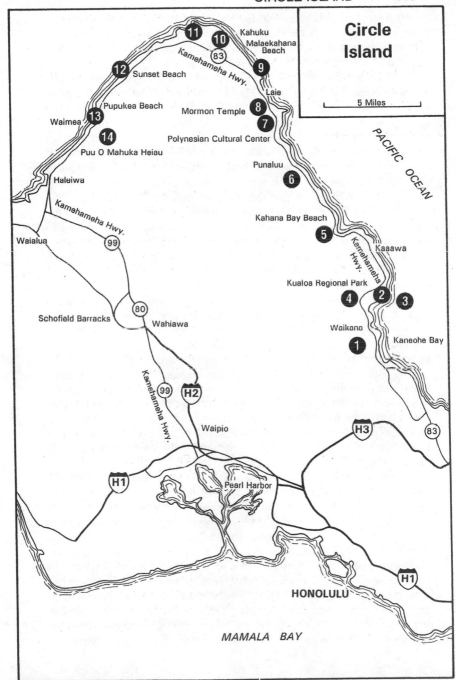

Circle
Island

5 Miles

PACIFIC OCEAN

Kahuku
Malaekahana
Beach

Kamehameha Hwy.

Sunset Beach

Laie

Pupukea Beach

Mormon Temple

Waimea

Polynesian Cultural Center

Puu O Mahuka Heiau

Punaluu

Haleiwa

Kamehameha Hwy.

Kahana Bay Beach

Waialua

Kaaawa

Kamehameha Hwy.

Schofield Barracks

Kualoa Regional Park

Wahiawa

Waikane

Kaneohe Bay

Kamehameha Hwy.

Waipio

Pearl Harbor

HONOLULU

MAMALA BAY

When you come back onto Kamehameha Highway from Kaneohe Bay Drive as though you are finishing Trip 10, turn right. After about a mile you will come to **Senator Fong's Plantation and Garden** (1) on the left at 47 Pulama Road, ☎ 239-8145. Now a nature preserve and bird sanctuary, this 725-acre park is the private estate of Senator Hiram Leong Fong, the first Asian-American to serve in the US Senate. The manicured gardens can be toured either via a special tram or on horseback. *There are five tram trips a day starting at 10:30 in the morning. Adults are $8.50, kids 5–12 $5.00. Horseback rides through the valleys and rainforest of the plantation range from one to four hours. These rides start at around $35 per hour.* Although Fong was a Republican Senator, in a show of bipartisanship he has named some of the valleys on his estate for Presidents Johnson, Nixon, Kennedy and Eisenhower. *There's a snack bar and gift shop.* ♿. ☎ *239-6775.*

Turn left on Kamehameha Highway. The road starts to really have the country feel as it winds through the trees. Way back against the steep *pali* are horse farms and some cattle ranches. Here and there along the road you will see farms, nurseries and roadside stands selling produce and flowers. Do stop, especially if you brought along the cooler for a possible beach picnic somewhere on the North Shore.

When the trees start to open up, you are approaching **Kualoa Regional Park** (2) on the right. It is open from 7–8. This open, grassy area is one of the biggest beach parks on the island. On weekends it accommodates literally dozens of families who come to swim, play in the water, picnic and camp. In spite of all that traffic, it never seems crowded.

The park faces one of Oahu's best known sights. The little cone-shaped island just offshore is commonly called **Chinaman's Hat** (3), or in Hawaiian, Mokoli'i Island. Geologically, it is a sea stack. The cone shape is the resistant part of the old Ko'olau volcano that remained as the rest of the mass was eroded away by the sea and time. While it looks temptingly close at low tide (it's only 600 yards offshore), it's advisable not to attempt to walk to the island. Better just to enjoy the view.

Opposite the park is **Kualoa Ranch & Activity Center** (4) at 49-560 Kamehameha Highway. This 4,000-acre working ranch started out as a sugar plantation. Around the turn of the century, cattle were brought in since sugar did not work out. Horseback riding in the 1970s gave visitors a chance to see the incredible beauty of the valleys and hills of the ranch. That single activity spawned what today has become a fascinating mix of agriculture, education, conservation and recreation. You can go on the ranch at no charge and enjoy just observing all the activities—or you can "pay for play" both on land and on the water. Singly or in various packages, you can have the fun of horseback rides, dune cycles, mountain biking, helicopter rides, scuba diving, sailing, jet skiing, snorkeling, canoeing or windsurfing. An example is the Secret Island & Snorkel Tour. Restaurant open for lunch daily. *Call 237-8515 for information about package rates and special events.*

A wide, gentle curve in the road after Kualoa Ranch signals **Kahana Bay Beach Park** (5). What makes this stretch of beach and the bay attractive for swimming is that it is so protected. It is set way back from the ocean and that makes it calm most of the time. Weekdays find the beach empty, except perhaps for some shore fishermen now and then.

At Punaluu, there are two rather large apartment/condo buildings. This tells you to start looking on the left for the **Sacred Falls State Park** (6), open from 7–6:45 The ancient Hawaiians believed that the pool beneath the falls was bottomless and merged with another realm where evil spirits lived. Though these spirits were continually trying to surface, they were held back by the plunging force of the sacred waterfall. To this day, it seems a perpetual struggle waged between the white waters descending from above and the dark mysteries ever rising from unknown depths. The area is a state park, and as its name suggests, is a sacred place to be respected. The hike in takes less than an hour.

Turn left when you come out of the falls. Enjoy the drive through country areas of small homes and farms. Watch the road, but enjoy the ocean which is right beside you for the next several miles. You will be tempted to stop your car and walk along the sand. Do it, then continue on to the:

*POLYNESIAN CULTURAL CENTER (7) 55-370 Kamehameha Hwy., Honolulu, HI 96762, ☎ 923-2911. *Open 12:30 p.m.–9:30 p.m. daily. Closed Sun. and major holidays. Adults $27, kids 5–11 $16. Snack bars. Treasures of the Pacific Shopping Plaza.* ⅙.

The 42-acre Center showcases the traditional lifestyle of Fiji, Hawaii, New Zealand, Marquesas, Samoa, Tahiti and Tonga. Villages typical of these Pacific islands are arranged around a picturesque lagoon. Double-hulled canoes navigate the lagoon daily taking visitors from one village to the next.

A leisurely walking tour, however, will get you up close and personal so you can get a complete village experience. Villagers in each area involve guests in demonstrations such as making *ngatu* or tapa cloth; climbing a coconut tree and then husking and opening the nuts; or pounding boiled taro roots into *poi*. Polynesians love games, a number of which are featured in the villages.

When it's time to eat, the Center offers samples of traditional island foods available in each village such as Hawaiian poi, or baked bananas. Besides these little samples, the Alii Luau takes guests back in time while they enjoy traditional Hawaiian food and entertainment. Hula dance favorites from the thirties and forties are blended with old-time *hapa-haole* music. Following dinner there is an extravaganza called "Horizons, Where the Sea Meets the Sky." This is big-time show biz with over 100 performers, 58 costume designs and 600 costumes in all. The luau, show and general admission are packaged under $60. *For reservations call 293-3333.*

After leaving the Polynesian Cultural Center (PCC), you may want to drive within the Laie area to see the **Mormon Temple** and **Brigham Young University** (8). These three attractions plus the shopping center and most of the roads belong to the church, thus making Laie essentially a Mormon Church-owned town. In 1865, the Church of Jesus Christ of Latter-Day Saints purchased 6,000 acres for $14,000. Through hard work and the right investments, the Church has turned what was a sandy and pretty desolate sugar plantation into a humming enterprise. It works like this: more than 30,000 students, mainly from Polynesia, have helped finance their college education at BYU-Hawaii while working at the PCC. Of the 1,000 people employed by PCC, 70 percent are BYU students. The PCC has hosted more than 24 million guests since it was opened in 1963.

Turn left again at the highway and after about half a mile, look on the right for **Malaekahana Beach Park** (9). It is open 7–7:45. After you park your car, consider a walk on this treasure of a North Shore beach. There is no reef on this part of the island, so the surf will come rushing in pretty strongly. This is a great beach for walking and sitting—and not so good for swimming. If you brought along a picnic, this is the right spot for it. Just offshore is a bird refuge called Goat island which you can walk to at low tide. If you go over, enjoy the curved white sand beach, but under no circumstances disturb the birds.

A right turn will take you into Kahuku about a mile down the road. At Puuluana Road turn right and make your way through what used to be plantation housing. The road stops at the **Kahuku Golf Course** (10). This rustic nine-hole course runs along a fabulous white sand beach. If you're inspired to try the windy and practically treeless course, clubs and a pull cart can be rented. Greens fees for 18 holes (the nine played twice) is $40. There's something intriguing about playing a non-resort course right along the beach with the ocean as a backdrop.

As you make your way along the highway, keep in mind that from the mountains to the sea was once all sugar cane. The winds and unpredictable rains made growing cane unfeasible, and it went away about 30 years ago. Many replacements have been tried. As the road rises, note on the right a sizable series of depressions. All these ponds once made up a huge aquaculture farm that grew wonderful salt water shrimp that was shipped all over the world. Still, the economics did not work and it ceased operation some time ago. Small truck farms can be seen along the left side of the road selling fresh fruits and vegetables. Try some.

The **Turtle Bay Hilton Hotel** (11) is worth a stop. The hotel sits on a point of land that can get pretty windy, but the point shelters Turtle Bay to the left where surfers and turtles (at times) ride the same waves.

After turning right coming out of the hotel, the road wanders along the shoreline for several miles until there appears an opening for the famous **Sunset Beach** (12). Surf movies, magazines and videotapes have all contributed to the fame of this beach. It is usually calm during the summer months, but in winter the waves build up in "sets" that can reach 20–30 feet. Just a short distance down the road is Ehukai Beach Park, and a bit farther still, Banzai Pipeline. The latter got its name from the shape of the waves—like pipes—created by a coral reef. Some amazing surfing legends have been made at "the pipe."

A suggested stop is at the **Pupukea Beach Park** (13) to inspect the tide pools. Unlike many other coastlines, Hawaii doesn't have much of this kind of shoreline. You will see all manner of snorkel and scuba skills at this spot.

Turn left up Pupukea Road. It climbs pretty quickly and twists and turns a bit, but the views start to get awesome as you go higher. About a mile up on the right, follow the signs to **Puu o Mahuka Heiau** (14). After nearly another mile, you will reach a plateau and opening. Before you are the remains of Oahu's oldest Hawaiian *heiau*, an open-air temple used for human sacrifices. The silence, the sweeping view and the gentle breeze from the ocean way below gives you a good sense of how sacred this spot was for the ancient Hawaiians.

If you continue up Pupukea Road, you will see some modest as well as estate-like homes. At the top on the right is the horse farm/estate of the man who developed the Kahala Hilton Hotel (now called the Kahala Mandarin Oriental Hotel as described in Daytrip 7).

From this point on, you should refer to Daytrips 13 and 14. Once you pass Haleiwa, follow the signs to Honolulu and eventually Waikiki.

Section III

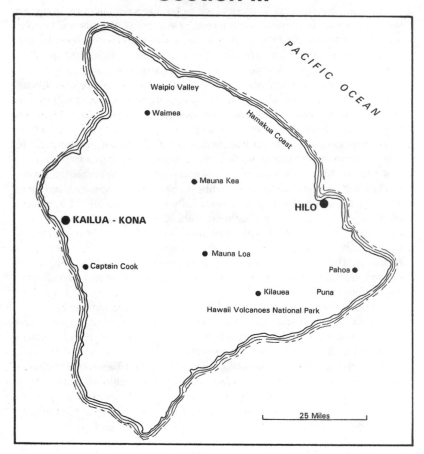

Waipio Valley

• Waimea

PACIFIC OCEAN

Hamakua Coast

• Mauna Kea

HILO ●

● KAILUA - KONA

• Mauna Loa

• Captain Cook

Pahoa ●

• Kilauea   Puna

Hawaii Volcanoes National Park

25 Miles

DAYTRIPS ON THE
BIG ISLAND OF
HAWAII

There's something fascinating about the Big Island being the newest in the Hawaiian island chain, and at the same time having brought forth two of the most dramatic changes to the entire state. Youngsters have a tendency to do that.

Those changes were, in order: The birth of Kamehameha the Great in the Kohala area and his warring success in unifying all the islands; and the arrival in 1820 of the first Americans as missionaries to civilize these tiny islands in the wide Pacific. A third event, the arrival of Captain Cook in 1779, also brought dramatic changes, but he landed first on Kauai.

Thus, the Big Island clearly has its place in the history of Hawaii. Adding to that is the continuing drama of its landscape. It changes almost daily when Kilauea Volcano erupts and sends lava charging to the sea. The Big Island has a clear place in science too, because atop a dormant volcano, Mauna Kea, sits about $1 billion worth of telescopes that scan the skies at night to bring back invaluable information about our solar system.

The east side of the island is decidedly unflashy. There are no mega-resorts with carved golf courses or trams to take you to your room. Fishing on this side is mainly of the commercial kind. But for culture and incredible floral beauty, nothing beats the Hilo side of the island. Two "must" destinations for visitors, Volcanoes National Park and Mauna Kea, however, are both much more accessible from the east side.

Almost always sunny, visitors from around the world flock to the *Kona* or west side to fish, swim, snorkel, golf, dive, explore—and much more. Many years ago Laurance Rockefeller spotted a white crescent beach among many miles of stark-looking lava fields on the west coast of the Big Island, and in one stroke created what has become a string of luxury resorts unrivaled anywhere in the world.

The Big Island is BIG compared with its neighbors. It is 65 percent larger than all the other Hawaiian Islands combined, and still growing thanks to Kilauea. It makes sense that driving distances are certainly greater. Agriculture plays a large role on the Big Island too. Cattle ranches are gargantuan—one is 225,000 acres. And we can't forget famous Kona coffee among many other crops grown here.

ACCOMMODATIONS:

Diversity is the word for accommodations all over the Big Island. Luxury resorts, as mentioned earlier, abound on the west side. But there are modest bed-and-breakfast places as well. There's plenty of middle ground in hotels and condos, too.

Aston Hotels and Resorts has two wonderful condominium resorts in Kona. The Royal Seacliff is a terraced oceanfront condo that sports fresh and salt water pools. Aston's Kona by the Sea was rated three diamonds by AAA. Both resorts, as condos, have full kitchens. *Aston's toll-free number is (800) 922-7866.*

In Hilo, the **Naniloa Hotel** offers reasonable accommodations. It is right on the bayfront with dramatic views toward Mauna Kea. *Their toll-free number is (800) 442-5845.*

GETTING AROUND:

There are tour companies that will take you to places you can't normally reach such as Waipio Valley, the top of Mauna Kea or onto private property offering rainforests and huge ranches. These are very worthwhile.

For general travel, a car is by far the best way to get around the island because it provides you flexibility. You can stop anywhere and poke around when you're on your own versus being on a tour group. **Budget** usually has plenty of vehicles of all descriptions. *Budget's toll-free number is (800) 527-0700.*

PRACTICALITIES:

All too often you see bright-red sunburned people who have overdone the sun in an attempt to take back a golden tan. Not only can it ruin your vacation, but it can threaten your life as well. Do not hesitate to use plenty of the strongest sunscreen. As the matter of fact, you will get a much more even and better tan with sunscreen. Sunglasses are a must too, especially when you are near the water.

There are lots of colorful and fun hats available in Hawaii. Get one and wear it regularly. Rubber sandals or slippers are good for certain things, but comfortable walking shoes are an even better bet.

Prepare to take everything out of your car when you stop to explore. Don't leave anything in the trunk either. Locking your rental car empty is the best idea.

VISITOR INFORMATION:

Hawaii Visitors Bureau, 75-5719 Alii Dr., Kailua-Kona, HI 96740, ☎ (808) 329-7787. Also at 250 Keawe St., Hilo, HI 96720, ☎ (808) 961-2126.

Destination Kona Coast, P.O. Box 2850, Kailua-Kona, HI 96745, ☎ (808) 329-6748.

Destination Hilo, P.O. Box 1391, Hilo, HI 96721, ☎ (808) 935-5294.

Kohala Coast Resort Associates, HCO2 Box 5300, Kohala Coast, Island of Hawaii 96743.

East Side Story/Hilo

Hilo, the island's capitol, curls around a crescent bay where Mauna Loa meets Mauna Kea. The town has always had a comfortable pace that visitors notice right away. In downtown Hilo, "talk story" (which means chit-chat) between residents and merchants is the norm.

Before the glitzy resorts came to the *Kona* side of the Big Island, Hilo was the trade and civic center of the island. It is still the government hub, but the major economic forces are now elsewhere.

The little town by the bay still has its charm; a blend of the old and the new. The contemporary state and county buildings are mixed together with tin-roofed one- and two-story wooden buildings housing Chinese preserved-fruit stores, Japanese *mochi* shops and soda fountains with the old-fashioned spinning stools. A good deal of downtown has been refurbished mainly through the national Main Street program. Revitalized businesses and buildings are springing up all the time.

Plunked just outside of the present downtown is a wide grassy area that once was filled with buildings, but was pretty well wiped out by the giant tidal waves the struck twice in Hilo. There's also a peaceful 30-acre Oriental park called Liliuokalani Garden. Designed and maintained in authentic Japanese style, it purportedly is the largest of its type outside Japan.

GETTING THERE:

By car, from the Hamakua Coast (which is north), Hilo is approached from Highway 19; from Volcano or the south, the town is approached on Highway 11.

By air, Hilo is served with 16 flights a day by Aloha Airlines. Hawaiian Air also flies into General Lyman Field.

PRACTICALITIES:

Hilo doesn't always like to admit it, but it does rain here more than most other places in the islands. The trade-offs are the waterfalls and the lush foliage. Keep in mind that it seldom rains for long periods of time, but a small umbrella could come in handy.

In spite of the moisture, bring along your sunglasses, sunscreen and comfortable walking shoes.

FOOD AND DRINK:

Harrington's (135 Kalanianaole St. by Reed's Bay) Housed in what looks like a little house are some terrific steak and seafood dinners. It can be cool since you're right on the water. Dinner only, daily. Reservations, ☎ 961-4966. $ to $$

Fiasco's Restaurant (200 Kanoelehua near Banyan Dr. on the Volcano Hwy.) Lots of big and juicy burgers, and a Bountiful Salad Bar that is an all-you-can-eat bargain. Open daily for lunch and dinner. ☎ 935-7666. $

Uncle Billy's Restaurant (87 Banyan Dr. in Hilo Bay Hotel) Tropical atmosphere with a hearty steak and seafood menu. Good Hawaiian entertainment with hula show nightly. Breakfast and dinner daily. ☎ 961-5818. $ to $$

Café Pesto (308 Kamehameha Ave. in the S. Hata Building) Pacific Asian cuisine including fresh seafood, pizza and pasta in a lively setting. Lunch and dinner daily. ☎ 969-6640. $ to $$.

SUGGESTED TOUR:

Numbers in parentheses correspond to numbers on the map.

Hilo is a town worth getting to know closely. Our suggested tour starts with walking and ends up with a short drive to take in the highlights outside of downtown.

To get started, find **Kalakaua Park** (1), surrounded on three sides by Kinoole, Waianuenue and Kalakaua streets. The statute to the king known as the "Merrie Monarch" for his love of dance and fun, commemorates his design of the first county complex at this very spot. The reflecting pond is in recognition of soldiers of all wars.

If you cross Waianuenue, you will be able to explore the recently-restored **Federal Building** (2) housing the post office and other fed agencies. Note the neo-classical design. Good, solid oak doors and lots of brass signify this as a very substantial structure.

When you cross Kalakaua going in the opposite direction, you will approach the **East Hawaii Cultural Center** (3), located in what was the old Police Station. This excellent exhibition space shows contemporary and local artists, and periodically has traveling shows from around the state. Upstairs is the Performing Arts Center and Concert Society where recitals are held frequently. *Call 935-8850 for a schedule. The Cultural center shows are free. Open from 10–4 Mon.–Sat.* ☎ 961-5711.

The next noteworthy structure going downhill on Kalakaua is the **Hawaiian Telephone Company Building** (4), next door to the Cultural Center. This

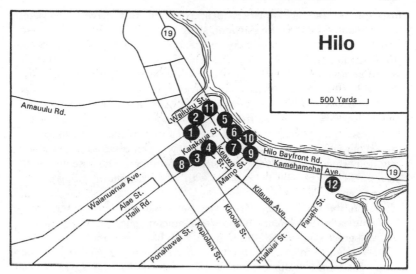

structure was designed by C.W. Dickey, who is credited with developing
Hawaiian Regional Architecture in the early 20th century. The most distinctive elements of this design are the high-hipped roof in green tiles, with
brightly-colored terra cotta tiles set in the building.

Another example of Dickey's work is at the corner of Kalakaua and
Kamehameha. The **First Hawaiian Bank Building** (5) with its parapet, fluted
columns and wrought-iron design was built in 1930. Although it is directly
on the bayfront, this sturdy concrete building withstood both the 1946 and
1960 tsunamis that caused 234 deaths and $50 million in damage. Partly
because of this fact and the generosity of the bank, the building has become
the Hilo Tsunami Museum. Photos of the devastation and stories of the hero-
ics during both catastrophes are stark reminders of the power of the sea.

As you walk along Kamehameha Avenue, in the next block is the **S.H.
Kress Company Building** (6). When it opened in 1932, floral designs,
batwing shapes and the terra cotta front contributed to introducing a new
kind of architecture—Art Deco. Restoration of the building was completed
in 1995, and it now houses a four-plex movie theater and nifty ice cream
parlor.

Turn right on Haili Street; at mid-block is the **Palace Theater** (7). Hilo's
Palace was built in 1925 for Adam Baker, son of the last Royal Governor of
the Island of Hawaii. The spacious lobby and auditorium are reminiscent of
the Art Deco days. Restoration of the Palace is still going on, and when completed will provide a performance venue for the blend of ethnic groups that
make up the Hawaiian Culture.

Cross Keawe and Kinoole, and then take a fairly long block to the **Ly-**

man Museum and Mission House (8) at 276 Haili. This marvelous museum was originally the Hilo Boys School, started in 1836 by Reverend Lyman. He was an enterprising missionary who taught native Hawaiian boys blacksmithing, printing and carpentry. The school operated for nearly 100 years. The Museum allows you to journey into Hawaii's interesting past by telling the story of the islands and its people through its extensive collection of artifacts. This is one of the best ways to learn about the state's multiculturalism. The museum also has an Astronomy Exhibit where you can learn how the ancient Hawaiians viewed their universe and used their knowledge of astronomy. In juxtaposition, you can discover how modern astronomers view our universe and see the instruments they use in their research. This is especially appropriate with all the astronomy going on atop Mauna Kea.

To tour the Mission House is to step back in time—into the Missionary Era of the early 19th century. A knowledgeable member of their interpretive staff will guide you through this home, which has been restored with many of its original furnishings. *The Museum and Mission House are open Mon.–Sat. from 9–4:30. Six tours a day. Adult admission is $5; kids under 17 $2.50, and seniors $3. Gift shop in the lobby.* ☎ *935-5021 for further information.*

Next we suggest you get in your car. If you travel along Kamehameha Avenue from Mamo going toward Wailuku Street, you will see in succession the **S. Hata Building** (9) that was built by the family in 1912 and confiscated by the U.S. government during WWII as property belonging to aliens. On the corner is the **Vana Building** (10), reminiscent of romantic Caribbean architecture with a tiled roof, plastered walls and arch windows. And finally, on the corner of Waianuenue is the **Koehnen's Building** (11). It was originally built for the Hackfield Company, one of the original Big Five that controlled commerce in the islands for nearly a hundred years. A thoughtful restoration emphasizes the exterior decorative details as well as preserving the koa walls and ohia floors.

Head out Kamehameha Avenue as though you were going to the airport. The first stop is the **Wailoa State Park Recreation Area** (12) at Kamehameha Avenue and Pauahi Street. The wide open areas are great for picnics, and sometimes you will see small boats fishing in Wailoa Fishpond. Proudly installed in the park recently is an Italian-made statute of King Kamehameha. The statute is usually festooned daily with huge leis around its neck and smaller leis at the base. Originally, the statute was to be a gift by the Princeville Corporation for its Kauai resort, but there was real resistance since Kamehameha never conquered Kauai as he did other islands (Kauai's King Kaumualii actually conceded the island to Kamehameha on his death). Visit the **Wailoa Visitors Center,** a worthwhile stop with its photos of Hilo's history, and changing exhibits. *Open Mon., Tues., Thurs. and Fri. 8–4:30, Wed. noon–8:30, and Sat. 9–noon. Closed Sun. Free.* ☎ *933-4360.*

The shoreline by **Liliuokalani Gardens** is worth a walk. Many small inlets, tide pools and a bridge across to Coconut Island for picnicking, wading and fishing make this fun for any age. Check out the **Suisan Fish Auction** weekdays at around 8 in the morning. If you walk a bit farther to Banyan Drive you will see several hotels and restaurants strung along this mile-long road with 50 giant banyan trees planted in the 1930s by famous people such as Babe Ruth, Amelia Earhart and so forth. All of the trees have plaques with the name of the person who planted it.

There's still another way to get around Hilo town called the **Hilo Sampan.** These open-air vehicles are found nowhere else in the world. They're old Chevys and Plymouths with custom made passenger compartments that hold up to eight. For many years they took Hilo residents around town for five- and ten-cent fares (their slogan is "Get There . . . Yesterday"). In 1994 they were brought back. Now you can take a two-hour ride from the Pier where cruise and cargo ships dock, through historic downtown and out to the University of Hawaii Hilo campus. *The current fare is $2.* ☎ *959-7864.*

If you've had enough of sightseeing and want some water activity, consider taking a dive with **Nautilus Dive Center** at 382 Kamehameha Avenue. They will take you to Hilo's best all-around dive site at Leleiwi Beach, which is about four miles from town. There's abundant sealife such as green sea turtles and tropical fish. The terrain on the ocean floor includes three lava arches. For introductory divers, the fee is $65 for tank, weight belt and the personalized attention of an instructor. They have many dives as well as rentals for kayaks and Boogie Boards. ☎ *935-6939.*

Trip 23

Puna/Pahoa

During this daytrip, we will explore the easternmost point of the Big Island. One of the roads we will take used to connect up with the Chain of Craters Road in Volcanoes National Park. Now there are barricades where the recent (those from 1983 to present) lava eruptions from Kilauea have flowed to the ocean, wiping out a couple of small communities as well as the road. Maybe the good news is that the Big Island is getting bigger as the steaming lava hits the ocean—creating new land. Is this landbanking for future generations compliments of Pele, the Hawaiian fire goddess?

Even though the Pahoa area hasn't seen an eruption in almost 40 years, there is evidence of earlier flows all around. At one state park, we'll see Ohia trees that were turned into lava trees toward the end of the 18th century. Then there's the lighthouse at the very tip of the island that was surrounded by lava, but was miraculously saved.

The east/south shore of the Pahoa area has many interesting shore stops, including a naturally heated pool we will visit on this trip.

GETTING THERE:

By car, get on Highway 11 going toward the Volcano National Park. About five miles out of town, turn left at Keaau and get on Highway 130. Follow this route to Pahoa town.

PRACTICALITIES:

Take the usual precautions when in Hawaii by having with you sunscreen, sunglasses, a hat and comfortable shoes. The other usual precaution is to leave nothing in your car or its trunk whether locked or unlocked.

FOOD AND DRINK:

Keep in mind that this is rural Hawaii, where street names and addresses are pretty casual. When you ask residents for their street address, they usually shrug and give you that quizzical "Are you a tourist?" look. These three restaurants are in Pahoa town—which is pretty small—along what is sometimes called Old Government Road.

Godmothers Restaurant (Pahoa Village) Long-time Italian eatery that serves breakfast, lunch and dinner daily. Good pasta dishes that will fill you up. ☎ 965-0055. $ to $$

Luquins Mexican Restaurant (Pahoa Village) The usual Mexican meals, but they also proudly serve American sandwiches. Try the fresh fish tacos and their specialty, Carnittos. Lunch and dinner daily. ☎ 982-9883. $

Pahoa Chop Suey (Pahoa Village next to Dairy Queen) Quite a long list of good Chinese dishes served in a rather plain atmosphere. That keeps the prices down. ☎ 965-9533. $

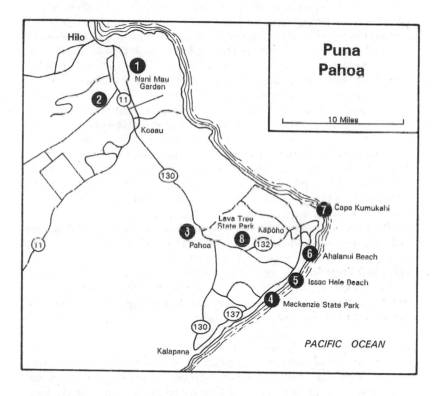

LOCAL ATTRACTIONS:

Numbers in parentheses correspond to numbers on the map.

The Big Island isn't called the Orchid Isle for nothing. A great way to see hundreds of varieties of orchids and other tropical plants and trees is to visit the **Nani Mau Gardens** (1). On your way out of town on Highway 19, after about three miles, turn left on Makalika Street. You will be rewarded with 20 acres of meticulously manicured floral gardens. You can walk, which is about 45 minutes, or take a tram for an extra $5 that takes about half an hour. Don't miss the Botanical Museum for an educational experience. There's a neat restaurant open for lunch and a gift shop. *Open every day from 8–5. Adults are $7.50, seniors $6 and kids 6–18 $4.* ☎ *959-3541.* ♿.

A bit farther up the road on the right, look for signs to the **Panaewa Rainforest Zoo** (2) and turn right at Mamaki Street. Go up about one mile. It is primarily an educational and recreational facility that is still under development, so don't expect a big city-type zoo with cage after cage of animals. The exhibits are designed to blend with existing terrain and vegetation, and the animals are exhibited in a natural setting wherever possible. The theme of the zoo is based on its location—in the Panaewa Forest reserve, which receives 125 inches of rainfall a year. There is a pleasant paved walkway leading through the zoo. *Donations for admission are requested—and needed. Open 9–4:15, daily except Christmas and New Years.* ☎ *959-7224.*

At the junction of the road at Keaau, turn left and get on Highway 130. Go ten miles and look for a sign to turn right to the little village of **Pahoa** (3), established in 1909. Sugar was king in this part of the island for many years, and Pahoa was the center. It's a great little one-street town with raised wooden sidewalks along false-front buildings. If you spend any time people-watching, you'll see a lot of hippie-type residents. It's hard to know if they've moved in recently, or never left.

If you keep going through Pahoa, it will take you back to the highway. Go right for another five miles and follow signs to **Kaimu**, which isn't there any more. It is here that you will run into the barricade erected by the National Park Service when the lava cascaded across the road in 1990. Sometimes you will see people walking on the lava that crossed the road, but DO NOT go beyond the barricades. It's enough to sit there for a while and realize the huge force of nature that wiped out two towns, many homes and, of course, the road.

Retrace your route and follow signs to **Kalapana**. Again, it isn't there any more. Turn right, and then when the road comes to a T, turn right again and shortly you will come to another barricade. Park here. On a tree there is a little sign that directs you one quarter of a mile across the lava to the "new" beach park. Native Hawaiians are creating another park with palm trees at the water's edge. It's nothing like the original Kapalana, but it's a beginning.

As you turn back again on the road you came in on, make special note of the five or six houses on the *mauka* (mountain side) that were spared from the onrushing lava. What is remarkable is that these lovely homes still stand with ominous black lava directly across the street on the *makai* (ocean side) as their silent, but unwelcome neighbor. These are brave souls who live in such a perilous neighborhood.

The route you are on is Highway 137, which is winding and narrow enough in places to be only one car in width. Be prepared for some roughness. But all of that seems okay because it is a beautiful drive. The trees are so thick in spots that the canopy overhead makes it quite dark.

About five miles along the road, turn right and pull into the **Mackenzie State Recreation Area** (4). The park is actually a large grove of ironwood trees fronting a sharp drop-off to the ocean. Be careful at the water's edge because the ocean has such force that periodically it will send spouts thirty feet in the air. What's interesting to note here is the separate layers of black lava revealed by the erosion of the sea. These layers are from successive eruptions. The facilities are minimal.

Turn right back on Highway 137. After a few miles you will come to an intersection pointing right toward **Isaac Hale Beach Park** (5) There's a boat ramp and small bay where you will see some swimmers and surfers. There's no beach to speak of, however the water in the area is warmed from geo-thermal steam below the surface. Some people say the reason for all the fishing boats at this spot is because the warm water means bigger fish. Fishermen will believe anything.

Keep your eyes open for a chain-link fence about three miles farther along the road. You're about to be treated to swimming in water heated from the volcano at **Ahalanui Beach Park** and its accompanying **Mauna Kea Pond** (6). There's a large yellow one-story house that the county bought along with the sizable pool right at the ocean's edge. The pool is fresh water heated to 93 degrees, and is a real treat for swimming. Apparently rainwater (at 36 degrees) collects at the 2,700-foot elevation of Kilauea and enters a lava tube which travels along until the water hits red-hot magma. At that point, the water is heated to 112 degrees. After it travels another six miles to the Mauna Kea Pond, it has cooled down to 93 degrees. Clear and nicely warm, swimming in the 20 yard long pool can be very therapeutic. *The park is open from 7–7 daily.*

Continue on until you come to an intersection of Highway 132. Turn right and go 1.5 miles across acres and acres of lava fields to **Cape Kumukahi Lighthouse** (7). The legend is that the keeper treated Pele (the goddess of fire) properly, and so she spared the lighthouse from the 1960 flow that in-undated about 2,000 acres. See for yourself how the lava parted just before the steel-skeleton lighthouse and made its way on either side on its way to the sea.

Head straight back on Highway 132 past rolling papaya fields and rows and rows of dendrobium orchids. Resist the temptation to help yourself.

At the next intersection, the road bears right and almost immediately on the right is the entrance to **Lava Tree State Park** (8). There's a paved walk-way that goes about three quarters of a mile through a peaceful wooded area with some huge trees. The lava tree monuments are dotted throughout the area. They were formed from a lava flow estimated to have taken place al-most two hundred years ago. Originally, this area was a stand of huge Ohia trees which were engulfed by the hot lava around 1790. The moisture in the trees was enough to cool the lava and encase the tree trunks. The rest of the molten lava flowed to the ocean. The trees have obviously rotted away, leaving some monuments twenty feet tall after all these years.

For a different experience in this part of the island, consider a 20-mile mountain bike ride along the Puna coast. Bikes can be rented at The Bike Hub in Hilo. This is called the **"Wild Orchid Ride."** Head south out of Hilo and take the Keaau turnoff (Highway 130). Turn left on Kaloli Road and go another 4.2 miles to Beach Road. Park here. This is a fun coastal ride through fields of wild orchids, rainforest canopy and mud puddles (if it's rained recently). The ride is fast and easy, starting out on red cinder and moving inland a bit. The dirt road ends on the pavement at Kapoho where you turn around. Or if you want a longer ride, continue on 137 for another 12 miles through Kapoho and into Kalapana. *The Bike Hub is open Mon.–Sat. from 9–5. Bikes rent between $20 and $30 a day. Call 961-4452 for reservations and information.*

Hamakua Coast/Waipio

If you fly along east shore of the Big Island heading into Hilo, two sights are very apparent. First are the sheer cliffs all along the coast with periodic deep cuts made by streams flowing down from Mauna Kea, and the huge amount of water dumping into the ocean from those cuts. Second is the massiveness of 13,796-foot-high Mauna Kea standing sentinel-like over what is usually called the Hamakua Coast.

Upslope from the cliffs used to be thousands of acres of prime sugar cane, but labor, processing and transportation costs got so high that all of the plantations have closed.

Keep your eyes peeled for the narrow band of highway that follows along the coastal bluffs and then dips down into the valleys. It is commonly called the Belt Highway and in many places follows the original King's Trail laid out by Kamehameha The Great. This will be our route all the way to Waipio Valley. Along the road, there are small plantation towns with interesting shops and restaurants. A couple of spectacular waterfalls and other attractions will make this a busy day.

GETTING THERE:
By car, head north from Hilo town on Highway 19.

PRACTICALITIES:
Sunscreen, sunglasses, hat, comfortable walking shoes and perhaps bug spray. Take everything with you when you leave your car, whether it's locked or unlocked.

FOOD AND DRINK:
What's Shakin' (on Scenic Route beyond Onomea Bay) Charming little plantation building serves up good pizzas and burgers plus their special tropical drinks like Hibiscus or Mango smoothies. Open daily 10–5. ☎ 964-3080. $
Jolene's Kaukau Korner (45-3625 Mamane St. in Honokaa) Pleasant local eatery with a mix of sandwiches, burgers and plate lunches.

Dine in or take out. Lunch and dinner Mon.–Sat., closed Sun. ☎
775-9478. $

Waipio Valley Café (bottom of the hill in Kukuihaele) Next door to a
marvelous little gallery, they serve light breakfast and lunch daily.
Pure Kona coffee and homemade ice cream are their specialties. ☎
775-0958. $

LOCAL ATTRACTIONS:

Numbers in parentheses correspond to numbers on the map.

As you leave Hilo on Highway 19, after five miles look for the blue highway sign that says "Scenic Route" and turn right. You will drop down closer
to the coast, although not exactly at sea level, as you go through heavy foliage and cross numerous streams headed for Onomea Bay.

About two miles along the road you will come to the **Hawaii Tropical
Botanical Garden** (1). This 20-acre private garden was gifted to a non-profit
foundation in the late 1980s. With over 2,000 different species of flowers,
palms and plants from around the world, the garden considers itself first and
foremost a tropical rainforest. It is dedicated to preserving rare and endangered tropical plants, endemic Hawaii plants and wildlife. A new Visitor
Center and entry takes you to the start of a self-guided walking tour of about
a mile. The walk wanders through ginger, haleconia, orchids, and past a
three-level waterfall and pools. Allow about two hours for your tour. *The
garden is open Mon.–Fri. from 8:30–5. Adult admission is $15. Kids under
16 are free. Call 964-5233 for further information.*

Back on the highway, turn right. After about three miles look for Route
220 on the left. This will take you up a fairly steep road past the old plantation town of Honomu to **Akaka Falls State Park** (2). At 65 acres, this park
includes a winding path (with some pretty steep ups and downs) through
bamboo, ginger, ferns and ti on its way to the falls. Akaka Falls is the upper and Kahuna Falls the lower of the two 400 foot cascades. The roar of
the water going over the sheer cliffs is pretty significant since these falls
are twice the height of Niagara. There are facilities at the park. *Open 7–
7 daily.*

On the way back down, be sure to stop in Honomu and have a freshly
baked peach/pineapple turnover at Ishigo's General Store. The little town
also has several attractive galleries, cafés and gift shops worth visiting.

As you turn left going back onto the highway, there will be several ways
to get down off the highway along the bluffs to the ocean below. The first is
Kolekole Beach Park (3), a half-mile down from the turnoff to the falls. For
Kolekole, look for the sign and turn left, which will take you down a long
switchback until you're practically under the highway far above. There's a
nice grassy area with a covered pavilion for picnicking. Full facilities. The
fresh water stream on the left has some pukas (openings) for swimming, but
only if it hasn't just rained.

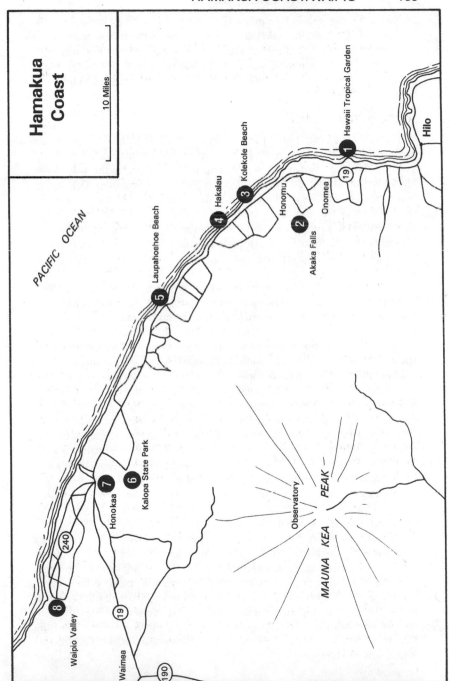

Hamakua Coast

10 Miles

PACIFIC OCEAN

Hawaii Tropical Garden
Hilo
Kolekole Beach
Hakalau
Honomu
Onomea
Akaka Falls
Laupahoehoe Beach
Kalopa State Park
Honokaa
Waipio Valley
Waimea
Observatory
MAUNA KEA PEAK

Re-enter the highway by turning left. About a mile down the road, look for a sign on the right for **Hakalau** (4). This is one of the nearly abandoned plantation towns along the Hamakua Coast. Large, silent buildings with boarded-up windows remind you of what was once a vibrant and productive area. The large white plantation manager's house on the left looks lived in, but that's about all. The rough road down to the water eventually comes to a cement path. It isn't advisable to drive on it, but you can walk out to the ocean on it.

Probably the best known park along the coast is **Laupahoehoe Beach Park** (5). There are signs on the right at about Mile Marker 27. A winding road will take you down to the park and the water. Along the way is the 1899 Laupahoehoe Jodo Mission with its distinctive design and elaborate decorations. It was restored recently. Visitors are welcome for a donation. While the two previous beach parks are fairly small, Laupahoehoe has broad lawns leading to a rocky coastline. Full facilities. A spot of beauty, it also has a good deal of sadness in its history. In the park is a monument dedicated to the 24 school children who lost their lives in the 1946 *tsunami* (tidal wave).

Look for **Paauilo Town** on the left after about five miles. Paauilo illustrates the plantation community in microcosm. The plantation manager's house is set back on a hill. The field managers' homes are below the highway, as are the workers' camp housing and the abandoned mill site.

While we have mostly paid attention to the ocean and its shoreline, now we will turn left and head inland at **Kalopa State Park** (6) around Mile Marker 39. Take the turnoff three miles up to a wonderfully cool and wooded area. The park is 615 acres total, but only about 100 acres are used at the present time. The park offers horseback riding, hiking, camping and cabins—and just plain relaxing. For information about camping or the cabins call 933-4200. The park is mostly about trees, so one of the hikes they have designed is a .7-mile Native Forest Nature Trail that makes a loop through Ohia, Kopiko, Strawberry Guava, Kukui and fern trees. This is guaranteed to be the only trail in the world paved in macadamia nut shells. Stations along the loop trail sound like names from a walk in Christopher Robin's Hundred Acre Wood—such as Guava Jam, Cricket Junction, Litter Bugs and A Strange Place. Full facilities.

About three miles down the road, Highway 240 bears right and heads into **Honakaa** (7). This is the major town between Hilo and Waimea. It's reason for being was sugar, but with that crop's passing, Honokaa is seeking a new identity. Since the first macadamia nut tree was planted here many years ago, the town has at times laid claim to being the mac nut capital of the world. The existing macadamia nut factory down the hill from the center of town seems an iffy proposition for making that kind of boast. Along the main street are a number of stores and galleries. Collectibles seem to be a specialty of Honokaa.

About eight miles farther on Highway 240—where the road ends—is **Waipio Valley** (8). This area is steeped in history, and is by far the biggest valley on the Big Island. About a mile wide and six miles long, it is surrounded by 2,000-foot-high cliffs on either side. This was once a retreat for Hawaiian Royalty. Perhaps because it was so secluded, or perhaps because of its rich soil and abundant water for agriculture, it was a favorite of Kamehameha I. It was here that Kamehameha The Great received custody of Kukailimoku, the war god of the kings of Hawaii. It was here also the Kamehameha engaged in the first naval battle in Hawaiian history that began his conquest and reign over the islands.

At one time, there were thousands of Hawaiians who lived and farmed in the valley and fished in the ocean at its mouth, but today there are only a handful of hardy residents. The sights include 1,200-foot waterfalls, lotus ponds, meandering rivers that flow through taro patches, wild horses and the rolling surf at the mouth of the valley.

Park above and walk down a short ways to the Lookout for a spectacular view from above. There are only two ways to get down into the valley: in a four-wheel drive or on foot. Be well aware that you cannot drive rental cars into the valley. If you don't have your own four-wheel (from a rental car agency that allows you to drive into Waipio), a good suggestion is to take the **Waipio Valley Shuttle.** This well-established company is located in Waipio Artworks (well worth a visit in itself) about a mile back from the Lookout in Kukuihaele. It runs four-wheel drive tours of the valley on Mondays through Saturdays from 8–4. *These tours are fully narrated and cost $35 for adults and $15 for kids 11 and under. Call 775-7121 for reservations.*

For horseback rides, consider **Waipio Naalapa Trail Rides.** *They have two departures a day on Mondays through Saturdays at 9:30 a.m. and 1 p.m. Call 775-0419 for reservations and check in at Honokaa Travel in town beforehand.* They will direct you to the parking lot at Waipio Valley Artworks. A four-wheel drive van will take you from there down into the valley where you will be met by an experienced guide, who during the two-hour ride will tell you about historical and spiritual places as you ride through streams, past taro patches and waterfalls. *The total cost including transportation into the valley is $75 per person.*

Trip 25

*Mauna Kea

Sometimes called "The White Mountain," Mauna Kea serenely dominates the Big Island with its 13,796–foot summit. The white designation comes from the fact that for many months during the winter, the summit can be deep in snow. Some intrepid souls even ski it.

This huge mountain has quite an industry at its summit. Presently there are nine major observatories—many of which are multi-national efforts—for viewing both the southern and northern hemispheres. By the year 2000, a total of 14 international observatories are planned to be in operation. Even now, Mauna Kea is considered to have the largest collection of astronomical observatories anywhere in the world.

There's good reason for this proliferation of scientific activity on the mountain. It has to do with a couple of major factors: Hawaii's isolation in the middle of the Pacific and its distance from any other major urban centers; and because the mountain is nearly 14,000 feet high, the night air has a clarity found in few other places in the world.

Most of this daytrip will be taken up with exploring the mountain.

GETTING THERE:

By car, get on Waianuenue in downtown Hilo. About a mile up this street, Kaumana Street bears left. This will turn into the Saddle Road. Don't expect smooth sailing from this rather rough road as it continues to climb. At the 28-mile marker, turn right on the Mauna Kea Access Road toward the Visitor Information Station, which is another six miles. Take your time. Total elapsed time from Hilo is a little over an hour.

By van, consider taking Arnott's Adventures, which has a state permit to take visitors beyond the Visitor Information Station to the summit. *Call 969-7097.*

PRACTICALITIES:

Check with your rental car company because some do not allow their vehicles on the Saddle Road. Be advised too, that two-wheel vehicles are okay to the Visitor Information Station (VIS), but if you decide to tag along on one of the supervised Summit Tours on the weekends, you are required to have a four-wheel drive vehicle since the summit road is quite steep and unpaved for about five miles beyond the VIS. *Mauna Kea road conditions are available by calling 969-3218.*

This may be a surprise because you are in sunny Hawaii, but warm clothing is needed for this trip whether you just go to the VIS, or go all the way to the summit. In winter, be prepared for especially cold, windy weather. In spite of the potential chilliness, take sunglasses and sunscreen.

There aren't many other places in the world where in such a short time period you go from sea level to 9,300 feet, which is the VIS altitude, or the summit which is almost two and a half miles up, so certain people shouldn't even consider the trip. Those under 16 are advised not to go as are those with respiratory problems, those with heart conditions, those who are overweight and pregnant ladies.

Because food, drink and gas are not available once you leave Hilo, it is essential to take food with you and to make sure you have plentiful gas.

FOOD AND DRINK:

Canoes Café (308 Kamehameha Ave. in the S. Hata Bldg. in Hilo) Outrigger canoe paddling is the theme. Owner Randy Botti makes his salads with hydroponically grown, pesticide-free greens. Fulsome sandwiches and wraps. Light breakfast and hearty lunches daily. *Kelepona* (telephone) 935-4070. $

Broke the Mouth (374 Kinoole in downtown Hilo) Energetic young couple started a bakery and restaurant that serves such specialties as herbal, smoked fish. Great local plate lunches too. They sell their own sauces and dressings. Light breakfast and terrific lunches Mon. –Sat. ☎ 934-7670. $

All Things Store (1976 Kaumana Dr.) This is the last chance to get food for your Mauna Kea adventure. Sandwiches, burritos, sushi, manapua and pork hash. Plenty of regular foodstuff. Try the Hilo Creme Crackers and Taro Chips. Open Mon.–Sat. 6–6, Sun. 6–4. ☎ 969-9208. $

SUGGESTED TOUR:

Five miles from Hilo are the **Kaumana Caves.** These two caves were created from the turmoil of the 1881 Mauna Loa eruption that left many lava tubes. These happen to be most accessible. A stairway leads down to one that looks about 50 feet high. You can venture into this one via a cement walkway and observe the ferns hanging from the ceiling. The second cave is best left unexplored.

On the trip up, you will pass through several climate zones, a phenomena not found in many other places in so short a distance. Hilo, where you

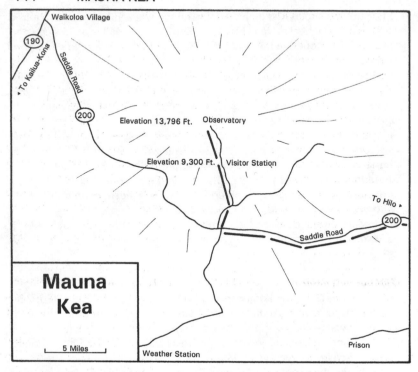

start, is surrounded by rainforests. At the top of Mauna Kea, you will be standing on subarctic tundra. In between, well, it's all pretty interesting. Be prepared to leave Hilo in sunny weather; about midway on the Saddle Road you may run into clouds or fog; and then as you approach the VIS, break into sunny weather again.

The road itself rocks and rolls through vast lava fields that are old enough to have stands of shrunken ohia and fern trees. At lower elevations, wild orchids, ginger and some anthuriums are plentiful along the roadside. At mile 19, the road surface becomes pretty rough for the next four miles.

Just before the 28-mile marker, as you turn left on Mauna Kea Access Road, there is a large working ranch. Mostly barren, open lava fields have by now turned to undulating grasslands with periodic stands of fir and pine. That change seems almost out of place since as you glance upwards the mountain is barren and has no vegetation. Watch out for cattle wandering on the road at this point.

*ELLISON ONIZUKA VISITOR INFORMATION STATION. On the slopes of Mauna Kea on Mauna Kea Access Rd. *Open Thurs. 5:30–10 p.m., Fri. 9 a.m. to noon, 1–4:30 p.m. and 6:30–10 p.m., Sat. and Sun. 9 a.m. to noon,*

1–2 p.m. and 6:30–10 p.m. Closed Mon.–Wed. Free. Full facilities. ☎ *961-2180.* &.

The Visitor Information Station (VIS) is relatively small, and the exhibits modest, but it is the knowledgeable people who make the trip worthwhile. Inside you will see several exhibits that provide a short lesson in galaxies; show how the observatories were constructed; demonstrate weather patterns on the summit including such key factors as tropical inversions.

Beyond the exhibits, however, the VIS has two excellent programs. One is **Star Gazing** in the evenings on Thursdays through Sundays. During these sessions, a tour guide such as Hugh Grossman will start with a video called *Mauna Kea: On the Verge of Other Worlds*, narrated by Johnny Carson. It describes the history of star gazing atop Mauna Kea. Very exciting stuff. As the skies darken, Hugh will take you outside to actually look through one of the center's two powerful telescopes. They have an 11" and a 14" Celestron Telescope, and with those they usually guide guests from Venus, to Mercury, to Mars and then to Jupiter, depending on the time of year. There is no charge for these marvelous sessions.

The second program offered by the VIS is a **Summit Tour** each afternoon at one o'clock on Fridays through Sundays. This program also starts with a video in which, among other things, you will learn that Mauna Kea was a victim of the Ice Age; a true phenomena of fire and ice. Many of the rocks on the mountain slopes have striations from glacial activity millions of years ago. It's hard to imagine given the thin air and cold, but you'll also learn that early Hawaiians probably lived atop Mauna Kea as craft specialists making adze-cutting devices, using the dense basalt rock found on the mountain. The video also points a finger at Europeans who came to the islands and brought cattle who became feral (wild) and devastated the forests on the lower slopes of Mauna Kea.

After the orientation video, Hugh lines up those with four-wheel drive vehicles for the 5-mile drive to the summit at 13,796 feet. Once there, you are in a mini United Nations. Presently, these countries—Britain, France, Canada, Argentina, America, Australia, Japan, Brazil and Chile—have joined hands to build nine huge telescopes to probe into the heavens. By the turn of the century, there will be 14 scientific installations at the summit.

Hugh (or one of his fellow tour guides) will take you into the W.M. Keck Observatory (known as Keck I), which is the world's largest optical telescope. It is eight stories high and was built of 150 tons of steel and glass. Can you imagine lugging all this material to nearly 14,000 feet? It's sister installation (known as Keck II) is under construction at the moment at a cost of $70 million. Keck I cost $80 million, to give you some idea of the commitment to science atop Mauna Kea. Dollars don't mean everything, but the Japanese observatory, which is expected to be completed by the year 2000, will probably cost $300 million when it's finished.

Why does all this exist in such a hostile atmosphere? The answer, according to the scientists, lies in the fact that these big telescopes can look way back in time. They can see to the edge of the visible universe and help answer such questions as: How did we get here?; where did our galaxy come from?; what is still out there? Sounds reasonable.

Depending on the time of year, Hugh or one of his colleagues will linger on the summit long enough to see one of the most extraordinary sunsets on Earth. Then it's back down from the summit to the VIS for the Star Gazing, if you are so inclined.

*Hawaii Volcanoes National Park

People in Hawaii take their legends pretty seriously. According to one of the better-known myths, Pele, the goddess of fire, wandered down the island chain after being kicked out of one volcanic home after another. She went from Kauai to Oahu, then to Maui. Her final home was in Halemaumau, the firepit crater of Kilauea volcano on the Big Island, where she still holds forth.

What's interesting is that scientific findings fit quite well with the legend since the lava rocks of Kauai are five to six million years old, while those of the Big Island are all less than one million years old. Who says we shouldn't take legends seriously?

Even today Pele is still spewing rock and fire. Kilauea has been erupting steadily since January, 1983. Mauna Loa, the mother volcano of Kilauea, last erupted at its summit and northeast flank in 1984. Hualalai's latest eruption was in 1801, however Mauna Kea has not erupted in 3,600 years. Whether it could or not is another question. With that quick background, it is understandable why the telescopes are all on Mauna Kea and not Mauna Loa.

People have been fascinated with volcanic activity forever. They want to see what goes on, and they can at the Big Island's Volcano National Park. The park has been called the "drive-in volcano," offering perhaps Hawaii's most dramatic visitor attraction.

GETTING THERE:
By car, Highway 11 from either the west or east sides.

By air, visitors can either fly in from Honolulu on Aloha Airlines or the other two inter-island carriers, or United has direct flights from the West Coast to Kona Airport.

By helicopter, leaving from the Hilo airport with Safari Helicopters provides more viewing time.

PRACTICALITIES:

Casual, comfortable shoes are fine for walking on some of the trails, but if you want to really take a hike in the park, take your hiking boots. We strongly suggest sunglasses, sunscreen, a hat and water.

Sometimes the sulfur fumes near the crater can be pretty strong, so if you have respiratory problems, it might be better to stay away from those areas.

FOOD AND DRINK:

Volcano House (at the very rim of the Kilauea Caldera in the park) It's almost impossible to concentrate on the food with the vast Halemaumau firepit smoldering right out the window. Free entertainment from the volcano. Breakfast, lunch and dinner daily. Gift Shop and 42-room hotel. ☎ 967-7321. $$–$$$

Kilauea Lodge (on Old Volcano Rd. in Volcano Village) Dinner nightly with European specials like duck à l'orange and lamb Provençale. Reservations recommended, ☎ 967-7366. $$–$$$

SUGGESTED TOUR:

Numbers in parentheses correspond to numbers on the map.

*HAWAII VOLCANOES NATIONAL PARK, 30 miles from Hilo or 96 miles from Kona to the park entrance on Highway 11. *Open 24 hours a day. Seven-day admission: car $5; hiker, bicyclist, motorcyclist $3. Kilauea Visitor Center open 7:45–5 daily,* ☎ *985-6000. Thomas A. Jaggar Museum, open 8:30–5 daily. Camping, hotel, restaurant, gift shop, art center, but no gas.*

The 229,000-acre park was established in 1916. The massive land area spreads down Kilauea's southern and eastern flanks like the lava that has flowed out of the crater over thousands of years. Across the highway, the park extends up the slopes of Mauna Loa to its 13,677-foot summit. Because the boundaries of the park include 30 miles of rugged coastline as well, the park is actually getting bigger almost daily as more lava surges to the sea.

Within the park are unparalleled scenic drives. If hiking is your thing, there are 150 miles of trails. A comprehensive Visitor Center, a museum, campgrounds and numerous scientific stations are spotted throughout the park. Those are the things we might expect. What probably isn't as expected are silent, smoldering firepits, pungent sulfur banks, steam hissing from deep vents and once-molten lava now encrusted into bizarre shapes and patterns.

It seems trite to say the park is a study in contrasts, but it's very true when you consider that the terrain goes from desert to arid expanses of lava to lush rainforest, and the climate climbs from cold to fiery hot.

By car, stop at the **Visitor Center** (1) for a worthwhile orientation that includes maps and films of recent eruptions in the center's 220-seat theater. The Center is about 4,000 feet above sea level. Across the road is the **Volcano House** (2), with a working fireplace and a dining room with the most

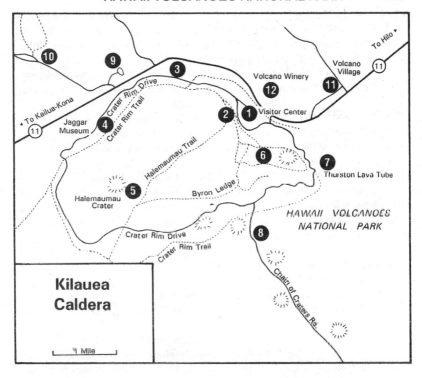

Kilauea Caldera

1 Mile

awesome view in the world. You can stay here in comfortable guest rooms that actually have heaters, and shop in their gift gallery.

A "must-do" is the 11-mile **Crater Rim Drive** (3) that will take you entirely around Kilauea's summit caldera. At times, it will seem like what we imagine the surface of the moon to be, with expanses of black *pahoehoe* lava folded over on itself. At times there will be sulfur banks that can repulse you with their odor. It surprises many to be driving along and see steam wafting up from a fissure in the ground. About halfway you will come to the **Jaggar Museum** (4), which shows the work of the Hawaiian Volcano Observatory. It has monitored these volcanoes since 1912 for two purposes—to increase the general knowledge of volcanic activity, and to try to lessen the hazards for people who live in the shadow of volcanoes.

Next is Pele's home, **Halemaumau Crater.** (5) It is Pele whose moods determine the area's level of activity—a tantrum here, a peaceful lull there. She is regularly appeased with gifts of gin, ti leaves, and ohelo berries tossed ceremoniously into the crater. Next is the **Kilauea Iki Crater** (6), and a must walk through the **Thurston Lava Tube** (7). The latter was formed when the hot lava folded over on itself and cooled quickly enough to form a large, open tube. This is the most accessible of many caves and tubes formed in much the same way.

If you backtrack a bit, it will bring you to the **Chain of Craters Road** (8). It is spectacular as you cross huge lava fields and go past many smaller volcanic craters. This dramatic drive affords a close-up look at the various lava flows that have marched to the sea. The road has been covered periodically from 1965 to 1979, but that adds to the excitement. Chain of Craters gives visitors direct access from Kilauea to the park's coastal section. You will eventually come to a barricade where the flows during the period 1983 into the 90s have buried the road and several small villages in between.

Hiking in Volcanoes National Park is a total treat because of the variety—from short and easy to very demanding. For instance, the Thurston Lava Tube hike is .3 of a mile with stairs at either end. The trail is paved and passes through deep fern forests. The mostly flat Devastation Trail is about one mile and takes you through trees and other growth that were flattened by one of the lava flows. Several challenging, but absorbing trails lead from the Crater Rim Trail. The Kilauea Iki Trail is about five miles and the Halemaumau Trail is 6.5 miles, and both take you through forest and lava desert. Only the very serious, well-prepared hiker should even consider the Mauna Loa Trail which is 36.5 miles and requires about four days round-trip.

If you like organized, guided hikes, **Arnott's Hiking Adventures** will take you on a special volcano hike that includes nighttime lava viewing. The volcano hikes are on Thursdays and Sundays. They pick up at your hotel before noon, take you to the park for lunch and then hike the 3-mile Pu Oo Trail. They usually return after 7. *The $50 fee includes park admission, lunch, drink, transportation and a guide. A terrific deal. Call 969-7097 for details since not every hike includes nighttime viewing.*

Camping is available at **Namakani Paio,** about three miles from the park entrance. At **Kipuka Nene** on Hilina Pali Road, camping is only permitted from October through June because of the nesting of the state's endangered bird, the Nene goose. Reservations are not needed, but are on a first-come-first-served basis. *Camping information is available by calling 985-6000.*

A couple of worthwhile attractions outside the park can be reached up Mauna Loa Road just beyond the golf course. The first is **Tree Molds** (9). The area demonstrates how hot lava encircles a tree, is cooled by the moisture in the trees, and when the molten lava flows away it leaves a stump rising many feet in the air. The tree rots and leaves a mold. **Kipuka Puaulu** (10) is a special bird park of calm beauty.

You might want to visit the little settlement called **Volcano Village** (11), about a mile from the park entrance going toward Hilo. Here you will find the second homes of many Honolulu residents, some nifty B&B's and the ever-popular **Volcano Winery** (12), said to be "the southernmost winery in the USA." It is located at the end of Volcano Golf Course Road. *Open daily, 10–5, with a winetasting room and a gift shop.* ☎ *967-7479.*

One of the best ways to view the volcano is from overhead. **Safari Helicopters** leaves from Hilo Airport, which saves time in getting to the volcano—thus leaving more time to view it. This company flies the newest ASTAR 'copters that have ample leg room, and they prepare a video of your trip. The pilot serves as your guide in going to areas where you actually see lava flowing. Their one-hour Waterfall/Volcano Safari flight costs about $140; a 45-50 minute flight to the same destination is a little over $100. This is an extraordinary experience. *Call 969-1259.*

Kailua-Kona

During this daytrip, we will concentrate on Kailua-Kona by walking a portion of the village and then driving around to close-by attractions.

The village has a rich history. *Alii* and other royalty governed and vacationed at this very spot. The town and surrounding area have seen substantial growth in the past ten years due in part to mainlanders settling in for retirement. The Kona airport has excellent nonstop flights directly to the mainland and Asia, which also accounts for the accelerating numbers of visitors and residents. All else aside, it's the near-perfect weather (even for Hawaii) brought about by the two big mountains that shield the west side of the Big Island from just about anything but sunshine.

This is a sports-happy town that hosts two of the biggest athletic events in Hawaii—the Ironman Triathlon and the Kona Billfishing Tournament. Both are world-class events that draw thousands.

Upslope of town is some of the best coffee grown anywhere in the world. We'll get to taste it, see it being grown, roasted and processed.

GETTING THERE:

On foot, find the King Kamehameha Hotel near the Kona Pier.

By car, for the *mauka* (mountain) portion of this tour see instructions below.

By bicycle, rentals are available as indicated below.

PRACTICALITIES:

Strong sunscreen, good sunglasses, beachwear—and you can add a hat and comfy shoes—are musts. Never leave anything in your car whether you lock it or not.

FOOD AND DRINK:

Oceanview Inn (75-5683 Alii Dr. on the bayfront) Linoleum floors and plain furniture take nothing away from this long-time standby for good Chinese, Hawaiian and American food. Breakfast, lunch and dinner daily. Closed Mon. ☎ 329-9998. $

Kona Inn Restaurant (75-5744 Alii Dr.) Shades of the old hotel in this casual dining room overlooking the lawn to the ocean. Good salads and steaks. Open for lunch and dinner daily. Reservations, ☎ 329-4455. $ to $$

Jamesons by the Sea (77-4652 Alii Dr. in Magic Sands Hotel) Atmosphere is the thing here. For lunch, there's a good variety of salads and sandwiches. Evening is called "Oceanside Sunset Dining." Reservations, ☎ 329-3195. $ to $$

Huggo's (75-5828 Ololi that parallels Alii Dr.) Woody goody building right on the waterfront. Prime rib and seafood specialties. Lunch Mon.–Fri. & dinner nightly. Reservations, ☎ 329-1493. $ to $$

Kona Ranch House (75-5653 Kuakini Hwy.) Just above town, this is a terrific family restaurant with excellent values. Breakfast, lunch and dinner daily. ☎ 329-7061 $ to $$

SUGGESTED TOUR:

Numbers in parentheses correspond to numbers on the map.

A natural place to start this walking tour along the bayfront is at the **King Kamehameha Hotel** (1). Inside the hotel are artifacts of ancient Hawaii worth checking out. The striking paintings of the area in the early 1880s will prepare you for your next stop. A short distance toward the water brings you to **Ahuena Heiau** (2) at Kamakahonu. Kamehameha the Great rebuilt this area between 1812–1813, and this was his final royal residence. The site was the focal point of all government activity from 1813–1819. This entire area was a compound of houses, plantings and fishponds supporting the needs of the royalty.

Next you might want to walk out on **Kailua Pier** (3). It has been an important site for the community since 1918, serving in the early days as the shipping and inter-island transportation hub. Today you will see game fish being weighed, outrigger canoe paddlers barking out their stroke count and even swimming and snorkeling at this very spot. Early in morning—in mid-October every year—after the starting gun for the Ironman Triathlon, the bay is a froth of 1,500 flailing competitors off on an odyssey of a 2.5-mile open-ocean swim, a 112-mile bike race to Hawi and back, and then a 26.3-mile marathon ending on Alii Drive.

They can have all that sweat. Why don't we just continue our calm walk along Alii Drive. On the *makai* (water) side is a special place known as **Hulihee Palace** (4). It is claimed that Hulihee is one of only three royal palaces in America. This one was built in 1838 by Governor John Adams Kuakini. It was originally constructed of native lava rock, coral, koa and ohia timbers and has been renovated over the years. The building exudes a peacefulness that drew Queen Emma and other royalty for vacations and relaxation. The furnishings are exquisite, especially the richness of the koa wood in bowls, tables, beds, rockers, chairs and more. You can make your own way around

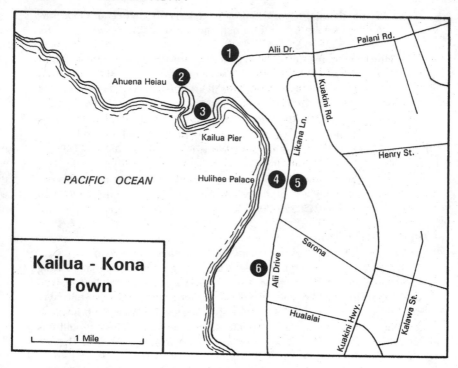

Alii Dr.
Palani Rd.
Kuakini Rd.
Ahuena Heiau
Kailua Pier
PACIFIC OCEAN
Likana Ln.
Henry St.
Hulihee Palace
Sarona
Alii Drive
Kuakini Hwy.
Kalawa St.
Hualalai

Kailua - Kona Town

1 Mile

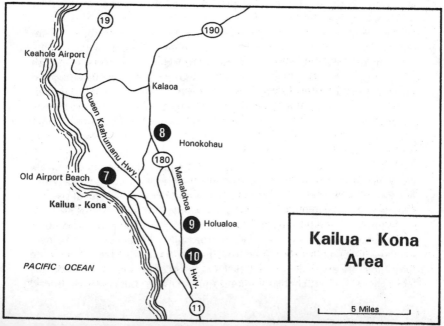

19
190
Keahole Airport
Kalaoa
Queen Kaahumanu Hwy.
Honokohau
180
Old Airport Beach
Mamalahoa
Kailua - Kona
Holualoa
PACIFIC OCEAN
Hwy.

Kailua - Kona Area

5 Miles

the palace, or there are knowledgeable guides. *Open 9–4 daily, closed holidays. Admission is $5.*

Across the street is the first Christian church in the islands, known as **Mokuaikaua Church** (5). At first it was just a thatched hut begun in 1820, but in 1836 John Adams Kuakini, the Big Island's Governor at the time, decided to rebuild the church using lava rock and native woods. The steeple and the shape of the church have a distinctly New England look. Take the time to go inside to see the extensive use of native ohia and koa for walls, pews and more.

Cross the Alii Drive again to the **Kona Inn** (6), mostly obscured now by a collection of small shops. If you walk past them to the old lobby, you will learn that the hotel was built in 1928 by the Inter-Island Steamship Company for its passengers staying in Kona. Originally, the hotel only had 20 rooms. It is no longer a hotel and the original rooms upstairs are now occupied by attorneys, a psychiatrist and a massage therapist. How times change. But the restaurant with its wide lawn down to the ocean will give you a good sense of the graciousness of an earlier era.

How about a treat only found in Kona? Follow these four simple steps: 1. There's usually a leis seller with his simple *plumeria* products displayed on the rock wall around the parking lot on the *mauka* side of Alii Drive, so go ahead and buy one of these for yourself or your mate; 2. find a cup of real Kona coffee; 3. get a copy of the local newspaper, *West Hawaii Today*; and 4. head for the rock wall on the *makai* side of Alii Drive to sit and relax and read in the sunshine. That's what Kona is about.

If you are more inclined to take a conducted walking tour of Kailua-Kona, the **Kona Historical Society** offers a 90 minute tour at 9:30 on Tuesdays through Saturdays. On Fridays there's an additional tour at 1:30. *Cost is $10. Call 323-2005 for reservations.*

Now it's time to find your car to explore some close-by attractions. Head out Kuakini Highway and go north about two miles. At the end is the entrance to the **Old Airport Beach Park** (7). Right next to the beach is the expansive old runway used by bicyclists, joggers, rollerbladers and walkers. The only planes that take off from this area today are of the model type at the far end. There's a roller hockey rink, picnic pavilion and facilities. The beach is fine, but the swimming isn't because of the rocky coastline. *Open 7–8 daily.*

An option for exploring from this beach park all the way along Alii Drive to Keauhou Bay is by bicycle. (For more about Keauhou Bay, see Daytrip 28). Bikes can be rented for about $20 a day from **Hawaiian Pedals** in the Kona Inn Shopping Village. The level round-trip is about 14 miles. *Call 329-2294.*

It's probably a good idea to stick to your car to go *mauka*, so retrace your steps from the Old Airport and at the intersection with Palani Road (Highway 190) turn left and follow that up about 4 miles to the intersection with

Highway 180 (Mamalahoa Highway). Just as you turn right, look for **Hawaiian Gardens** (8). While this is primarily a nursery, they have Kona Coffee plants for close inspection. They also have certified orchids that can be shipped home should you want to do so. *Open 8–6 Mon.–Fri., 9–4 Sat. & Sun.,* ☎ *329-5702.*

This narrow, winding road takes you past several handsome old homes, ranches and coffee farms. Soon you will come to the old town of **Holualoa** (9). It has several quaint coffee shops serving pure Kona Coffee. Enjoy the art galleries, shops and sights down toward the ocean from this vantage point.

If you continue a mile past the intersection with Hualalai Road, on the left is **Holualoa Kona Coffee Company** (10) at 77-6261 Mamalahoa Highway. The sign at the driveway says Maikai Ranch. Drive up the hill to a two-story white building, which is the mill. They welcome visitors when they roast coffee on Monday and Thursday mornings. *Call 322-9937.*

To get back to Kona, return to Hualalai Road and take that into town.

Kailua-Kona South

Give yourself plenty of time to fully enjoy this excursion. There are good water places to visit and activities to enjoy along the coast; and then it's up to higher elevations or *mauka* (mountain in Hawaiian) for great views. There's lots of history, including the landing where the first European stepped foot on Big Island soil. Apparently he was fun for the natives for awhile, and then something happened on his second trip and they did him in.

GETTING THERE:

By car, take Alii Drive south from Kailua-Kona.

PRACTICALITIES:

It's almost required that you go in the water somewhere along this coast, so take your bathing suit and a towel. Here's the double mantra again: sunglasses, sunscreen, a hat and comfortable shoes—and don't leave a thing in your car or its trunk whether it's locked or not.

FOOD AND DRINK:

Teshima's (in the center of Honalo town on Hwy. 11) Their specialty is Japanese food. Try the tempura prepared real Japanese-style. Local foods are *bentos* (box lunch) and *saimin*. Breakfast, lunch and dinner daily. ☎ 322-9140. $

Aloha Theater Café (in Kainaliu on Hwy. 11 in the theater) As expected, this eatery offers a theatrical presentation of its salads, burgers and sandwiches. Breakfast, lunch and dinner Mon.–Sat., Sun. brunch. ☎ 322-3383. $

Wakefield Gardens and Restaurant (on Refuge Rd. and Rodeo Rd. in Honaunau) Set in a neat tropical setting, with its own short garden tour, this eatery serves the best homemade pies. They even have an avocado cream pie. Small gift shop. Open daily for lunch. ☎ 328-9930. $ to $$

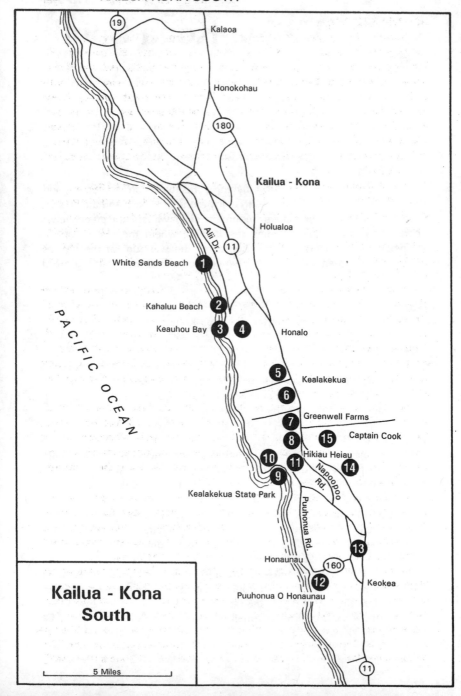

Kailua - Kona
South

5 Miles

SUGGESTED TOUR:

Numbers in parentheses correspond to numbers on the map.

As you head south on Alii Drive, about 3.5 miles from Kailua-Kona village is one of the most well-known beaches on the Big Island. It's official name is **White Sands Beach Park** (1). Actually, this beach is more commonly called "Disappearing Sands," or "Magic Sands" with good reason—every year in the winter or high surf months this beach goes away. But usually around April the sand comes back, leaving a nice pocket of white beach. The ocean can be tricky here, and while you may see divers and surfers, they are probably very experienced water people. The best advice is to just take a look.

About another mile farther south on Alii is **Kahaluu Beach Park** (2). This one is worth a stop to snorkel, swim or just sun yourself. Snorkeling is popular here because of the variety of fish and their large population, and because of the calm water created by the breakwater built by the early Hawaiians. This park has full amenities including lifeguards, showers, a pavilion for picnics, snorkel and mask rentals—and even a lunch wagon called "Beach Bites." *Open daily 7–10. No camping.*

Next is Keauhou, which was an important ancient settlement where Hawaiians, like visitors today, enjoyed the beauty and perfect weather of the region. The huge landowner in the area is the Bishop Estate. Follow Alii Drive, which turns into Alii Highway. Turn right at Kaleiopapa Street, which takes you to **Keauhou Bay** (3), a neat little pocket of water with a little beach. Keauhou is revered as the birthplace of Kamehameha III. There is a wooden pier that can be a good vantage point for viewing sea turtles. Water activities include snorkeling, scuba diving and rafting.

Sea Quest Rafting Adventures leaves from Keauhou in hard-bottom, rigid-hull craft to take visitors to the calm waters of Kealakekua Bay. Along the way you will see the rugged coastline up close with its accompanying lava tubes and caves. Snacks and snorkel stuff, including masks are included. The tour in the morning is four hours and the one in the afternoon three hours. *Tours start at $44. Call 329-7238.*

On the same street is the **Kona Surf Hotel** (4). This striking hotel conducts nightly feedings of Manta ray. The ritual can be viewed from the hotel's salt-water pool deck. It's amazing to watch these graceful sea animals, with wing spans up to 10 feet wide, glide along in the lighted water in front of the resort scooping up the plankton attracted by the lights.

Retrace your steps and get on Kamehameha III Road, heading up to Highway 11. There are several super scenic spots along the way. At the top bear right; a few miles down the road is Kainaliu town. The dominant feature here is the **Aloha Theater** (5) built for silent movies in 1929. The theater has been restored and today offers a wide variety of productions. There's a gift shop and restaurant in the building. Next, travel about 3.5 miles to the **Kahanahou Hawaiian Foundation** (6) on the right. For 30 years this small, non-profit foundation has been fashioning traditional Hawaiian implements that range all the way from nose-flutes to children's toys. There's a gift shop where many of the products can be purchased. *Open daily. Donations are greatly appreciated.* ☎ *322-3901.*

Next is the village of Kealakekua, where the bustle of a modern business and banking center blends with the rustic peacefulness of an old, rural community. The grass shack of Kealakekua, made famous in the song of the same name, today is a gift shop with small botanical garden next door. Look for signs to **Greenwell Farms** (7), where you can take a free 20-minute tour of their coffee farm that has been going since the 1850s. It's a good place to buy Kona coffee at the source. *The farm is open from 7–4 Mon.–Sat.,* ☎ *323-2862.*

Fronting the farm on the highway is the old **Greenwell Store** (8), built by Henry Nicholas Greenwell about 1875. The old building, listed on the State and National Registers of Historical Places, is the site of the **Kona Historical Society Museum.** Artifacts of the Greenwell Ranch and old photos of the area give a good perspective to the early days of Kona District. *The museum is open Mon.–Fri. 9–3, closed Sun. and holidays. Donations of $2 per person are encouraged. Call 323-3222.*

Another mile down the highway is the turnoff to Kealakekua Bay. Napoopoo Road is a narrow, winding route that descends about four miles to the bay with terrific views on the way down.

The bay itself is a marine preserve called the **Kealakekua Underwater State Park** (9). It got this designation because it is one of the rare places in the world where spinner dolphins swim close to shore to rest, breed, birth and nurse their young. You will see swimmers and snorkelers in the bay, but don't disturb the dolphins under any circumstances.

Across the bay (accessible only by boat) is a white obelisk that marks the spot where Captain James Cook landed in 1779, recognized as the first European to step foot on this island. **Captain Cook's Monument** (10), was actually erected by the British government during the last century, and amazingly the ground is still owned by Britain. The ancient Hawaiians revered Cook and showered him and his crew with gifts and supplies. They purportedly held many ceremonies in his honor. The good captain reciprocated by entertaining the natives with music and fireworks and tours of his ships.

Cook sailed off after all these good times only to return a short time later to repair storm damage to one of his ships. Again the natives welcomed him as the reincarnation of their great god Lono. However, animosities broke out between the Hawaiians and the British following a beef over a boat stolen from one of Cook's ships. The dispute escalated into a battle on the beach, and Cook was killed in the early morning of February 14, 1779.

The **Hikiau Heiau** (11) in the vicinity is a sacred temple where it is said

Cook was celebrated as a deity. It is also where Cook presided over the burial of one of his seamen making that ceremony the first Christian burial in Hawaii. The *heiau* cannot be entered.

If you travel along narrow Puuhonua Road from the bay, you will come to a place of quiet, simple beauty. In old Hawaii, people were governed by the strict and sacred laws of *kapu*. Under these laws, rulers and other royalty were sacrosanct—commoners could not get close to a chief or walk in his footsteps. The people believed that if the *kapu* was broken, the gods would punish them with a natural disaster like a lava flow, famine or giant wave known as a tsunami. Thus the penalty for kapu-breaking was the ultimate—death.

There was one salvation for the kapu-breaker. If he could reach a *puuhonua* (a place of refuge) by land or sea, he could be spared. At a *puuhonua*, made sacred because it was associated with the burial site of royalty, a kapu-breaker would be absolved by a *Kahuna* (priest) and returned shortly to normal life.

Continue south to:

*PUUHONUA O HONAUNAU (12). *The Visitor Center is open daily from 7:30 to 5:30. There is a brochure for a self-guided tour. Admission is $2. Since this is a sacred place, there is no picnicking, smoking or sunbathing. Call 326-2326 for further information.*

Several *puuhonua* still exist in the islands, but this one was restored by the National Park Service in the early 1960s. It is called Honaunau. In addition to being a place of refuge, it was also the residence of the ruling chief whose palace grounds adjoined the refuge. Between those grounds and the sacred place is the Great Wall, a massive hand-built, mortarless barrier of lava rock 1,000 feet long, 10 feet high and 17 feet wide. Within the *puuhonua* are two *heiau* dating from before 1550, and a third built around 1650. The latter with its wooden images served as a temple mausoleum until 1818, housing the bones of at least 23 chiefs. Kamehameha II abolished the kapu system in 1819.

In one *hale* (thatched house) you can see some of the arts and skills of old Hawaii such as *lauhala* woven into baskets and mats. What is most memorable is the peacefulness of this sacred place. The ground is almost all sand, with many palm trees among the *heiau* remains. The sea washes up against the rocky coastline and all your senses tell you this is some place very special.

On the left of the *puuhonua* is a recreational area with picnic grounds and modest facilities. What is fun is walking along the lava rock shore where you can inspect dozens of tidepools. If you have rubber slippers, you can actually walk into the pools for a closer look. *No camping. Open 7–8 Mon.–Thurs., 8–11 Fri.–Sun.*

On the way out, take Highway 160. Several miles up you will see signs to the **Painted Church** (13). St. Benedict's Catholic Church is an ornate, wooden structure built between 1899 and 1904 by a Belgian missionary named father John Velge. He painted intricate murals and frescoes inside that are worth a visit.

Turn left when you get to Highway 11. At approximately mile marker 110 is the **Amy B.H. Greenwell Ethnobotanical Garden** (14), operated by the Bishop Museum. This 15-acre garden is landscaped to reflect the plant life of the area before 1779 when Captain Cook arrived. There are remnants of the Kona Field System. You can take a self-guided tour any time it's open, or a guided one at 10 o'clock on the second Saturday of each month. *Open 7–3:30 Mon.–Fri. Suggested donation of $2. Call 323-3318 for more information.*

At the stoplight in Captain Cook, turn right where a sign says Konawaena High School. Just up the road on the right is a very attractive small church. Besides the simple aesthetics, the significance of **Christ Church** (15) is that it was built on land donated by Henry Nicholas Greenwell (see Daytrip 31). The old cemetery contains headstones for him and his wife. Presently, there are 10 Greenwells who belong to the church.

Kailua-Kona North

If you look right going north on Highway 19 around the airport and beyond, you may not think there's much going on this side of the Big Island. But by nosing your way along the shore on your left or *makai* (ocean) side, that notion quickly disappears. Tucked among all the thousands of acres of lava stretching for miles are interesting beaches—from little skinny ones to broad and long ones. For history buffs, there are *heiau*, petroglyphs, ancient fishponds, and the remains of the Kings Trail that mostly runs right along the water's edge.

World-class hotels dot this coastline bringing all manner of the rich and famous—and ordinary people too—for golf, tennis, beaches, pools, horseback riding, shopping, dining and riding with dolphins.

So don't let the folded black *pahoehoe* or the brown crumbly *a'a* lava that stretches for miles fool you. Frankly, there's so much to do on this trip that you will have to make choices along the way.

GETTING THERE:
By car, as you leave town, get on Highway 19 going north.

PRACTICALITIES:
Leave fairly early in the morning to take advantage of only a portion of all there is to see and do on this wonderful coast. Take beachwear and suitable beach gear, like a mat for sitting or sunning. Sunscreen, sunglasses, a hat and comfortable shoes are a given. You may want to leave your car several times during the day, so leave nothing in it (trunk or otherwise) locked or unlocked.

FOOD AND DRINK:
Sam Choy's (before the airport turn right on Hinalani, right on Kanalani and left on Kauhola St.) Not easy to get to, but this is the one that brought Sam his fame. Great taste. Big portions. Very popular. Lunch & dinner Tues.–Sat. ☎ 326-1545. $ to $$

Roussels Waikoloa Village (from Hwy. 19 turn right on Waikoloa Rd.

and go to the Village Golf Club) This is authentic French Creole. Their okra gumbo is tops. Open for lunch daily and dinner Tues.– Sat. ☎ 883-9644. $ to $$

Kawaihae Harbor Grill (At the intersection of Hwys. 19 and 270, go left to town. It's on the right). Old Hawaii building houses a terrific seafood house. Try the lobster grown down the road at Keahole plus other local seafood. Open daily for lunch and dinner. ☎ 882-1368. $ to $$

Café Pesto (Kawaihae Shopping Center) Their slogan is "Pizza, Pasta and Pesto." And they do a terrific job at each. Great for families. Lunch and dinner daily. ☎ 882-1071. $ to $$

SUGGESTED TOUR:

Numbers in parentheses correspond to numbers on the map.

When you start in Kailua-Kona, go up Palani Road and turn left at Highway 19. About 2.5 miles down the highway from the junction is the entrance to **Honokohau Small Boat Harbor** (1). Take the left and go down to the water. The attractive harbor has all manner of ocean activities, and it's only a matter of choosing whether you want to dive, kayak, fish, watch whales, go below the ocean's surface, sail or whatever. Maybe you want to do it all.

To demonstrate the magnitude of sport fishing in the Kona area, it is estimated that there are nearly 200 boats in this harbor. Generally speaking, a half-day will cost around $60 and a full day just under $100 per person. Charters are considerably more. Most boats provide everything including tackle, ice and bait. No license is required. You might consider calling **The Charter Desk** at ☎ 329-5735. They will recommend the right boat for you based on what you want and your skill level.

Another option would be to take a voyage with Dan McSweeny on one of his **Year Round Whale Watching** cruises. Dan, a marine mammal biologist, is very knowledgeable about the six varieties of whales that inhabit Hawaii's waters. He guarantees you will see either whales or dolphins or both year round, or you get another cruise free. He goes out on Tuesdays, Thursdays and Saturdays during the lighter visitor seasons from 8:30 to noon. During the December-to-May period, when the whales proliferate in Hawaiian waters, he goes out daily. *Cost is $44.50 for adults and $29.50 for kids under 11. Call 322-0028 for reservations.*

If science is your thing, turn left at the sign for the **Natural Energy Lab of Hawaii** (2) just before the airport. The state established this unique facility on 870 acres in 1974. The primary mission was the Ocean Thermal Energy Conversion (OTEC) in which cold water from 2,000 feet down was pumped up to be mixed with the warm surface water for energy production. The cold water turned out to be nutrient rich, and this lead to a thriving algae and aquaculture industries. Lobsters, clams, shrimp and mushrooms are

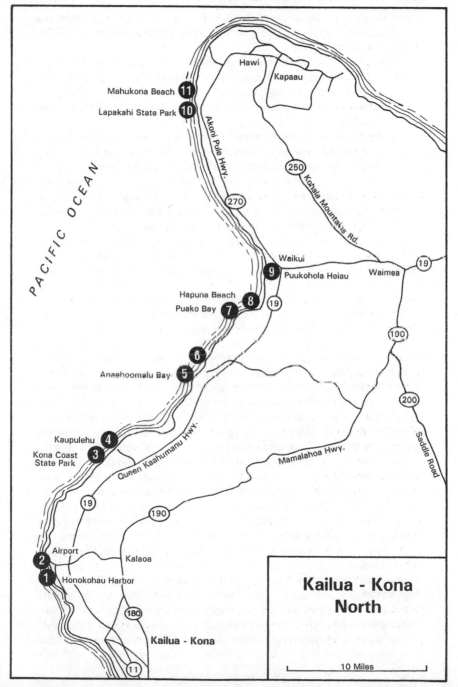

Kailua - Kona
North

10 Miles

grown here. *The gates are open from 8–6 daily. On Thursdays, there is a two-hour tour of OTEC at 10 o'clock. Call 329-7341 for reservations and information.*

About three miles north from NELH is the **Kona Coast State Park** (3). There is a sign on the *makai* (ocean) side of the road. Go almost 1.5 miles over a rough road to a salt and pepper beach that's great for picnicking and snorkeling. Swimming is over by the red house. *No facilities. Gates open 9–8. Closed Wed.*

While we have been concentrating on the water and shoreline north of the village, we must now pause and pay due respect to the third of the Big Island's five volcanoes, 8,271-foot-high **Hualalai** standing silently above the massive spread of lava at her feet. To do that, turn left about 15 miles north of town for the Four Seasons Resort, a total oasis among stark black lava, master-designed by Hawaii's pre-eminent land planning firm, Belt Collins. At the resort is the **Kaupulehu Cultural Center** (4), which celebrates the ancient *Kaupulehu ahupuaa*, a land division that reached down from the Hualalai volcano to the land on which the hotel sits. Interesting paintings depict ancient Hawaiians engaged in such activities as house building, weaving, fishing, hula dancing and more. They also provide a handy brochure for a self-guided tour of sites at the resort that include trails, petroglyphs, rock boundaries and the anchialine ponds in front of the hotel. *The Center is open daily 10–8. Admission is free. Call 325-8520.*

At about 24 miles north from Kailua-Kona is **Anaehoomalu Bay** (5), better known as "A Bay." It has quite a collection of things to see and do. Turn to the left on Waikoloa Beach Drive and go about a mile, then turn left. Just ahead is public parking. The hotel on your right, the Royal Waikoloan, had to be built back from the beach in order to preserve the existing fishponds. This is a wonderful family beach set in palm trees. The water is almost always calm. Lots of water toys are for rent so you can play to your heart's content. If you walk along the beach going north, or to your right facing the water, you will come to the King's Trail that is pretty much open all the way to the Hilton some distance away. Originally, this trail circled the whole island. There is a local hiking group that has covered almost 50 miles—in increments—of the trail along this coastline.

As you retrace your steps on the road you came in on, turn left at the intersection and on your right are the **King's Shops.** This is one of the most innovative collection of shops in the islands, and while relatively small, is worth a visit.

Now turn right again and head for the 1,200-room **Hilton Waikoloa Village Resort** (6). This was the last Hawaii mega-resort built by Chris Hemmeter, who you might recall from Daytrip 7 as the high-flying developer who built himself a $65-million residence on Diamond Head on Oahu and never put his head down on a pillow in the place. In this case, he had 62 acres to play with, and that he did. The hotel reflects his grandiose ideas with gondolas floating along nearly a mile of winding waterways and lagoons, and a tram to take guests to their rooms.

A unique feature of this resort is a program called **Dolphin Quest** where, under careful supervision of marine mammal experts, you can be in the water with dolphins. It is stressed that these are educational experiences in which you can learn about the amazing capabilities of these intelligent sea creatures. *Programs are available every day, but reservations are required for children 5–19. Adults are chosen by lottery. Cost is $ 150 per couple for "Dolphin Doubles." "Adult Dolphin Encounter" is $95 per person. Call 885-2875.*

For a family, there is enough at Waikoloa to keep everyone busy, including golf. If you are so inclined, you can play the Beach or King's courses for $120 a round. With a special Fins & Fairway Golf Pass for slightly more than $20, you can play those same courses for $80, or the Waikoloa Village Course about five miles away for $50. *Call 325-6171 for more information.*

At about mile marker 69 there are signs to **Puako Bay** (7), which is on your left. This is quite a beach community. As you drive along, you will see several entries to the water marked "Beach Access." The shoreline is rocky with many tide pools, but what makes this area interesting is that it is a Green Sea Turtle Marine Preserve. This endangered species at times comes up on the rocks to feed on algae and bask in the sun. If you are fortunate enough to see one, DO NOT disturb them. They are protected by State and Federal laws.

Back on Highway 19 (Queen Kaahumanu Highway) look for signs to the **Hapuna Beach State Park** (8). Of all the beaches in the Big Island, this one ranks among the best. As a matter of fact, *Sunset* magazine rated it among the top four in all of Hawaii. They say it's because of the shaded grass and picnic tables along a gorgeous strand of white sand. There are lifeguards and full facilities. Excellent boogie boarding, but watch out for strong currents and undertow. There's a snack bar where you can rent needed beach and water equipment. *Park is open 7–8.*

Turn left on Highway 19, and from here on we will visit some of Hawaii's best-preserved and most valuable archeological sites. To get there, turn left at the junction with Highway 270 and head toward Kawaihae.

Look for signs to the **Puukohola Heiau National Historic Site** (9), just before the harbor. Legend has it that Kamehameha The Great built this war temple when he was told that in order to unify all the islands he must dedicate such a structure to the war god Kukailimoku and sacrifice a major chief. He did both. The massive stone platform is 100 by 225 feet and dominates its hillside location. It was built by Kamehameha in 1791. The federal government declared it a national historic monument in 1972. There is a small Visitor Center. You may not enter the *heiau* unless you are Hawaiian, but there is a path surrounding it. *Puukohola is open daily from 7:30–4. Admission is free.* Next door is **Spencer Beach Park.**

Next on this tour is the **Lapakahi State Historical Park** (10), about 14 miles farther on Highway 270. Lapakahi is an ancient seaside village encompassing 265 acres of this dry coastline. A good brochure helps visitors on a self-guided tour through the village proper, where you will see the remains of house sites, common buildings and shrines. Some of the village is reconstructed to give you a good feel for life in an ancient Hawaii village starting in about 1300. *It is open daily from 8–4. Admission is free. There is usually a guide on site.* ☎ *882-7218.*

The final stop on this daytrip is **Mahukona Beach Park** (11), a mile beyond Lapakahi. As you take the road down to the water, you will pass a big, rusted tin shed on the right that held sugar brought from Kohala by railroad. As a matter of fact, at the bottom of the road is an old building that can be rented that has a sign over the door, "Hawaii Railroad, 1930." The remains of an old sugar shipping pier still stands jutting out into the bay. Sugar and the railroad are both long gone.

Waimea and the High Country

Some people have said that good portions of the Waimea area remind them of Scotland—cool air, rolling soft green pastures, rocky crags, wisps of fog and periodic stands of deep green trees. What may be hard to compute, however, is that there are gorgeous white sand beaches just ten miles away instead of the cold and steely coastline of the Highlands. But this is the tropics, and Waimea definitely has that high country feeling—albeit with a decidedly ranch atmosphere.

Waimea does things small and big. On the one hand, there are many quaint little houses huddled on the hills above town and on the other, there is the 225,000-acre Parker Ranch stretching for miles all around the place.

The town is also host to the only private boarding school in Hawaii. The Hawaii Preparatory Academy's buildings and grounds, mostly designed by the renowned Honolulu architectural firm of Ossipoff, Snyder and Rowland, is like a small college campus.

GETTING THERE:

By car, take Highway 19 from Hilo and Honakaa. From Kona take Highway 190 (Mamalahoa Highway).

PRACTICALITIES:

As mentioned, Waimea can be cool at night and in the mornings, so a light sweater is advisable. It warms up during the day, so take your sunglasses, sunscreen and hat. Use a fanny pack, back pack or both so you leave nothing in your car, locked or unlocked. If you plan on horseback riding, take suitable clothing.

FOOD AND DRINK:

Maha's (in the Spencer House in Waimea) Cozy setting for light breakfast and luncheon salads made from local produce. Fresh fish daily. Afternoon tea is fun. Open for breakfast and lunch daily, closed Tues. ☎ 885-0693. $

Merriman's (in Opelu Plaza on Lindsey Rd. in Waimea) They call it Hawaii Regional Cuisine. Grown in the area, try the Kahua Ranch Lamb or the Ulupalakua Ranch Filet Steak. Lunch Mon.–Fri., dinner daily. Reservations, ☎ 885-6862. $$–$$$

Paniolo Country Inn (near the Junction of Hwys. 190 and 19 in Waimea) Down-home cooking for hearty cowboy appetites. Hamburgers, pizza, salads, steaks, of course. ☎ 885-4377. $–$$

Bamboo (center of town in Hawi) Casual dining in an old hotel that housed early sugar workers. They blend East and West for an "Island Style" that includes Thai, Hawaii, American. Lunch and dinner Tues.–Sat. Brunch Sun., closed Mon. ☎ 889-5555. $–$$

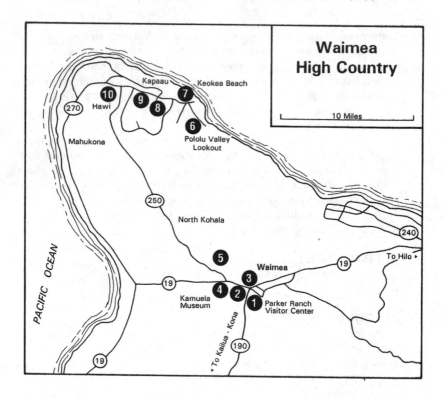

LOCAL ATTRACTIONS:

Numbers in parentheses correspond to numbers on the map.

Any way you come into town, stretching nearly as far as the eye can see toward Mauna Kea and an equal distance to the hills on the other side, is the Parker Ranch. At 225,000 acres, (consider that at one time it was double that size) it takes up most of the northern part of the island. A working spread with 50,000 head of cattle, the ranch had its beginnings in 1847 when John Palmer Parker, a young Massachusetts sailor, jumped ship in the islands in the early 1880s.

The ranch started small. King Kamehameha I befriended Parker and gave him two acres in which to corral the wild cattle that were roaming the slopes of Mauna Kea. It didn't hurt that Parker married the King's granddaughter, because very gradually this savvy Yankee expanded and expanded until he and his descendants turned the spread into one of the largest privately owned ranches in the nation.

A good way to get to know more of this story is the go to the **Visitor Center** (1) at the back of the Parker Ranch Shopping Center at the junctions of highways 19 and 190. (Lots of things in Waimea understandably have the Parker Ranch name attached). Here you will be enthralled with the Museum that features items and accounts of the 150-year history of the ranch. There's an informative video presentation as part of the package. *Open daily 9–5 except major holidays. Adult admission $5, kids 4–11 $3.75.* ☎ *885-7655.*

Head back on Highway 190 for about a mile; on the right are signs to the **Historic Parker Ranch Homes** (2). They are an interesting pair of bookends to the first Parker and the last Parker (sixth-generation Richard Smart) to run the ranch. **Mana Hale** was originally built away from town by the ranch's founder John Parker in the 1800s. It reflects functional New England design with small pane windows and a sloping slate roof. What is totally non-New England is the handsome interior made of Hawaii's gorgeous native koa wood. The koa was artfully taken out of the original and built into this replacement. Next to it is **Puopelu** with sweeping lawns and formal gardens. In the 1960s and 70s Richard Smart took this home, originally built in 1862, to its zenith as an 8,000-square-foot edifice with magnificent furnishings. It is also home to his outstanding French Impressionist and Chinese collections. Here in cowboy country you will find a Renoir, a Chagall, a Degas and at least a hundred paintings, plates, glasses and scores of other art treasures of equal cachet. *Open daily 10–5, except major holidays. Adults are $7.50 and kids 4–11 $5.00. The best deal is a "twofer" of the Visitor Center and both Historic Homes: $10 for adults and $7.50 for kids.* ☎ *885-7655.*

If you retrace your steps back into town, next to McDonalds is historic **Spencer House** (3). It was the first frame house in Waimea, built by a sea captain in 1852. Captain Spencer became rich growing onions and other veggies in Hawaii's high country and shipping them off for the California gold miners. Today it houses two treats. **Cook's Discovery** is a general store featuring a rich collection of made-in-Hawaii arts, crafts, edibles, collectibles and Hawaiian-language games and learning materials. *Open daily 10–6.* ☎ *885-3633.* Next door is **Maha's Café.**

As said earlier, this is cowboy country and if you're hankering to ride a horse, an excellent place to saddle up is at the **Mauna Kea Stables.** Take the road opposite the Spencer House for about a quarter of a mile to the stables. They can accommodate equestrians of all abilities since the stable manager carefully matches each rider with a suitable mount. The thrill is to ride across green rolling pastures on the Parker Ranch with such scenic highlights as ancient stone corrals and breathtaking vistas of snow-capped Mauna Kea and its sister peaks Mauna Loa and Hualalai. One hour in all this splendor astride a well mannered horse is about $35; two hours runs about $60. *Riders must be at least eight years old. Call 880-1111.*

Now retrace your route on Highway 190. At the major intersection, turn right on Highway 19. You will pass some very lovely high country homes. Just past the junction of 19 and Highway 250, on the left is the **Kamuela Museum** (4) founded by Albert and Harriet Solomon. She's a direct descendant of the Parker Ranch founder. This privately-owned museum houses an unusual collection of artifacts originally owned by Hawaiian monarchs and later displayed in Iolani Palace. There are other artifacts from around the world as well. *Admission is $5 for adults and $2 for kids under 15. Open 8–5 daily.* ☎ *885-4724.*

Head back to the intersection and turn left on Highway 250. Spread out before you on the right is the spacious campus of the **Hawaii Preparatory Academy** (5). The school was started in 1949 on Parker Ranch land as an Episcopal School. It has grown so that today there are about 600 students with about 150 day students. The campus includes a small chapel—built almost entirely of native materials—which is one of the most unusual religious structures in these parts—or anywhere else for that matter. Kids actually like to go to church here. It is not advisable to wander around the campus on foot when school is in session.

When you turn right to get back on Highway 250 headed for North Kohala, the road will climb considerably from Waimea, which itself is nearly 2,500 feet above sea level. Enjoy the ranch country as the road winds through ironwood trees. During nearly the entire trip the view on the left, downslope across brilliantly green pastures to the sea way below, is spectacular. Note the gentleman ranches lined with white fences. As you glide down toward Kapaau, you are headed into Kamehameha The Great country. After you turn right on 270, on your right is the king's statute. This is the one that was lost at sea and then miraculously found.

Head out on 270 all the way to the **Pololu Valley Lookout** (6). This is a spot of vast beauty, with the sea pounding away down below at the feet of towering cliffs. You can see a series of valleys marching along the coast and over one of the highest ridges is Waipio Valley, the largest on the Big Island. It is possible to take a footpath all the way from the Lookout to the ocean below, but it's a pretty arduous hike.

As you head back on the highway it's possible to reach the water in an easier fashion by driving down to **Keokea Beach Park** (7). The road is about a mile down that takes you to a grassy area with picnic tables. Most of the bay is surrounded by sheer cliffs, but there is a small lagoon for snorkeling and safe swimming. *Facilities. Camping is permitted.*

About three miles farther on the road, look on your left for signs for what's called the **Bond Historic District** (8). The Bonds were missionaries who came from New England to this very remote outpost in the Kohala District of the Big Island in the mid-1880s. Today, the last of three Kalahikiola Congregational Churches still stands as a monument to adaptation of New England design to Hawaii ways. The original thatched *Halau* (church) collapsed and was replaced by a wooden building in 1845, which also didn't withstand the vagaries of the Kohala-district weather, including strong winds. So the present church was built in 1855 of two-foot thick stone. Even this one got a huge crack in the front wall that couldn't be repaired. Yankee ingenuity built an attached wooden steeple tower over the damage.

You can tour the Bond Historic District, which includes the grounds of the Homestead (a wonderful collection of New England-style buildings), the church and an early Kohala Girls School with one of the Bond descendants. *Tours Mon.–Sat. from 9:30–4:30. Admission is $14 for adults and $7 for kids under 14. A self-guided tour with accompanying brochure is $6 for adults and $2 for kids under 14.* ☎ *889-0883.*

As you head back through Kapaau, keep in mind that this was sugar country for nearly a hundred years. As is true in so many other areas of Hawaii, with sugar fading or gone completely, there is an ongoing search for replacement crops or a similar economic engine. One such activity that utilizes some of the sugar infrastructure left behind (when it all ended in this area in 1975) is the **Kohala Mountain Kayak Cruise** (9). The kayak trip is down a portion of an engineering marvel called the Kohala Ditch. The story of building the ditch is a fascinating one. The original idea was to carve out an immense water highway from the rainforests of North Kohala to grow plentiful sugar cane in the fertile but essentially dry lowlands. Six hundred immigrants began their labors in 1906. In a fairly short time period they carved and scraped and literally hacked the ditch through rock, along sheer cliffs and over streams.

Today, you can leisurely float down a safe 2.5-mile section of the ditch in super-safe inflatable kayaks with a guide who is well informed of the Hawaiian history, culture and legends of the Kohala area. It is an experience of a lifetime. Stop at the Sakamoto Store in Kapaau where the tours originates. *They run two tours a day. Cost is $75 for adults and $50 for kids under 15.* ☎ *889-6922 for reservations.*

Keep going on the highway that will take you into quaint **Hawi** (10), just down the road. Enjoy the shops, galleries and restaurants in this old sugar town. Continue on Highway 270 south and get on Highway 19 at Kawaihae Harbor. This will take you directly back to Kona.

Trip 31

Nature Day on a Private Ranch

How does a young man who started out following the family tradition of farming and beekeeping in California end up organizing and running one-of-a-kind eco tours on the Big Island?

The answer goes through Boulder, Colorado, where Rob Pacheco went to college. As a student, he served as the chief beekeeper in a lab at the University of Colorado and hung out most of the time with a bunch of biology students. Even though he was an English major, Pacheco was hooked on biology and the natural world.

While a beekeeping job originally brought him to Kona after college, the lure of Hawaii's incredible natural world was too much for him, so in 1993 he started his company, Hawaii Forest & Trail. There's not another one like it in the Hawaiian Islands. There are two secrets to Rob's company—first is his boundless knowledge and enthusiasm for the Big Island's forests, birds, insects, geography and history, and second is his ability to take visitors onto inaccessible, private lands.

The experience is worth every minute during this daytrip.

GETTING THERE:

By van is actually the only way to get to the areas where Hawaii Forest & Trail takes you since these are private lands. They pick up at three locations: Kona Airport; the King's Shops in Waikoloa and Lanihau Center in Kailua-Kona.

PRACTICALITIES:

We'll quote from the company's own materials: "All you need to bring is a pair of comfortable walking shoes, your camera gear (with plenty of film) and a desire to see, explore and enjoy Hawaii's native world the way it was meant to be experienced . . . naturally!" A light jacket isn't a bad idea.

This full day, including pickup, continental breakfast, lunch, beverages, gear and outerwear is $110.

Rob offers three more eco-tours. First, there's the **Rainforest Discovery** on the Puu Oo Ranch off the Saddle Road on the slopes of Mauna Kea. If you have ever dreamed of venturing into a wild tropical rainforest, this trip is for you. It departs at 7 a.m., returns around 6 p.m., and costs $130.

The **Valley Waterfall Adventure** is on private property too, that goes along an incredible trail carved into cliffs a thousand feet above the valley floor. A full day is from 8–4 and costs $110. A half-day is from 7:30–12:30 or 12:45–5:45 and costs $79. The **Volcano Tour** is filled with information about this spectacular National Park. The cost is $130. Kids 5–12 for full day tours are $95.

Call (800) 464-1993 or locally 322-8881 for reservations. All tours are designed for all ages and abilities and run daily if there are enough passengers.

FOOD AND DRINK:

Buns in the Sun (Lanihau Center in Kailua-Kona) Bakery and deli that shines. Try the sticky buns and many other treats. Terrific sandwiches with fresh breads, of course. Breakfast and lunch daily. ☎ 326-2774. $

THE TOUR:

Today we're going to spend practically the entire day exploring Hawaii's incredible natural world on a 44,000-acre private, working ranch above the town of Kailua-Kona. Palani Ranch is one of three ranches on the Big Island still owned by the Greenwell family.

Henry Nicholas Greenwell began the family dynasty when he came to the islands from Britain in the mid 1800s and assembled a huge tract of land by buying parcels up and down the Kona coast. Cattle was the major product of the ranch, but Henry started to grow citrus as well. Things were going fairly well until a blight came along that practically destroyed all the fruit and trees. He tried to replace the citrus with other crops like rubber, but he was pretty determined to grow fruit. So off he went to visit a well-established orange plantation in the West Indies to find out how to overcome the blight. The plantation owner's daughter, Elizabeth Caroline, caught his eye, and so Henry came back to the islands with a wife, but no cure for the citrus blight.

On their return to Hawaii, Henry and his new bride and set about starting a family that eventually grew to 10 children. The ranch prospered and expanded to raising sheep along with cattle. Henry died first and Elizabeth Caroline died several years later, leaving the original ranch divided among three sons. All three ranches still exist, headed by Greenwells.

Rob tells you this charming tale of the early Greenwells as the van makes its way up Palani Road, named after Frank Greenwell (*Palani* is Frank in Hawaiian, and he was one of the three inheritors of the original ranch). It's hard to imagine this very busy road was once a narrow trail used to drive his cattle down to the pier in Kailua town for shipment to Honolulu.

After the van turns right at Mamalahoa Highway, it twists and turns along the narrow winding road and finally stops at a locked, steel gate. Rob opens it—and you have now entered a world of incredible natural beauty, a world of silence except for the proliferation of bird sounds—and now and then, the moaning of fat cattle among the soft green pastures. You are unlikely to see or hear another human, except for your fellow tour members, for the next six hours. What you will encounter are sights of un-equaled beauty seen by few others, since Rob has exclusive rights to take visitors to Palani Ranch.

The ranch road is pretty jostly as you steadily climb through the pastures dotted with assorted fruit trees like mango, guava, avocado and breadfruit. The four-wheel-drive vehicle you are traveling in, however, is top-of-the-line with special suspension Rob had installed on the mainland.

Just when you think you've had enough of the jouncing over the narrow ranch pathway, Rob pulls over onto a level spot under the shade of a giant mango tree. Soon he is at the back of the van unloading a table which he covers with a *palaka* cloth. There are stools. A fruit compote is opened with fresh tropical treats artfully arranged with orchid blossoms sprinkled about. You are at about 2,500 feet and the view down to the ocean is enthralling. The group hardly says a word for several minutes, and then the exclama-tions start. The chatting continue for some time; this is when you begin to get to know your fellow passengers.

Rob pulls back onto the road and starts to tell about the Kona Field Sys-tem. He says the early Hawaiians were the ones who originally cleared miles and miles of these slopes to build a vast system of terraces where they grew food that supported a large population at one time. He points out that wa-ter has always been of prime importance, starting in ancient Hawaii, and to-day Palani Ranch has about 50 miles of piping to bring water to their cattle.

The terrain remains rolling bright green pastures, but now the lovely ohia trees are more prevalent. He points to an unusual example of the adapt-ability of these trees: it has branches that look like a weeping willow tree. He says in all his experience in this part of the island, he has never seen one like it. He slows the van and points to a "stilt" tree. If you separate your fin-gers and hold them downward on a table, that is what the bottom of one of these unusual trees looks like.

He explains that when a tree falls over in the tropics it usually becomes a "nursery" tree meaning that it makes a great host for other trees to begin life in. The nursery tree rots away leaving the stilted roots of the new tree that grew around the fallen trunk. Sometimes there are straight lines of trees that all grew out of one long nursery tree.

Periodically, Rob slows the van nearly to a stop and his eyes dart upward when he spots an unusual bird species. He knows their Latin and Hawaiian names, and shares his excitement by grabbing binoculars and handing them around.

Over on the left is a neighboring ranch that contrasts sharply with Palani. Instead of vast open pastures, it has rows of apple banana trees, coffee trees, mango and ginger. As you climb, you note the many stone walls all built without mortar. One particularly imposing wall appears in the distance on the right, and Rob explains that it separates Palani from Bishop Estate land. Because the estate land has not been grazed by cattle, it is a nearly perfect example of a Hawaiian *Mesic* (moist) forest that has grown on this side of the island from time immemorial. Being an expert, he rattles off some Latin-sounding names, but he tells everyone to relax because we will get to examine the forest at closer range during a three-mile round-trip walk we are about to take.

Rob stops the van at an opening in a stone fence. We are now at the 3,000-foot level, and the mists have started to flow up the slopes of Hualalai making it chilly and more mysterious. Rob makes it clear that this will be a 1.5-mile walk and not a hike. The first thing is to slip on "gaiters," which are little cuffs around your shoes to keep out burrs and leaves and possible pebbles. Hawaii Forest & Trail is all about details—not only in their service, but also in their knowledge. The walk goes right along the stone wall separating the Bishop Estate land from Palani. Rob is full of tales and stories and information as vast as from how a particular native Hawaii tree got its shape, to the state of the rare Hawaiian *apapane* bird, to how to find the happy faced spider under a particular leaf. His patter about the natural world is almost non-stop. It is fascinating. After the walk, he breaks out an outstanding lunch.

There are many more treats in store for this group—including a visit to an old single-family compound at the 5,000-foot level that was served by its own Catholic church. You have to experience walking through a special lava tube with a light around your forehead yourself.

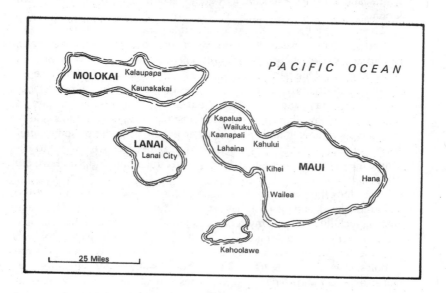

DAYTRIPS ON
MAUI, MOLOKAI
& LANAI

Maui actually changed it's nickname awhile back. It used to be called "The Valley Isle," but now is called "Maui—The Magic Isles." The reason is because Maui County actually encompasses three islands—Maui, Molokai and Lanai. Previously, there was little interplay for visitors between these islands, but now it's possible to have fun on all three. Each island is decidedly different from its nearby neighbor, as we will find out.

Maui itself has enduring popularity among the Hawaiian islands—and beyond. For several years, Maui has been voted "Best Island in the World" in the annual *Condé Nast Traveler* Reader's Choice Award. This particular rating was based on the responses of 35,000 subscribers to the magazine, and these individuals really know travel.

Some people claim it is Maui's diversity—the island's uncanny ability to dazzle and soothe almost at the same time. The dazzle comes from some of its extraordinary resorts situated on beaches that can calm the nerves and soothe the spirit. Molokai and Lanai, much smaller than Maui, are decidedly rustic and low-key, and more and more people are looking for that vacation style—at least for part of their vacation time.

GETTING TO MAUI, MOLOKAI AND LANAI:

You can reach Maui from any other major neighbor island in Hawaii, and of course, from Honolulu where **Aloha Airlines** has 29 flights daily to Kahului Airport. There is a second airport in west Maui at Kapalua, where Aloha Airline's sister airline, **Island Air** has 10 daily flights. It also flies to Hana Airport from Honolulu and Kahului twice a day. Aloha and Island Air can be reached toll free at (800) 367-5250. **Hawaiian Airlines** also has frequent service to Maui from Honolulu. **United Airlines** has two daily non-stop flights to Maui from both Los Angeles and San Francisco. **Delta** and **American Airlines** serve Maui non-stop from Los Angeles daily.

Island Air serves Molokai from Honolulu with 12 daily flights and Lanai with 10 daily flights. Hawaiian Air has flights to these two islands as well. Lanai can be reached in numerous ways over water from Maui as we will learn in these daytrips.

ACCOMMODATIONS ON MAUI:

There is a vast array of places to stay on Maui. There are over 60 hotels with about 10,000 rooms offering just about every price. Bed-and-breakfast inns have sprung up all over the place, and at last count, numbered over 40. Topping the list, in numbers at least, are condominiums with 103. **Aston Hotels & Resorts** has seven properties on the island, three in Kaanapali and four along the east shore from Kihei to Wailea. Aston's toll-free number is (800) 321-2558.

On Molokai, there is a hotel at the east end called the Kaluakoi Hotel & Golf Club, and a unique tent-a-lo (that's a combination of tent and bungalow) experience in the hills and near the water at Molokai Ranch. Lanai has two world-class hotels at either end of the island and a funky little old-fashioned hotel in town.

GETTING AROUND:

There is no public transportation system on Maui—except for resort shuttles and a nifty old train. Certain ground tours are available from **Polynesian Adventure Tours**. Call their toll-free number, (800)622-3011, for more information. As with most Hawaiian Islands, a rental car is the most frequently used method of getting around. **Budget** has a wide selection of cars, Jeeps and vans available at the Kahului, Kapalua and Molokai airports. Budget's toll-free reservation number is (800) 527-0700. On Lanai, Jeeps can be rented from Lanai City Service. Call (808) 533-3666.

PRACTICALITIES:

Amazingly, you will see some young people who were born in Hawaii surfing or boogie boarding with sun-reflective clothing. This is a new, and as yet not widely used practice, but the doctors and scientists are adamant about sun protection at all times. Sunglasses are also a must. Except for swimwear, ocean toys like snorkeling gear, boogie boards and the like can be readily rented. Take everything out of your car whether you lock it or not.

VISITOR INFORMATION:

Maui, Molokai and Lanai Visitors Bureau, 1727 Wili Pa Loop, P.O. Box 580, Wailuku, Maui, HI 96793, ☎ (808) 244-3530.

Wailea Destination Association, 3750 Wailea Alanui, Wailea, Maui, HI 96753, ☎ (808) 879-4258.

Kihei Destination Association, P.O. Box 962, Kihei, HI 96753, ☎ (808) 874-9400.

Kaanapali Beach Resort Association, 45 Kai Ala Drive, Kaanapali, Maui, HI 96761, ☎ (800) 245-9229,

Kapalua Resort, 500 Bay Drive, Kapalua, Maui, HI 96761, ☎ (808) 669-0244.

Molokai Visitors Association, P.O. Box 90, Kaunakakai, HI 96748, ☎ (808) 553-3876.

Destination Lanai, P.O. Box 700, Lanai City, HI 96763, ☎ (808) 565-3924.

Information on camping, hunting and hiking:

Department of Land & Natural Resources, Division of Forestry, 54 South High Street, Wailuku, HI 96793, ☎ (808) 243-5353.

*Haleakala—
"House of the Sun"

Responses from 40,000 readers of *Consumer Reports* magazine who visited national parks over a recent three-year period rated Haleakala in the top ten of all the parks in the nation. On an island with a multitude of spectacular places to visit, it is Maui's top attraction.

Haleakala viewed from the Maui isthmus is a mighty green giant with broad shoulders and lush pastures rolling down from its summit. Once inside the park, the view of the cavernous, eroded crater shows hues of brown and gold and red with almost no vegetation. The contrast is startling.

No matter how it is viewed, Haleakala has a tendency to draw you to it. Early Hawaiians felt that draw and made their way to its summit regularly. Legends abound about Haleakala. The best known is the one about the young boy Maui, the mischievous demi-god, who made his way to the summit to await the first signs of the sun. As the rays came over the rim of the crater, Maui lassoed each one to a nearby tree thus slowing the movement of the sun so his mother could have more sunlight to dry her *kapa* cloth. The sun complied and that is how Haleakala has become known as the "House of the Sun."

GETTING THERE:

By car from Lahaina, get on Highway 30. Bear right at Highway 380 and then right again on Highway 37. Follow signs to the park.

From Kihei and Wailea, get on Highway 31 and turn right on Highway 311. If you want to take a shortcut, just past the HC&S sugar mill, look for signs to Hansen Road. This winding road through the sugar cane will bring you to Highway 36, where you will turn right and then right again for Highway 37. Follow signs to the park.

The distance to the park summit from the intersection of Highways 36 and 37 is 38 miles. Leave plenty of time to get there.

PRACTICALITIES:

There is no gas or food in the park, so fill up before you leave or bear off to Pukalani on the way up on Highway 37. There are places to buy food on the upper reaches of the highway leading to the park.

It can be very hot on Maui's isthmus or along the shoreline, but cool once you get inside the park, so take a parka or sweater, especially in the winter and for sunrise or sunset viewing. If you plan to hike in the park, wear appropriate shoes, and take a backpack for water and food.

Even though you are at about 10,000 feet above sea level, put on sunscreen and wear sunglasses. Water is a necessity. Don't leave anything in your car, locked or not.

FOOD AND DRINK:

UpCountry Café (7-2 Aewa Place in Pukalani) Fun cow theme with many appropriate dishes. Da Moo Cow Wow is pork, teri chicken, mahimahi, spam and rice. Local residents hang out for breakfast & lunch Mon.–Sat. Dinner Wed.–Sat. ☎ 572-2395. $

Kula Sandalwood Restaurant (Haleakala Hwy. in Kula) This is worth the view and the fairly standard food is good. Sunrise breakfast and lunch daily. ☎ 878-3523. $ to $$

Sunrise Market & Protea Farm (Haleakala Hwy. above Kula) Family-owned working flower farm specializing in protea (they will ship). Variety of pastries, sandwiches and picnic makings for your park trip. Open daily. ☎ 876-0200. $

Kula Lodge (Haleakala Hwy. in Kula) Premier lunch and dinner spot in a lovely lodge setting. Sweeping views downslope of Haleakala and across to the West Maui mountains. They specialize in locally grown beef and seafood dishes. Lunch and dinner daily. Reservations ☎ 878-1535. $$ to $$$

SUGGESTED TOUR:

Numbers in parentheses correspond to numbers on the map.

*HALEAKALA NATIONAL PARK, P.O. Box 369, Makawao, HI 96768, ☎ *572-9306. Park entrance open every day 24 hours a day. Two Visitor Centers open 7:30–4, Mon.–Fri. Both centers are ♿. Gift shops at each. $10 per car.*

This full daytrip can be approached a number of different ways. Some visitors are insistent on driving to the summit for the spectacular sunrise; others are content to spend a normal day exploring this huge park; and still others try to time their visit for the sunset. All ways are good ways, but no matter how you want to do it, call either 877-5111 or 871-5054 for weather information. It can be sunny, cloudy, wet, windy and, as one park ranger was overheard to say, "the weather changes by the second." Going up the slopes

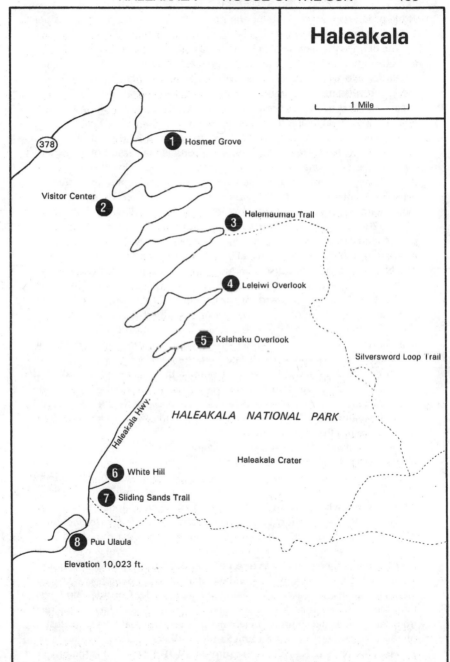

Haleakala

1 Mile

378

1 Hosmer Grove

Visitor Center

2

3 Halemaumau Trail

4 Leleiwi Overlook

5 Kalahaku Overlook

Silversword Loop Trail

Haleakala Hwy.

HALEAKALA   NATIONAL   PARK

Haleakala Crater

6 White Hill

7 Sliding Sands Trail

8 Puu Ulaula

Elevation 10,023 ft.

of the mountain means the temperature will drop about three degrees per 1,000 feet in elevation.

The drive to the summit of Haleakala has been compared to driving from the sub-tropical beaches of Mexico to the forest of Alaska—all in two hours instead of two weeks. As the road winds upward, the changes in climate, mood and vegetation are dramatic. Palm trees at sea level give way to pines, eucalyptus and even giant redwoods. Seemingly endless rolling pastures hold contented cattle and frisky horses.

Just after passing through the entry gate at about 6,500 feet above sea level are signs to **Hosmer Grove** (1). This forest is the result of an experiment by Ralph Hosmer, who was the territorial forester in 1904. He introduced pine, cypress, fir and cedar along with eucalyptus as a needed watershed and to see if a timber industry could be started. There are picnic tables, camping sites, facilities and a pleasant nature walk through the trees. The 5,320-acre **Waikamoi Preserve** of rain forest and alpine shrubland on private land can be hiked on either Mondays or Thursdays at no charge with a park ranger. It starts at the grove at 9 in the morning and takes three hours. The Nature Conservancy also conducts hikes on the second Saturday of each month. Space is limited, so call 572-7849. Donations are requested.

The **Park Headquarters and Visitor Center** (2) is a half-mile up from the grove at the 8,000-foot level. It has an information desk, maps and a gift shop. The park ranger can answer almost any question and provide trail maps and a list of Programs and Activities. A pond nearby is often the home to some of Hawaii's endangered state bird, the nene goose.

About 3.5 miles above the Visitor Center is the **Halemaumau Trailhead** (3). The first mile of this trail is fairly level through native shrubland to the rim of the crater. Next are two miles of steep switchbacks that descend 1,400 feet to the valley floor. The views are stunning and offer a look at the cloud forest as well as the barren crater.

Two worthwhile lookouts are next. **Leleiwi Overlook** (4) is at 8,800 feet above sea level, and offers views on a clear day from the Hana Coast to the Kihei shore. **Kalahaku Overlook** (5) was the first visitor stop long before the park was opened. In 1894 a small overnight shelter was built to house those intrepid souls who came by horseback to Haleakala. Today this spot is known for its different view angle of the crater and for a good selection of silverswords, a rare plant that only grows on Maui and the Big Island.

A stop at the second Visitor Center at the 9,700-foot level is worthwhile because located next to it is **White Hill** (6). A short footpath leads around the hill, which has a rich history with several sleeping shelters used by ancient Hawaiians. Be cautious walking at this altitude. Consider, however, that at two different times of the year there is a bike race and a running race from sea level to the summit of Haleakala. These are real "crazies." Just to one side of the Center is the **Sliding Sands Trailhead** (7).

Puu Ulaula (8) or Red Hill is the summit. At 10,023 feet, it is the highest point on the entire island of Maui. Here the full sweep of the huge one-million-year-old volcanic crater is visible. At seven miles long and two miles wide, the gaping, barren space exhibits rich colors of reddish brown, gray, black and even green. Cinder cones dot the floor, and as you look deeply into the crater, you can make out the various hiking trails that wander among the cinder cones.

Hiking in Haleakala is very popular, and you will find 32 miles of marked trails. An example of a half-day hike is Sliding Sands to Ka Luu o Ka Oo, five miles down to the crater floor. Images of multi-colored cinder cones, ever-changing clouds and silversword reward hikers willing to make this trek. An example of a good all-day hike is from Halemaumau to Silversword Loop; a 10-mile hike. Park rangers offer a guided Cinder Desert Hike on Tuesdays and Thursdays at 10 o'clock, which is about two miles long and takes two hours. It starts at Sliding Sands Trailhead. In addition to guided hikes, park rangers also offer 30-minute Natural and Cultural History Programs three times daily in the morning at the Summit Building.

There are three very popular cabins in the crater that can be reserved by writing to the park at the address at the beginning of this trip, or by calling the park phone number. Near these cabins are also camping sites that can be reserved the same way.

If hiking is not your thing, but you want to go down into the crater, **Maui Mule Ride** will take you on a guided ride on a gentle animal in one of three ways. The Aloha Ride is two hours and goes down Sliding Sands 1,400 feet. Cost is $90. A 4.5-hour picnic ride descends 3,000 feet to the crater floor and includes a picnic for $140. An all-day Panlolo Ride across lava flows, over cinder cones and past mysterious Pele's pig pen and paint pot, including lunch, will cost $175. *Call 244-6853 for reservations.* There are horses to take you down in the crater, too. **Pony Express Tours** has a variety of half- and full-day rides. *Call 667-2200 for more information.*

If you drove up to the crater during daylight hours, no doubt you saw several dozen bundled-up bike riders coasting down the Haleakala Road. This is a very popular activity for visitors. Most of these bike companies start at the top and travel the 38 miles down to sea level. Slickers and gloves are provided, as are protective helmets and specially-equipped bikes. **Maui Downhill** offers five guided downhill safaris from $48 to $115. *Call 871-2155.* **Aloha Bicycle Tours** does it slightly differently. They include the downhill run, but from outside the park entrance. Riders are free to go at their own pace and instead of going to sea level, they go through Keokea in upcountry and out to the Tedeschi Winery, where lunch is served. *Cost is $89. Call 249-0911 for reservations.*

Trip 33

Upcountry

There's something special about Upcountry Maui—that broad area on the slopes of Haleakala above the central plains. It is a belt of rolling hills and misty pastures, of ranches and farmland with small towns dotted here and there. It seems like another world from the beaches and hustle and bustle of the resorts along the coastal areas. The temperature alone tells you this is different than the rest of Maui. On the higher reaches of the Upcountry section of the mountain, residents occasionally scrape frost off their windshields in January and even February.

Kula, Makawao, Paia, Keokea are small towns that have all contributed to the rich lore of Upcountry. This is cowboy country with a rip-snorting rodeo every 4th of July. These upper slopes grow some world-famous produce and flowers. If you haven't had Maui onions, do so. And Upcountry Maui's protea blossoms can be found fresh and dried all around the globe.

GETTING THERE:

By car, from Kihei and Wailea, get on Highway 311, which will run into Highway 36 (Hana Highway). From Kaanapali and Kapalua take Highway 30 to 380, which will connect with Highway 36 (Hana Highway).

PRACTICALITIES:

Even though it may be cool in Upcountry, be sure to cover exposed areas with sunscreen. Sunglasses and a hat are necessities. There is a terrific mountain bike ride and a great hike in a redwood forest, so take substantial shoes if you decide to do those activities. Take everything out of your car whether you choose to lock it or not.

FOOD AND DRINK:

Paia Fish Market (110 Hana Hwy. in Paia) Lots of fish as the name suggests, plus burgers and pasta. Casual dining includes salads too. Daily lunch & dinner. ☎ 579-8030. $ to $$

Haliimaile General Store (900 Haliimaile Rd.) Old store and post office in a quaint sugar and pineapple town has been transformed into an excellent eatery with lots of fresh greens and unique dishes like Thai Ahi Tartare. Lunch Mon.–Fri., dinner daily. Sunday brunch. Reservations, ☎ 572-2666. $, $$ and $$$

Polli's (1202 Makawao Ave., in Makawao) Famous for its full offering of Mexican dishes, they also serve burgers and salads and ribs—for all appetites. ☎ 572-7808. $ to $$

Grandma's Coffee House (on Hwy. 37 near mile marker 16 in Keokea) Since 1918, famous hang-out for Upcountry's many artists and writers, Grandma's grows their own coffee just down the road. Excellent pastries and sandwiches. Open daily for breakfast and lunch. ☎ 878-2140. $

LOCAL ATTRACTIONS:

Numbers in parentheses correspond to numbers on the map.

As you head along the Hana Highway, about five miles from Kahului you will come to **Paia Town** (1). While this is not technically in Upcountry, it is a good entrance to the whole area. To visit the town today with its many galleries and quaint shops, you'd never know that it was a sugar town at one time, with a railroad and central station. Take the time to browse around the shops.

In the middle of town, turn right on Baldwin Avenue. A short distance up on the right is the old **HC&S Sugar Mill.** While not overly attractive to look at, it is one of four of this endangered species left operating in all of Hawaii. The road twists and turns as you climb to higher ground. About two miles up, you will practically run into the **Holy Rosary Church** (2) with its Father Damien Memorial (he founded the leper colony on Molokai—see Daytrip 44) and posts with pictures of the Stations of the Cross. Another couple of miles and you again practically run into another imposing sanctuary, which is the **Makawao Union Church** (3). It looks like it could be in the English countryside—except for the palms out front. This gothic beauty, designed by Hawaii's famed C.W. Dickey, is built of locally quarried lava rock. The oak interior, however, was imported from England. It is on the National and Hawaii Register of Historic Places.

Be sure to stop at the **Hui Noeau Visual Arts Center** (4), another mile up at 2841 Baldwin Avenue. What makes this artists' haven especially noteworthy is that it occupies the historic Upcountry estate, Kaluanui. The gracious two-story Mediterranean-style home was designed in 1917 by Mr. Dickey, who left his mark on the church just mentioned, as well as many other famous buildings in Hawaii. This lovely old Baldwin mansion has just been restored to its original magnificence. Also located on the property are the picturesque stables and tack room, and a large carriage house, all now used as various artist's studios. The landscaping combines local flora with European design concepts. Two of Maui's largest and oldest Cook Island

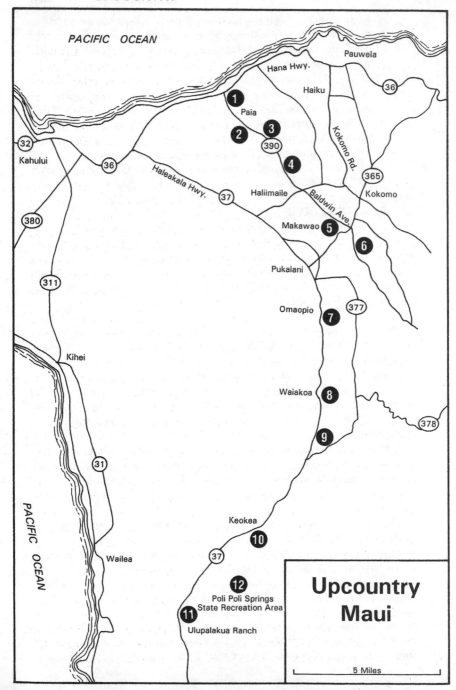

PACIFIC OCEAN

Pauwela

Hana Hwy.

Haiku

36

1

Paia

32

Kahului

36

2   3

390

4

Haleakala Hwy.

37

Haliimaile

Baldwin Ave.

Kokomo Rd.

365

Kokomo

380

Makawao   5

6

311

Pukalani

Omaopio   7   377

Kihei

Waiakoa   8

9

31

378

PACIFIC OCEAN

Keokea

10

37

Wailea

12

Poli Poli Springs
State Recreation Area

11

Ulupalakua Ranch

Upcountry
Maui

5 Miles

pine trees can be found near the house. *Gift shop. Open 10–4 Mon.–Sat. Donations. Call 572-6560 for current classes and shows.*

Another mile and you will enter **Makawao** (5), which in Hawaiian means "forest beginning." There's a vibrancy about this cowboy town that perhaps comes from its Portuguese and Chinese heritage. For food, Makawao is second to none with its famous cream puffs, homemade Portuguese sweet bread and the area's fruity jams and jellies. Today, the streets are lined with art galleries and nifty little shops and boutiques. In spite of all that gentrification, up Olinda Road is a cowboy nirvana known as the **Oskie Rice Rodeo Arena** (6). The arena is the home of the famous 4th-of-July rodeo, but they also hold other rodeo contests during the year. *Call the Maui Roping Club at 572-2076 for a schedule.* Adjacent to the rodeo arena is the well-known **Polo Grounds.** *The season is from August through November, on Sundays at 1:30. Admission is $3. Call 572-7326 for more information.*

Retrace your steps back into Makawao and turn left at Highway 365 (Makawao Avenue). Follow that out to Highway 37 (Kula Highway). At mile marker 10 in Omaopio is the **Enchanting Floral Gardens** (7). In this 15-acre garden you can see 1,000 colorful flowers and tropical plants. Protea and other Kula flowers are for sale, and they will ship. Great picnic spot. *Open daily 9–5. Adults $5, kids 6–12 $1.* ☎ *878-2531.*

Just before Waiakoa and beyond mile marker 11, turn left to Lower Kula Road. (Strange since it's actually above the road you're on.) This will take you to the distinctive **Church of the Holy Ghost** (8). This unusual octagonal church was built in 1889 by Portuguese artisans, and was restored several years ago to its original luster. The church's gilded altar and museum-quality Stations of the Cross were hand-carved in Austria and then shipped in sections around Cape Horn. The pieces were reputedly hauled to upcountry on oxcarts. The church is on the National and Hawaii Register of Historic Places.

Farther down this road, look for Poli Poli Road on the left. Take this hilly, winding and narrow road about two miles. On your left is the **Kwock Hing Society Building** (9), built in 1907. The two-story structure was used by the large early Chinese population as both a meeting and religious hall. Next to it is a one-story brown building that years ago functioned as a kitchen, gambling hall and opium den. Both buildings are no longer in use. Bear right on Middle Road, then right on Cross Road to return to Highway 37.

Turn left, and you will find in succession the **Ching Store and Gas Station, Fong's Market and Keokea Gallery,** and **Grandma's Coffee House.** All are worth a visit. Mrs. Ching sells reasonably-priced protea blossoms and other cut flowers from her gas station. This is the heart of Maui's Chinatown, known as Keokea.

As you continue out Highway 37, it becomes hilly and fairly narrow. A short distance from the Ching Store, look for the **Sun Yat Sen Monument.**(10) When a teenager, the famous Chinese leader hid out in the Upcountry area because of problems back home. He eventually went to Honolulu and graduated from Iolani School (see Daytrip 5). This is a good picnic area.

Next is the **Tedeschi Winery** (11) on Ulupalakua Ranch. Besides Hawaiian Pineapple Sparkling Wine and Maui Blanc Pineapple Wine, the winery also produces champagne, Maui Blush, Maui Splash and Rose Ranch Cuvee (the Rose Ranch designation was another name for Ulupalakua Ranch). The tasting room is in a New England-style building that was used by King David Kalakaua as a vacation retreat during the early days of the ranch. *Gift Shop, food and facilities. Free guided tours of the winery are offered 9:30– 2:30. The tasting room is open 9–4.* ☎ *878-6058. Free sips of wine for sampling.*

As you head back on Highway 37 from the winery, watch for signs to Highway 377. Bear right and then right again on Waipoli Road. It's about 20 minutes up a winding, steep and narrow road to the **Poli Poli State Recreation Area** (12). Almost the entire time you will be driving through Kaonoulu Ranch, a 10,000-acre *ahupuaa* (traditional land division) that reaches from the rim of the crater down to Kihei in South Maui. Henry Rice, the ranch's owner, is generally considered to be the unofficial Mayor of Upcountry since he is the fourth generation of the family to run the ranch. He advises not to pet the bulls on the way up to Poli Poli since this is open cattle range.

The reward for making the trip over the rough road is a large and dense forest of Monterey pines, eucalyptus and redwoods. The park is crisscrossed with trails including the delightful 1.7-mile Redwood Trail that starts at the 6,200-foot level. For the more ambitious, a trail leads uphill to Haleakala National Park. There is a picnic area, facilities and water.

If you want to experience Upcountry on a mountain bike, **Chris' Adventures Bike or Hike** has either a 34-mile morning ride or a 22-mile afternoon ride that includes crater viewing and a short hike plus riding to the winery and beyond to the remote lava fields of Laperouse Bay. They provide an island-style gourmet picnic breakfast or lunch. Cost is $79 for the morning ride and $59 for the afternoon ride. Chris offers bikes or hikes on Kauai and the Big Island too. *Call 871-2453 for Maui tours.*

Heavenly Hana

Hana has been saved from major development by a road optimistically called The Hana Highway. This pleasurably scenic route covers 52 serpentine miles winding around about 600 curves. The one-lane bridges number in the 50s. That makes the going slow. And that's what Hana is all about—slowing down the pace.

Many macho drivers decide they can tackle the road in less time than the recommended three hours to cover the distance. But why? You might miss the spectacular scenery on both sides of the road that includes waterfalls splashing down fern-covered cliffs and plunge pools that invite the swimmer—as well as hundreds of ocean vistas that are truly breathtaking. The profusion of fruit trees and flowering plants cast a tropical aroma that is found in few other places on Earth.

Along the way to Hana town are state parks for picnicking, botanical gardens open to the public and an occasional fruit stand selling snacks and dispensing gossip and local lore.

Do not ask of Mauians, "What is there to do in Hana?" When you ask that question, you have missed the point of this daytrip.

GETTING THERE:

By car, from the Lahaina side, take Highway 30 and bear right at 380. This will take you to Highway 36, which becomes 360 and is the Hana Highway. The distance from Lahaina is about 80 miles and it will take you from 3.5 to 4 hours to reach Hana town.

From the Kihei/Wailea side, take Highway 31 and turn right at Hansen Road just after the HC&S Sugar Mill. This will take you right to Highway 36, which becomes 360 or the Hana Highway. The distance is a little over 65 miles to Hana town and it will take about 3.5 hours to get there, depending on how often you stop.

No matter where you start from, plan to leave early so you can get in the "Hana Spirit," which is laid-back and easy going.

Rent-a-Local is a neat service whereby a driver drives your rental car over The Hana Road. This has three great advantages: you can customize your trip any way you like, you don't need to pay attention to the road and can enjoy all the sights, and the driver can take you to spots most visitors don't see. *The cost is $199 for two people, $25 for each additional. Call 877-4042.*

PRACTICALITIES:

Gas up before you start since there are no stations beyond Paia. However, once you reach Hana, there is fuel. Picnic stuff can be purchased in Hana. Sunglasses, sunscreen, a hat and water are very good ideas. Leave your car empty of possessions when you leave it—locked or unlocked.

FOOD AND DRINK:

Hecock's (505 Front St. in Lahaina) Hearty breakfasts with three-egg omelets their specialty. Try the scampi omelet. Good lunch sandwiches and burgers. Dinner is a variety of Italian dishes, well prepared. ☎ 661-8810. $ to $$.

Maui Coffee Roasters (444 Hana Hwy. in Kahului) 100% pure Hawaiian coffee from Kona, Maui, Kauai and Molokai. Light breakfast and lunch daily. ☎ 877-2877. $

Hana Ranch Restaurant (Hana Hwy. in town) Take-out breakfast daily. Big buffet lunch served in the dining room daily. Fri. and Sat. night dinners. Wed. is pizza night. ☎ 248-8255. $ to $$

LOCAL ATTRACTIONS:

Numbers in parentheses correspond to numbers on the map.

There is so much to see along this road that it is impossible to include it all. These are the highlights. Drive very carefully, but when you see something that interests you, don't be afraid to pull off and explore.

Before the original highway was built in 1926, to come from Hana into town was a two-day ride by horseback, or you could take the steamer that took a whole day. After the first 20 miles or so, the road becomes very winding and narrow in spots, although it was improved and "widened" in the early 1990s.

As you leave Kahului, the highway is wide and well paved. It narrows slightly beyond Paia, but still seems easily traveled with speed limits around 40 mph. Don't be fooled. At mile 19 when the sign says, "Narrow, winding road next 30 miles," that's when you drop all thoughts of being a road warrior and kick into low speed—mentally and otherwise.

Here you will start to see inviting waterfalls and roadside pools. At mile marker (mm) 2, look for a trail on the *mauka* (mountain) side of the road that leads to **Twin Falls** (1). While there is a lovely pool that looks good for swimming, you will probably see a No Trespassing sign. A few miles beyond is the tiny village of **Huelo** (2), where fresh fruits are sometimes sold along

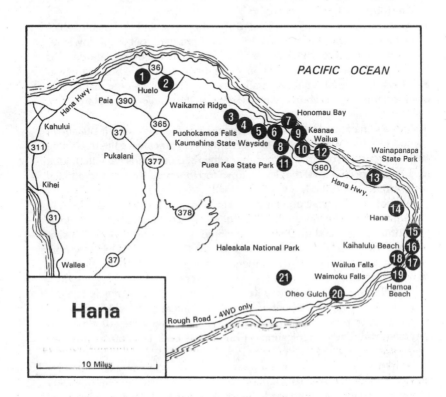

Hana

the roadside. Another New England-style church built in 1853 highlights this quaint stop.

At about mm 9 is **Waikamoi Ridge** (3), where you will find picnic tables and a nature trail. Above this area is a closed preserve, but in this lower region you can explore a bamboo forest and other native plants. At mm 11 is **Puohokamoa Falls** (4), which is a lovely setting for a picnic beside the waterfall and large pool. There are trails on either side of the pool that lead to other waterfalls. Just a short distance farther on the *mauka* side is **Haipuaena Falls** (5).

Kaumahina State Wayside (6) at mm 12 has facilities, and it sits above the coast in a pleasant grove of trees. From here, you can see the upcoming peninsula sticking out into the ocean. As the road descends the gulch, look for a *makai* (ocean) road that leads down to **Honomau Bay** (7) and a black sand beach.

At about the halfway point (mm 16) to Hana, on the right is the Keanae Arboretum (8). In the lower portion are ginger and heliconia and other flowering ornamentals and fruit trees, all marked. Look for the Polynesian section that includes what are thought to be the 24 plants brought from the South Pacific by the original settlers to the islands. A more ambitious hike/walk for another mile will take you into a rainforest.

Take the *makai* road down to **Keanae Peninsula** (9), which gets as close to an old Hawaiian settlement as they come. Interesting old homes amid palms and taro patches lead out to a windy point along the coastline. It is very peaceful. The Congregational Church was built in 1860 by missionaries.

At mm 18 is a lookout and a road leading down to another old community called **Wailua** (10). Banana and taro are still grown in neatly arranged patches along the road. Today, the Keanae/Wailua area is one of the major commercial wetland taro farming regions in the state. St. Gabriel's Church was built in 1870.

Look for **Puaa Kaa State Park** (11), where you will find a waterfall, restful picnic areas and facilities. Just beyond mm 25 is a rough road on the left that leads to **Nahiku** (12) with a high-up, stunning view of the coast. The crash of the ocean on rocks way below sends spray up the bluffs all along the coastline. The Nahiku Church was built in 1867.

Beyond the airport is **Wainapanapa State Park** (13). This area has a rich history that involves the two caves found here. According to legend, the beautiful wife of a cruel Hawaiian warrior fled him and hid in the caves. He searched the mountains, valleys and seashore only to discover her when he stopped to bathe in the clear water of the caves. Overcome with anger, he murdered her—and that is why every year during spring, millions of red shrimp appear in the caves and it is said this is a testimony to that tragic event. The jagged coastline is not suitable for swimming, but a wonderful

three-mile hiking trail leads into town along the rugged shore. There are picnic tables, showers and full facilities. Twelve cabins can be rented. *Call 243-
5354 well in advance to reserve one.*

Bear right on the road that will take you into **Hana** (14). Today's population of 2,000 is about half Hawaiian. There were many more people
in the late 1880s when six sugar plantations were operating in the area.
The last plantation closed in 1946, ending an era of bustling activity and
good employment. A retired entrepreneur from San Francisco, Paul Fagan
(the memorial on the hill in the middle of town is a tribute to Mr. Fagan),
came to the rescue by buying up 14,000 acres of land for a cattle ranch.
He also started the Kauiki Inn, which has become the five-star Hotel Hana-
Maui.

Near the turn-off to Hana Bay is the **Hana Cultural Center** (15). Here
you will find Hana artifacts and the recently-built *Kauhale O Hana*, which
is an authentic Hawaiian living complex exhibiting housing and gardens of
pre-contact Hawaii. *Open daily 10–4. Admission is $2.* ☎ *248-8622.* At
Hauoli Street and the Hana Highway is the recently-restored **Wananalua
Congregational Church** (16), built in 1838. This is still another example of
the missionary-style New England church.

Plan to go down to Hana Bay, where you will find a black sand beach,
snack shop and pier. You can take a two-hour guided **Kayak and Snorkel
Trip** of the bay that costs $59. *Call 248-8211.* Rising to the right is Kauiki
Head, which can be climbed via a short trail. Also on this hill is a cave in
which Queen Kaahumanu was born in 1768. She was the favorite wife of
King Kamehameha. If you come back up to Ua Kea Road, turn left and follow it practically to the end. Straight ahead are the casually elegant Sea
Ranch Cottages of the Hotel Hana, Maui. Look for the trailhead that will take
you above **Kaihalulu Beach** (17).

When you get back on 360 (the Hana Highway) going south out of town,
look for the **Hasegawa General Store** (18), made famous by Paul Weston
and his song about this store. Started in 1910, the store has survived many
ups and downs of the area including a devastating fire. There's little you
won't find in this wonderfully complete family store.

Nearby are the **Hana Ranch Stables** that offer one-hour guided rides
three times a day. You can experience the ranch and coastline on Mondays
through Saturdays astride a gentle mount for a cost of $35. Call 248-8211.
If you would like to explore underground lava tubes, **Hana Cave Tours** offers a two-hour tour for $59 or a full-day tour for $119. Call 248-7308.

A short distance out of town is **Hamoa Beach** (19). James Michener described it as "The only beach I've ever seen that looks like the South Pacific
was in the North Pacific."

If you are determined to go beyond Hana town, about 10 miles out of
town is **Oheo Gulch** (20), which is not a very glamorous name for the **Seven**

Sacred Pools. This is also the southern extension of **Haleakala National Park** (21) (see Daytrip 32). Up the trail are two waterfalls—Makahiku that drops 200 feet and Waimoku that falls twice that distance.

The road beyond this point is very rough. It is a good idea to turn around here and head back the way you came.

Kihei Explorer

A string of sleepy Hawaiian Villages with outrigger canoes once lined the shore of this sunny stretch of the east side of Maui. Kamehameha had an ancient fishpond at Kalepolepo rebuilt for his exclusive use. The story goes that it took 10,000 men to complete the project. Some fishpond.

Because Lahaina is fairly close, Hawaiian royalty sojourned regularly at Kihei, basking regally on the breeze-swept shore and enjoying the clear, usually calm water.

There's nothing sleepy about this coast now, however, and it won't cost a king's ransom to visit. Kihei is well stocked with reasonably-priced condos. Here you'll also find a string of small shopping malls, a bustling farmer's market, activity centers and a host of family restaurants.

Most remarkable about Kihei are the long stretches of sandy beach with views of two uninhabited Islands, a sparsely inhabited neighbor island and West Maui, which from this angle looks like a separate island, but isn't.

GETTING THERE:

By car, from the west side, take Highway 30 to Highway 31. At the intersection with Piilani Highway, follow Kihei Road. From central Maui, get on Punene which turns into Mokulele or Highway 311. As you drive along Piilani, there will be signs to Kihei.

PRACTICALITIES:

We have said time and again that to have a terrific vacation with a modest tan, always wear sunscreen—from the moment you leave your room, and not just on the beach. Protective eyewear is also advisable. Take a hat too. If you like the water, take along your swimsuit. A pair of rubber slippers will make sense as we go along. Whether you lock your car or not, leave nothing in it or the car's trunk.

FOOD & DRINK:

Stella Blues Café (1215 S. Kihei Rd.) Fun family place. The East Coast Scramble includes eggs and lox and onions. Toby's Tofu Tia is a wrap sandwich with lots of goodies. Breakfast, lunch and dinner daily. ☎ 874-3779. $ to $$

Ukelele Grill (575 S. Kihei Rd. in the Maui Lu Resort) Feels like old Hawaii in this former showroom. Ever try saimin for breakfast? It's noodle soup. Dinner offers a spectacular salad bar and tasty entrees. Breakfast and dinner daily. ☎ 875-1188. $ to $$

Antonio's (1215 S. Kihei Rd. in Longs Center) This is reasonably-priced Italian food at its best. The Lasagna Con Carne is tops. Many pasta dishes. Dinner daily. ☎ 875-8800. $$

Buzz's Wharf (in Maalaea Harbor) Wonderful spot overlooking the small boat harbor. Sandwiches and salads for lunch daily. Dinner leans toward fresh fish. Papeete Steamed Fish is their award winner. Beef too. Reservations, ☎ 244-5426. $ to $$

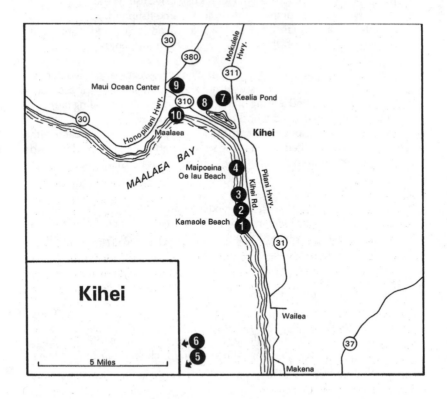

LOCAL ATTRACTIONS:

Numbers in parentheses correspond to numbers on the map.

We hope you like oceanside exploring, because that's what this daytrip is all about. This is not your usual beach stroll, however, because the beach at Kihei goes on for several miles—with a few interruptions here and there. That's not to say you can't stop for refreshments, or if you are so inspired, jump in the ocean.

The best place to start your tide pool exploration and shell collecting is at **Kamaole Beach Park III** (1) near the Kihei Boat Ramp in South Kihei. The tide pools at the beginning of the beach teem with fish of many sizes and colors. The rocks can be slippery and rough on the feet, so a simple pair of rubber slippers will make this adventure more pleasurable.

As you walk along the sandy shore, you will come to **Kamaole Beach Park II** (2). Both this one and the park before have grassy areas above the beach and full facilities. The water here comes in straight along the beach, and as a consequence, many tiny shells can be found at the waterline. Periodically, bigger shells will show up, but generally they are about fingernail size. What some people do is collect a cup full and place them in colored water. If you are especially patient, you can find shells with small holes and string what is called a "puka-shell" necklace. Better collect two cupfuls if this interests you.

Although it is not quite seamless because of rock outcroppings that restrict easy access at high tide, nonetheless, you can make your way to **Kamaole Beach Park I** (3) for the wrap-up of your tide pool and shelling experience. As you walk back the way you came, you will have covered a little less than two miles by the time you get back to your car in the parking lot of Kamaole III.

Drive north on Kihei Road past the various shops, restaurants and condos until you are nearly at the end, and on the left look for **Maipoeina Oe Iau Beach Park** (4). The park is fairly small, but has nice grass and full facilities. This area is considered a windsurfers' paradise, especially in the afternoon when the wind picks up.

This is the beginning of another two miles of beach walking, and if you are so inclined you may want to continue your beachcombing for shells and even glass balls used by Japanese fishing boats to hold their nets. As you make your way along, you may have noticed a couple of miles offshore a tiny semi-circular island that at night has a navigational beacon on it. This is **Molokini Island** (5). It is actually another Hawaii volcano that didn't rise nearly as high as its neighbors. When the ocean, rain and wind began eroding it millions of years ago, about a third fell eventually into the ocean. The cove created by this weather action provides unsurpassed diving and snorkeling in crystal-clear calm water. It became so popular that the state turned it into a Marine Life Conservation District where no netting or taking of fish is allowed, and has now regulated how many boats may go to Molokini. You should consider a water tour out to this island. Nobody can land on it.

A bigger neighbor to Molokini is uninhabited **Kahoolawe** (6). This 46-square-mile island has had a difficult past. Early Hawaiians inhabited Kahoolawe and the island has a rich history, but available water has always been a problem. In the 19th century, Queen Kaahumanu banished Catholics and prisoners to the island. Goats and sheep were introduced at one point, and after humans left about 70 years ago, these voracious feral animals practically striped the island of vegetation. At the start of WWII, the Navy took over the island for target practice, and they continued shelling it until 1990.

In the 1980s, Hawaiian activists started to demand the return of Kahoolawe. In one daring attempt to land on the island while the Navy still used it for target practice, two Hawaiians set out on surf boards at night. While the closest points between Maui and Kahoolawe are only seven miles apart, these are tricky waters and the intrepid paddlers were never heard from again.

But the Navy at last has given it up. Astonishingly, the U.S. Congress voted $450 million to clean the island of exploded and unexploded ordnance. Who knows what its future will be after that work is finished.

To the north is Lanai with only 3,000 residents. (Daytrips 41 & 42).

Next, we suggest you get in your car and travel north onto Highway 31 (North Kihei Highway). For about two miles there are no buildings on either side of the road because this is **Kealia Pond National Wildlife Refuge** (7), a salt-water marsh that is refuge for the Hawaiian stilt and coot, birds that are on the endangered species list. It is also a nesting and breeding refuge for the magnificent and rare 200-pound Hawaiian Hawksbill turtles. Between mile markers 1 and 2 look for the **Wildlife Boardwalk** (8). This newly-constructed raised walkway extends for nearly a mile loop and takes you through the wetlands for viewing water birds, the turtles, and whales. And speaking of whales, this is a great spot to view them during the winter months of December to April. Nearby is the:

*MAUI OCEAN CENTER (9), 192 Ma'alea Rd., Wailuku, HI 96793, ☎ 270-7000. *Open daily 9–5. Adults $17.50, kids 3–12 $12. Snack bar and open-air restaurant. Big gift shop.* ⚫.

We suggest you now make your way to this state-of-the-art aquarium and marine park. Set on three acres, several buildings—almost like a campus—hold exhibits of superb quality. Highlights include living coral displays, colorful tropical reef fish species, large "open ocean" and game fish, several species of sharks, green sea turtles, sting rays, eels and jelly fish. This new facility has sister operations in the U.S. Virgin Islands, Australia, Bali and Israel. All the marine life in the facility is indigenous or endemic to the Hawaiian Islands. The Whale Discovery Center has full-size models of humpback whales so you can study what you can see live right offshore during the winter months. Visitors of all ages can enjoy a computerized arcade of interactive learning whale stations, all included in the admission price. Of special note is the Underwater Walk through a re-created lava rock cave that leads to a massive deep-water cavern; its 750,000 gallons makes it the biggest aquarium in the state. Tiger sharks, large tuna and creatures of all sizes and colors swim above, beside and under your feet as you are in a transparent tunnel.

Since you are right next to **Maalaea Harbor** (10), stop in at this small fishing village, the site of the only remaining Shinto Japanese shrine in Hawaii dedicated to the fishing god *Ebisu Sama*. This harbor is a mecca for water activities including scuba, snorkeling, whale watching, sport fishing and sunset dinner cruises. **Pacific Whale Foundation** runs five-hour snorkeling trips daily to Molokini that also includes turtle watching at Turtle Arches near Wailea. *Cost is $39.50. Call 879-8811.* From December through April **Trilogy** will take you for an afternoon whale-watching and snorkeling adventure. They serve an Hawaiian-style barbecue lunch, provide snorkel gear and let you listen on hydrophones for whale songs. *Cost is $55 for adults and $27.50 for kids 3–12. Call 661-4743.*

For a classy sunset dining experience aboard a smooth and stable ship, consider **Navatek II**. They have seated service with linens, flatware and glassware. Live music enhances the already incredible sunsets. Very good food. *Adults are $87 and kids 2–11 are $55. Call 661-8787.*

Trip 36

Wonderful Wailea

As you enter Wailea, the feeling you get is that whoever designed this resort did it right—right from the beginning. There is a sense of calm that perhaps comes from the rolling green golf courses strung along the roadside of the entire resort. The custom homes on the *mauka* (mountain) side of the road seem just right. Not too ostentatious. The five hotels spaced out on the *makai* (ocean) side seem to fit very nicely too.

Nature has been good to Wailea, blessing the resort with a mile and a half of shoreline notched into five crescent beaches, fringed in palms and splashed by gentle surf. People have been good to the resort too, since in recent years more than a billion dollars have been lavished on upgrading everything from the sports facilities to the flowers that grow beside the road.

By contrast, Makena is Maui untamed, the spirit of the unchained. That is not to say that Makena is without a spectacular hotel. The Maui Prince is called "a precious pocket of civilization." The two beaches in Makena are among the finest anywhere.

GETTING THERE:

By car, from the airport take Highway 380 and turn left at Punene Road. This will bend into Highway 311 (Mokulele Highway). At the intersection, take Piilani Highway, which will deliver you straight to the resort. From West Maui, take Highway 30 and turn right at Highway 31. Then take the Piilani Highway.

PRACTICALITIES:

There's plenty of sun and water along this coastline, so put on lots of sunscreen and those protective sunglasses. A hat is fun. Wear comfortable shoes. Load up your fannypack or backpack so you leave nothing in your car, locked or unlocked.

FOOD AND DRINK:

The Clubhouse Restaurant (at the Golf Clubhouse of the Blue Course in Wailea) One-price breakfast will fill you up. Lunch offers good sandwiches. Try the chili and rice. Dinner has Italian-style pizza, prime rib. Open daily. ☎ 875-4060. $ to $$

Sandcastle at Wailea (3750 Wailea Alanui in the Wailea Village Shops) Big burgers and salads, plus complete dinners with fish and beef. The pizza is highly recommended. Open daily for lunch and dinner. ☎ 879-0606. $ to $$

Bella Luna (555 Kaukahi in the Diamond Resort) Lanai dining with a view that is extraordinary. This is the highest spot in Wailea for the best sunsets. Excellent but reasonably-priced Italian-style food. Open daily for dinner. Reservations, ☎ 879-8255. $$

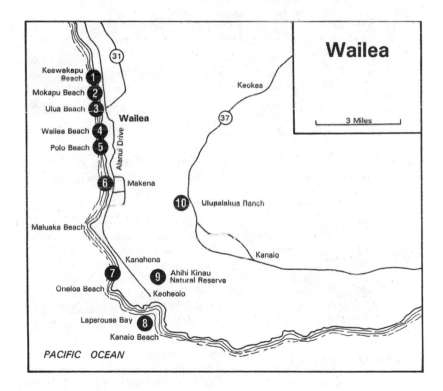

LOCAL ATTRACTIONS:

Numbers in parentheses correspond to numbers on the map.

A good place to start exploring this resort is the mile-and-a-half footpath along the shoreline. It has a nice flow to it because of the master planning of the entire space. There are only five hotels tucked into a space three times the size of Waikiki—with a few condominiums mixed in.

If you are a morning person, walking along the shore of Wailea in the sunny warmth of winter—when the air is still and the ocean calm—it is possible to hear whales singing out on the ocean. It is a haunting, unforgettable experience. It happens at Wailea because the conditions are just right.

The first beach (of five) you come to is **Keawakapu Beach** (1), fronting the Wailea Ekahi Condominium. The white sand along the **Renaissance Beach Resort** is called **Mokapu Beach** (2). This hotel, situated on 15.5 acres of tropical gardens offers lei-making, pineapple cutting demonstrations, hula lessons and garden tours. It is here that, if you take the road along the right side of the resort *mauka* and connect with Wailea Ike Drive, it would take you to the **Wailea Tennis Club.** This 11-court tennis complex overlooking the entire resort has a stadium court that features terraced seating for 1,000. Rates are $25 per hour for Wailea guests and $30 for the general public. Call 879-1958 for courts.

Back along the shoreline, the next beach in front of the Wailea Elua Condo and part of the **Aston Wailea Resort**, is called **Ulua Beach** (3). This one and its next-door neighbor, Wailea Beach—across some black lava fingers—have been named among the top ten beaches in the U.S. by *Condé Nast Traveler* magazine. Remember, that's in the whole country.

The 22-acre grounds of the Aston include the Luau Garden, where four times a week (Monday, Tuesday, Thursday and Friday evenings starting at 5) the hotel puts on what is considered Wailea's best luau. The whole evening is very complete including the Imu ceremony, traditional Hawaiian music and entertainment, Mai Tai and lei greetings—and of course, superb luau food. *Adults are $55 and kids 6–12 are $28. Call 879-1922 for reservations.*

The Aston also has distinguished itself by offering the **Hoolokahi Hawaiian Cultural Program** run by Bill Boyd, who is the hotel's full-time Director of Hawaiian Culture. These daily Hawaiiana programs are open to guests, Maui residents and hotel employees. There are classes and demonstrations in such cultural activities as lei making, Hawaiian quilting, and weaving offered Mondays through Fridays in the main lobby. There are small charges for these classes, mostly for materials. Call Bill at 874-7822.

The path is great for people-watching in the morning, especially at the tiny Jog 'n Java Coffee stand in front of the Aston. If you get a chance, stop and have coffee and watch the power walkers along the pathway.

The **Grand Wailea Resort & Spa** is next, and it features a spectacular nine-story atrium filled with ten thousand seasonal flowers and plants. The superlatives go on: there is $30 million worth of commissioned art and $15 million worth of water features. The spa is certainly grand too at 50,000 square feet.

Wailea Beach (4) wraps around in front of the Aston, Grand Wailea and the **Four Seasons Hotel** as well. Several of the guest amenities about the latter hotel need to be mentioned. Their VIP poolside service pampers guests with butler-passed cold face towels, ice water and chilled Evian spray misters to refresh sunbathers. To wrap up this beach walk, across Wailea Point is **Polo Beach** (5), which partially fronts the **Kea Lani Hotel.**

Because of the angle of the land, Wailea is also all about sunsets. From your hotel lanai, or even sitting on one of the five beaches, be sure to leave plenty of time for nature's dramatic splash of color at day's end.

Wailea has three championship golf courses—Blue, Gold and Emerald—and two clubhouses, making it one of the largest golf facilities in Hawaii. The entire resort has made a commitment to preserving the environment. This is best demonstrated on the Gold Course where the landscaping uses indigenous foliage bordered by old Hawaiian stone walls. With that in mind, the Gold Course is the priciest at $100 for Wailea guests and $130 for the general public. Blue and Emerald are $85 for guests and $130 for the general public. *For reservations call 875-7450.*

Now it's time to get in your car and move on down the road to Makena. Right past the Maui Prince is a road that turns at a sharp right angle. Take that and it will lead you a short distance to what's popularly called **Little Makena** (6). This is the perfect crescent white-sand beach, with some surf coming in. The grassy area and facilities are topnotch since the hotel provides them. One of the best ways to go over to Molokini is to take the 46' **Kai Kanani** right from this beach, Tuesday through Saturday mornings. They call it the "Short Cut" because this snorkeling and diving haven is so close. You get a light breakfast and deli-style lunch included in the $65 cost. *Call 879-7218.*

Farther down the track is Oneloa, which most people call **Big Makena** (7). It got the "Big" designation because it's about 3,000 feet long by nearly 100 feet wide. It is a pristine beach without a trace of development. Crystal clear water and soft breezes make this one a favorite.

At the end of the road and about five miles from Wailea is **Laperouse Bay** (8). It was along this shore that French explorer Jean-Francois de Galaup, Compte de Laperouse, became the first non-Polynesian to set foot on Maui in 1786. He wrote that the people "hastened alongside in their canoes, bringing articles of commerce, hogs, potatoes, bananas, taro with cloth and some other curiosities." The bay where he landed was given his name.

Laperouse is mostly rock with little sand, so swimming is difficult, but the ocean is great for snorkeling. There is a sign for the **Ahihi Kinau Natural Reserve Area** (9), the trailhead for a path that leads out onto the peninsula and along the shore. In 1851, missionary Henry Cheever rode a mule along 20 miles of this same trail, and he wrote that it was built by convicts of adultery, thus he called it a trail "which Sin has wrought."

The anchialine ponds with brackish water are the most striking feature of the peninsula; the bright colors are very unusual, running from orange to green, caused by the endemic algae found in them.

About 50 years after the arrival of Laperouse, an American sea captain, James Makee, had a run-in with one of his drunken sailors in Honolulu Harbor. He got slashed up pretty badly, but managed to survive. He came to Maui to settle down and started a sugar plantation and ranch—Ulupalakua. The reigning monarch, King David Kalakaua, would sojourn at the ranch, and ships from around the world came to Makena Landing to visit the successful American rancher.

Ulupalakua Ranch (10) is the huge expanse of rolling green hills reaching up from the shoreline to the top of Haleakala. (see Daytrip 33). If you want to explore some of that open, but private, space on horseback, **Makena Stables** offers introductory rides for $99 and a Laperouse Bay lunch ride of five to six hours for $160. These rides are spectacular. *Call 879-0244 for reservations.* If you want to try shooting clay pigeons, **Papaka Sporting Clays** up in the ranchlands has 30 stands adaptable to every level of shooter. *Open daily from 8:30 'til dusk, their rates go from $75 to $120. Call 879-5649 for reservations.*

*Central Maui—
"The Valley Isle"

The broad green plain between the sculpted West Maui mountains and the massive slopes of Haleakala gave Maui its nickname, "The Valley Isle." The early Hawaiians called the isthmus *Kula-o-ka-Mao-Mao*.

Wailuku, Maui's county seat, is older than its sister city Kahului. Sometimes called sleepy and picturesque, Wailuku is the birthplace of some of Maui's most famous citizens, among them Keopuolani, the most sacred wife of Kamehameha the Great.

Neighboring Kahului is much younger and unencumbered by history. It was primarily built in the 1950s by Alexander and Baldwin to provide affordable housing for its many sugar workers toiling in the huge plantation that stills spreads out over the central section. It has become Maui's population center with subdivisions and shopping malls.

GETTING THERE:

   By car, from the airport, bear right and that will connect you with Highway 32, which takes you into the heart of town. From Kihei/Wailea, take Highway 31 and turn right at Highway 30. From Kaanapali, take Highway 30 all the way to Wailuku.

PRACTICALITIES:

   There are some good hikes in the area, so take appropriate shoes if you choose this activity. For horseback riding, take long pants. Sunscreen, sunglasses, a hat and water are also good items to have along. Strip your car and carry things with you whether you lock or not.

FOOD AND DRINK:

   Since we are in Central Maui, which is pretty far removed from the major resorts and their hotels, this selection of Wailuku restaurants is decidedly low-key. Any one of these will provide you with a good chance to mingle with residents.

   Maui Bake Shop and Deli (2092 Vineyard) This is a hangout for residents who snap up the baked goodies. Great sandwiches to eat there or for picnics. Open Mon.–Sat. for breakfast and lunch. ☎ 242-0064. $

Sam Sato's (1750 Wili Pa Loop) This is a regular for people who live in Central Maui. Japanese food primarily, including monju. American dishes too. Open Mon.–Sat. for breakfast and lunch. ☎ 244-7124. $

Chums Family Restaurant (1900 Main) The name says it all for this family-style eatery. Soups, sandwiches and more will keep everyone happy. Open daily for breakfast, lunch and dinner. ☎ 244-1000. $

Bentos & Banquets by Bernard (85 N. Church) A true mix of local and American foods for all tastes. *Bentos* are basically box lunches of local foods convenient for picnics. Open for lunch Mon.–Fri. ☎ 244-1124. $

LOCAL ATTRACTIONS:

Numbers in parentheses correspond to numbers on the map.

Behind Wailuku the land narrows and curls into the mountains, forming the most magnificent valley on the island, Iao, Maui's Valley of the Kings. This whole area is rich in history, starting with the ancient Hawaiians. Two hundred years ago, one of the most famous battles in Hawaii's history was fought here when Kamehameha The Great conquered the island and added it to his Hawaiian nation.

To start this trip, keep going toward the mountains on Highway 32, which gets narrower and turns into Iao Valley Road. Follow this up about four miles to **Iao Valley State Park** (1) to view the famous Iao Needle, a 1,200-foot green monolith that pierces the mist. This striking formation was formed over 10,000 years ago by the forces of wind and water. At the head of the valley is a natural amphitheater, which is the caldera of the original volcano that formed Maui. From the parking lot there is a short walk with some steps to a viewing stand, where the needle is most dramatic. Hikes in the valley will take you through stands of giant tree fern, ti and ohia, and past stream beds where moonstones sparkle and wild orchids line the banks. *The park is free and is open from 7–7. Facilities.*

Just down from the needle is a worthwhile nature experience for young and old:

*HAWAII NATURE CENTER (2), 875 Iao Valley Rd., Wailuku, Maui, HI 96793, ☎ 244-6500. *Open daily 10–4. Adults $6, kids $4. Gift shop.* ♿.

This wonderful facility lets you get your hands on Maui by providing adventuresome and educational exhibits where you become part of the whole experience. A towering glass solarium presents ever-changing views of the

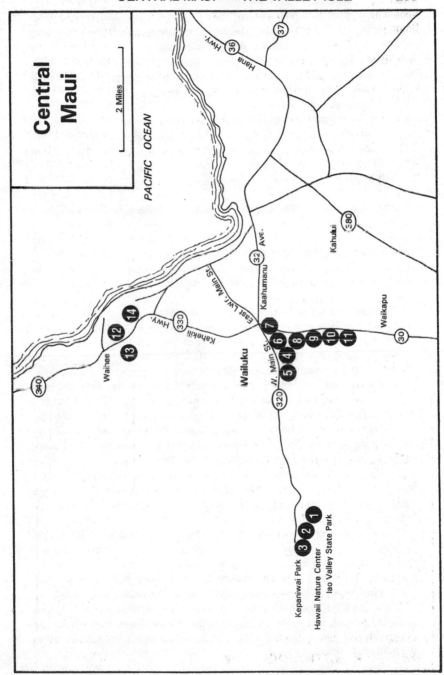

valley as rushing water flows over rock formations into touch pools and aquariums of native stream life. There are rainforest explorations, dispersal arcade games, live insect and stream animal exhibits—and best of all—a dragonfly ride where you are the insect. The exhibits are organized around five concepts—isolation, interdependence, biodiversity, dispersal and adaptation—that makes these islands so unique.

You may also want to take the Center's Nature Walk. It is a 1.5-hour interpretive stroll lead by an environmental educator that will take you on ancient footpaths into a Hawaiian rainforest. *Advance reservations are required by calling 244-6500. The Nature Walk is packaged with admission to the Center and a special T-shirt for a total of $24.95 for adults and $22.95 for kids 8–12.*

Adjacent to the Nature Center is **Heritage Gardens—Kepaniwai Park** (3), named for the 1790 battle in this valley in which Kamehameha conquered Maui. It is a collection of ethnic gardens and pavilions representing the various groups that make up Maui's chop-suey mix. Included are Hawaiian, Chinese, Japanese, Portuguese, Filipino and American gardens and small representative houses. *Covered picnic areas. Open daily all hours. Free.*

Tropical Gardens of Maui is on the left side of the road as you come out of the valley. This four-acre facility has many tropical plants, trees and bushes that grow well in the wet climate of Iao Valley. Iao stream runs through the property creating a nifty waterfall. *Tours of the garden are available for $3. Open Mon.–Sat. 9–5.* ☎ *244-3085.*

Next is a short walking tour to rediscover Wailuku town. This area was the center of power and population in pre-historic Hawaii. Things changed dramatically in the early 1800s when the missionaries came and brought their religious beliefs, Western skills and implements, and new agricultural methods. By 1860, another change had taken place with the start of a booming sugar industry. That brought thousands of immigrants.

The road out of the valley turns into Main Street, and before that bisects with High Street, where you will find probably one of the most significant historic sites in Wailuku, called the **Bailey House Museum.** (4) This two-story coral block structure was built in 1833 on the royal compound of Kahekili, the last king of Maui. It has a fascinating collection of landscape paintings of Maui done by the Reverend Edward Bailey over a 30-year period. Besides the art, the large collection includes 1,000 Hawaiian artifacts and over 400 missionary-era artifacts. *Gift shop. Open 10–4 Mon.–Sat. Adult admission is $4, seniors $3.50 and kids 6–12 $1.* ☎ *244-3326.*

If you walk back up Main Street and peek through the foliage next door to Bailey House, you'll see the old **Wailuku Plantation Manager's House** (5), which will give you some idea of how sugar moguls lived. It served as the manager's residence as well as the social and administrative hub of the plantation. Wide lawns, three lanais, a four-car garage and servants' quarters are among the features of this private residence designed by the famed C.W. Dickey. Do not enter.

As you wander back down Main Street, after Bailey House is the **Alexander House** (6). This nicely designed residence was built in 1837 as the Alexander Mission Home. One of the succeeding residents, Sam Alexander, teamed up with H.P. Baldwin to form Alexander & Baldwin, one of the Big Five powerhouses in Hawaii's mercantile, shipping and sugar industries. Today A&B owns HC&S Sugar on Maui. (see Daytrips 3 and 20). At the corner of Main and High streets you will find **Honolii Park** (7), which honors John Honolii, the first Hawaiian missionary to come to Hawaii as a Christian. He translated for other missionaries.

Stately **Kaahumanu Church** (8) was built in 1876 and is named for the Queen who wanted to learn Christian ways. The church is built over the site of a *heiau* associated with Kahekili. The **Territorial Building** (9), which is next on South High Street, was designed by C.W. Dickey, who many describe as the most influential architect in Hawaii's history. It should be noted that he was the grandson of William Alexander, father of Sam who started Alexander & Baldwin. This is Dickey territory since he designed the next building too, which is the **Maui Public Library** (10). Our final structure on this short walking tour is **Wailuku Union Church** (11), built in 1911 as "an English-speaking Christian Church."

If you've had enough of history, you may want to shoot out South High Street about two miles to the **Maui Tropical Plantation.** Many of Hawaii's better-know fruits and flowers—like pineapple, papaya, macadamia nuts, coffee, anthuriums, orchids and more—are growing on display. *Admission is free. If you want to take a 30-minute narrated tram ride through the fields and groves, the cost is $8.50 for adults and $3.50 for kids. Gift shop and tropical nursery. Open daily 9–5.* ☎ *244-7643.*

We suggest retracing your route and turning right on East Main Street and then left on North Market Street. This will take you out a few miles to the village of **Waihee** (12) on Highway 340.

Several activities that require exercise are available in the area. For hiking, turn up Maluhia Road for about a mile, which will bring you to the **Waihee Ridge Trail** (13). The 2.5-mile trail climbs the windward slope of West Maui to a peak overlooking Wailuku. The ascent is from 1,000 to 2,600 feet, and the views are awesome. No water or facilities. For horseback riding, **Mendes Ranch** will take you on three-hour ride with a BBQ picnic through pastures and the lush Waihee Valley taro patches. *Operates Mondays through Saturdays. $130 per person. Call 871-5222.* For golf go to the **Waiehu Municipal Golf Course** (14), a wonderful 72-par oceanfront course open daily. *18 holes weekdays is $25; weekends $30. Carts and clubs can be rented. Call 243-7400 for starting times.*

You can discover West Maui from the air on **Sunshine Helicopters**, located at Kahului Airport. Their West Maui Deluxe Tour will take you to the "Wall of Tears" waterfall and around to the resorts of Kapalua, Kaanapali and Old Lahaina Town. The 30-minute flight is $99. An expanded West Maui Molokai Tour does all of the above, but also includes whale watching (in season) and the incredible north shore of Molokai. This flight is 60-70 minutes and cost $179. They also offer Hana/Haleakala for $135 and a Circle Island Special for $179. The owner is a decorated Viet Nam Vet with over 30 years of flying. *Call 871-0722 for reservations and additional information.*

Lahaina Prowler

This little seaside town is probably as well know as Honolulu—and with good reason. The first invasion was the booming sandalwood trade with China, when dozens of ships tied up at Lahaina and the Hawaiian chiefs stripped the hills of this fragrant wood. It was once the royal capital of the Hawaiian Kingdom and the seat of power for the Kamehameha dynasty in the early nineteenth century. Then Lahaina became the lusty port of the Yankee whaling fleet. As many as 400 ships at a time were berthed in the harbor, spilling 1,500 sailors ashore at any given time. You can imagine the mayhem. It is said the whalers felt there was no God west of the Horn, and conducted themselves accordingly. Among the miscreant sailors was Herman Melville, who wrote the classic *Moby Dick.*

The real conflict came when a band of puritanical missionaries arrived from New England around 1820 and tried to spoil the party. The New England missionaries were a determined lot however, and they pressed on with their good works—such as building the first high school west of the Rockies (Lahainaluna School thrives to this day), installing the first printing press, and changing the course of Hawaiian history through their language, customs, buildings and religious beliefs.

Precious remnants of Lahaina's Hawaiian birthright and its whaling and missionary eras are very evident to this day. Approximately 55 acres of the town have been set aside as historic districts, containing several sites designated as National Historic Landmarks.

GETTING THERE:

By car, take the Honoapiilani Highway (Route 30) from either Kahului or Kaanapali.

PRACTICALITIES:

Lahaina can be very warm, especially in the summer months. So dress lightly, wear a hat, put on those good sunglasses and sunscreen. Parking is a bit of a problem, and the parking lots are several blocks from Front Street, so be prepared to walk. And since this is a walking tour, wear comfortable shoes. Don't leave anything in your car.

FOOD AND DRINK:

Cheeseburgers in Paradise (811 Front St.) What a spot, right on the water, for the greatest burgers around. They serve very good-vegetarian dishes too. Try the chili cheese fries. Breakfast, lunch & dinner daily. ☎ 661-4855. $ to $$

Kimo's Seafood, Steaks and Grog (845 Front St.) For 20 years this eatery right on Front Street has recaptured the lusty sailor era of Lahaina. Fresh fish, pasta and steaks served in a whaling era atmosphere. Lunch and dinner daily. ☎ 661-4811. $ to $$

Longhi's (888 Front St.) This Maui landmark has been around for two decades, serving excellent steaks and seafood. Their Ahi Torino is a signature dish along with Steak Longhi. Breakfast, lunch & dinner daily. Dinner reservations, ☎ 667-2288. $, $$ & $$$

David Paul's Lahaina Grill (127 Lahainaluna Rd. in the Lahaina Inn) They write the menu daily, but have standards like Kona Lobster Crab Cakes and Clay Roasted Garlic-Garlic Chicken. Dinner daily. Reservations a must, ☎ 667-5117. $$ to $$$

SUGGESTED TOUR:

Numbers in parentheses correspond to numbers on the map.

The best way to get your arms around Lahaina is to take a walking tour of the town's many historical sites. The Lahaina Restoration Foundation has an excellent map featuring a short tour that covers 13 historical sites and a long tour that has another ten or so.

Some of the highlights you won't want to miss are included here. At the corner of Front and Dickenson streets are two missionary buildings. The first is the **Masters' Reading Room,** a unique coral-block and fieldstone building built in the early 1800s. It is not open to the public. Next door is the two-story **Baldwin Home** (1) built in 1834 by one of the first and certainly most notable Protestant missionaries, Dr. Dwight Baldwin. It has thick coral walls, stone and hand-hewn timbers. The building's most noteworthy architectural features are overhanging eaves for sun protection and a second-floor verandah. *Open daily 10–4. Guided tours. Adults $3, families $5, kids free.* ☎ *661-3262*

Tied up at the end of a stubby street opposite the Baldwin Home is the brig **Carthaginian** (2). This is a replica, since the original was lost at sea in 1972 on its way to Honolulu for dry-docking. Imagine hundreds of these small, fast square-riggers anchored or tied up at Lahaina during the height of the whaling and trading eras. Aboard you will find special whale exhibits and an original whaleboat discovered in Alaska and brought back to Lahaina in 1973. *Open daily 10–4. Adults $3, families $5, kids free.*

One of the most recognizable landmarks in this picturesque town is the **Pioneer Inn** (3). With its broad red roof extending over a wide second-story lanai, deep green walls and white trim, this was the only place of accom-

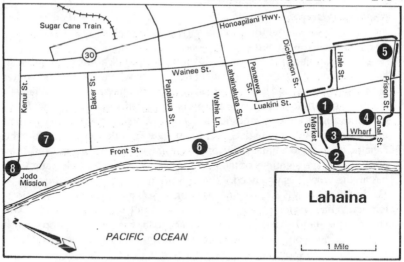

modation from the time it was built in 1901 until the late 50s. It has been expanded and today houses a combination of shops and restaurants. You can still stay at the Inn for about $80 a night. ☎ *661-3636.*

What would Lahaina be without the gargantuan **Banyan Tree** (4)? Just think—this 60-foot-high giant was only eight feet tall when it came from India in 1873 and was planted by William O. Smith to commemorate the 50th anniversary of the missionarys' arrival in Lahaina. The missionary ways and the banyan have lasted pretty well over all these years. The tree casts its shadow over two-thirds of an acre. Make time to enjoy it.

Go up Prison Street; at the corner with Wainee Street stands **The Old Prison** (5). Its Hawaiian name is *Hale Paahao,* which means "stuck-in-irons house." It was built in the mid-1880s by convict laborers. Most of the inmates were there for desertion from ships, drunkenness, working on the Sabbath or dangerous horse riding. *Take a free self-guided tour daily from 8–5.*

You might consider visiting three more worthwhile historical structures by car. The **Wo Hing Society Building** (6) at 858 Front Street was built in 1912 as a gathering spot for Lahaina's large Chinese population. It contains a large collection of Chinese artifacts, and upstairs in the temple is Maui's only Taoist altar open to the public. *Open 10–4. Donations.* A short drive will take you to the **U.S. Seaman's Hospital** (7) at 1024 Front Street. For a while it was Kamehameha II's residence, then it was a hospital, and then a vicarage and girls school for the Episcopal Church. Today it is used for commercial offices. Closed to the public, but well worth a look. Farther down Front Street, turn left at Mala Wharf Road, where you will find the distinctive **Jodo Mission Cultural Park** (8). It was built in 1968 to commemorate the arrival of the first Japanese immigrants 100 years earlier. The park includes the traditional three-tiered shrine and a 7,000-pound stone Buddha, reportedly the largest outside Japan.

It's impossible not to talk about whales when you talk about Lahaina. From late November through April the giant humpback whales make their winter home in Lahaina's (and the surrounding) offshore waters. They come here to mate and give birth to their young. This endangered species is known for its gentleness, its oceanic gymnastics and its haunting song. You won't want to miss these monsters of the deep. **Pacific Whale Foundation** leaves from the Lahaina Harbor three times daily for two-hour whale-watching cruises. They guarantee whale sightings or the next trip is free. A comfortable catamaran has all the amenities you need. All profits are used to help save the oceans. *Adults $30, kids $17. Call 879-8811.* **Atlantic Submarines** has a one-hour afternoon Whale Watching Adventure Combo during whale season. First, you cruise more than 100 feet below the surface to take inventory of tropical fish and corals found only in Hawaii. Then there is an exciting surface expedition to observe Maui's splendid whales. *Cost is $99. Call 871-0722.*

Both of these operators have several other cruises as well. And fun on the water around Lahaina doesn't mean just whale watching. There are about a dozen water activities from parasailing to regular sailing available in Lahaina Harbor. Some of the following might be fun. You can go fishing with **Finest Kind Sport Fishing,** which has three different boats. They have caught the most marlin on Maui for ten years straight. Finest Kind supplies all bait and lures. Bring your own food and beverage. *Cost is $135 for a shared boat for a full day (8 hours). A half day (6 hours) shared boat is $110. Call 661-0338 for reservations.* **Kamehameha Catamaran Sails** offers a daily two-hour snorkel tour of a shallow reef where the fish are so friendly they can be hand fed. Full instruction and equipment provided. *Cost is $50. Call 667-0680.* **Zip-Purr Charters** has a six-hour Lanai snorkel sail/whale watch on Tuesdays, Wednesdays, Thursdays and Saturdays. The trip starts with a delicious breakfast and narrated (seasonal) whale watch and dolphin search on the way to Lanai. They stop at two pristine snorkel spots known as Turtle Reef and Containers. A terrific lunch is served midway. Boogie boards, optical lenses, snorkel equipment and underwater cameras are available. *Cost is $85.95 for adults and $79.95 for kids 4–12.* They also offer sunset dinner cruises and scuba diving adventures. *Call 667-2299 for reservations.*

Sunny Kaanapali

In ancient times, Kaanapali was a royal retreat for the rulers of Maui. They liked the perfect three-mile stretch of white sand beach, gentle waves and warm sunny days. Maui's "royals" surfed, raced their outrigger canoes and feasted on luaus that lasted for weeks. Part of the rolling Kaanapali Golf Course was once a sizable bowling green where the *alii* played *ulu maika*, a form of lawn bowling using heavy lava rock balls.

In more recent times, the land from the beach to the sweeping West Maui mountains was largely sugar cane. Amfac, the owner of all that land, wisely saw the greater potential in hosting visitors than growing a commodity crop like sugar. As a result, Kaanapali was the first resort in Hawaii in the early 1960s where a single landowner planned it from stem to stern. It has become a model for other planned resorts around the world.

Amid several world-class hotels and condominiums is a unique shopping center with two whaling museums. From November until as late as the end of May, the waters off Kaanapali teem with majestic whales. Indeed, Maui is one of the few places in the world where you can watch whales from the shore—and Kaanapali is one of the best.

GETTING THERE:

By car, get on Highway 30 from either direction.

There is a **West Maui Shopping Express** that runs between all the Kaanapali hotels and into Lahaina about ten times a day. $1 for adults each way.

By train, you can go from Lahaina to Kaanapali (about five miles) on the **Sugar Cane Train** which offers an entertaining and scenic ride through sugar cane fields. A singing conductor acts as a guide. *Ten roundtrips daily, at $13.50 for adults and $7 for kids 3–12. Call 661-0089.*

PRACTICALITIES:

As one of the sunniest spots in all Hawaii (and that's saying a lot), make sure you protect yourself by using sunscreen even before you go to breakfast; wear sunglasses whenever you are outdoors. If you use your car, take everything with you whether you lock the car or not.

FOOD AND DRINK:

Reilley's (2290 Kaanapali Parkway in the Clubhouse) The grilled Ahi sandwich is a favorite. They are big on steaks, including a 22-oz. bone-in rib steak. Kona lobster too. Breakfast, lunch and dinner. Reservations suggested, ☎ 667-7477. $ to $$

Hula Grill (on the beach in Whaler's Village Shopping Center) Plantation ambiance. Look for two beautiful antique koa canoes. Oh yes, the food. Dim sum, big tasty salads, pasta, seafood—all great. Lunch & dinner daily. ☎ 667-6636. $ to $$

Basil Tomatoes (in the Royal Lahaina Resort at Kaanapali) Their Italian Grille prepares some excellent steaks, fresh fish and chicken. Fresh pasta dishes are tops. Dinner daily. Reservations suggested, ☎ 662-3210. $ to $$

Leilani's (beautiful beachfront location in Whaler's Village Shopping Center) Lower Beach Grill for lunchtime burgers, sandwiches and salads. Upper dining level for serious fish and steaks for dinner. Open daily. Reservations, ☎ 661-4495. $ to $$

LOCAL ATTRACTIONS:

Numbers in parentheses correspond to numbers on the map.

For this trip, we suggest a wondrous stroll along the beach and among the many hotels that are dotted along the Kaanapali Resort. If you start at the south end, the first hotel is another Hemmeter production called the **Hyatt Regency Maui** (1). Hemmeter (see Daytrips 7 and 29) was quite a visionary, and the elaborate pool he designed and built includes water slides, a swinging rope bridge and a swim-through grotto and bar. This was also the first of many grand hotels where Hemmeter began his practice of filling the place with art—this time it was about $2 million worth. Note the museum-quality sculpture, antique screens, paintings and carvings spaced all over the hotel. The concierge desk will give you a 24-page booklet so you can take a self-guided tour of their artwork.

A unique feature of this hotel is a program for guests called, **"Close Encounters with Maui's Cosmic Skies."** It is rooftop star gazing led by the hotel's director of astronomy who helps participants see star clusters, galaxies, planets, moons and much more through stationary binoculars and "Big Blue," the hotel's 16-inch high-powered telescope. There are three nightly shows. *The cost is $12 for adults and $6 for kids 12 and under. Call 667-4727 for more information.*

Next on our walk along the beach is the **Maui Mariott** (2). Its large open atrium makes a wonderful place for a light meal where you can gaze out at the sparkling ocean. Along this hotel's beachfront walk is the ultimate relaxer called **Paradise Body Works** where a half-hour massage is $15, up to an hour for $70. Tennis is also available right on the beach at the Marriott.

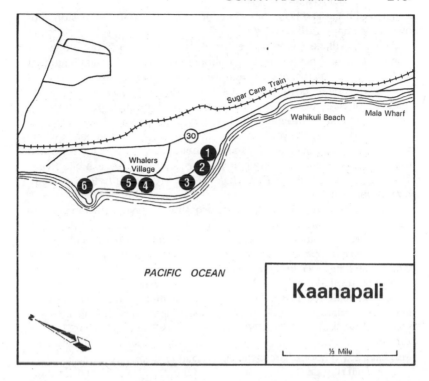

The charges are $12 per person all day. Bikes can be rented here too for $10 per hour or $30 per day, plus lots of water toys.

Unlike the first Hemmeter hotel we visited, which he built from the ground up, the next on our list is the **Westin Maui** (3) which was one of his best refurbishing jobs. Seeing its potential, he took a rather ordinary beachside hotel property and waved his magical wand over it. Not all will agree, but the transformation via another elaborate multi-level pool system, garden walkway through pools and lagoons with swans, abundant artwork and a general sense for good style is pretty astonishing. Mr. Hemmeter doesn't own either of these hotels any longer. He sold these and several other Hawaii properties at the top of the Japanese investment invasion in Hawaii, and went off to build gambling halls in New Orleans and Colorado.

Tucked back a short way from the beach walk is **"Dig Me Beach Activities."** (The name comes from a volleyball term, when players dive to save a ball and thus Dig Me). Besides volleyball at the beach, they offer 90-minute windsurfing lessons for $49 where they guarantee you'll get up. Windsurf rentals start at one hour for $20. Surfing lessons are $49 for 90 minutes with the first hour for instruction and the last 30 minutes on your own. *Open daily. Call 667-1964.*

Whalers Village Shopping Center (4) is next on our foray along this stunning beach. What is there to say about the many world-class boutiques and their pricey merchandise here except maybe it's great fun to shop and look? A star attraction of the center is the **Whale Center of the Pacific** made up of **Hale Kohola** (which tells the fascinating story of whales) and the **Whalers Village Museum** (which tells the history of whaling in Hawaii). In these two neat spots, you can come eye-to-eye with a humpback whale and even take a squeeze of whale blubber. There are many "see and touch" displays, and guests are invited to handle these exhibits freely. There is a small gift shop. *The Whale Center is open daily 9:30 a.m.–10 p.m. Admission is free.*

From December through April, the beautiful **Trilogy** catamaran pulls up right in front of the shopping center to take visitors on a Sunset Whale Watch. The two-hour cruise starts at 3:30 in the afternoon and includes sodas, snacks, hydrophones for listening to whale songs and of course, great whale watching. *$45 for adults and $22.50 for kids 3–12.* ☎ *874-2666.*

As you stroll along the the beach walkway, the next hotel you come to is the **Kaanapali Beach Hotel** (5). If ocean activities interest you, the **Teralani**—a 53' catamaran—pulls up to the beach right in front of the hotel and you simply walk aboard. *They offer a picnic/snorkel/sail daily from 11–3:30. All snorkeling equipment, lunch and open bar are included for $69. They also have a two-hour Champagne Sunset Sail for $35.*

Our final stop on this walking tour is at the newly refurbished **Sheraton Maui** (6), which was one of the first along this strip. As a result, the rehab ran about $130 million, and now the whole place has a renewed and fresh feel to it. New lobby, new restaurants and newly redone rooms. The hotel is nestled up against famed Black Rock. As the name implies, this hunk of rock jutting out into the ocean was once a shipping point for cattle and sugar before the hotels were built. Long before that, Kahekili, the last Chief of Maui, earned a reputation for leaping feet first from 300-400 foot cliffs. At Black Rock, he reputedly made his most impressive leaps, not only because of the distance, but also because it was a sacred place where souls of the dead leaped into their ancestral spirit land.

This ancient tradition is carried out daily at 6:15 in the evening when a brave cliff diver begins the ritual by lighting torches poolside at the Sheraton. He continues his ascent up Black Rock by lighting torches all the way up the steep staircase until he reaches the top. He then tosses his lei into the ominous waters below, waits until the waves are precisely as he wants them—and then takes his breathtaking miraculous plunge. Dôn't miss it.

You, too, can soar into the sky with **Parasail Kaanapali**. These people are so skilled that they launch you and bring you back into the boat without so much as getting wet. Imagine soaring as high as 900 feet above the water along the resort with Lanai and Molokai as the backdrop. They have an early bird special for $28.50. *Call 669-6555.*

While our focus has been totally on the beach and water so far, take a moment to look *mauka* (toward the mountains), for there you will see the majestic West Maui mountains. These giants actually give life to Maui by providing most of the island with its fresh water. At the center is Puu Kukui Crater, a 5,788-foot peak that is the second rainiest in Hawaii, with approximately 400 annual inches of rainfall.

Within those mountains lies the 1,264-acre **Kapunakea Preserve** run by the Nature Conservancy of Hawaii. The Conservancy describes Kapunakea as, "a biological and cultural wonder that harbors an astonishing variety of indigenous natural communities and many of the plants that were indispensable to everyday life in ancient Hawaii." The material from the Conservancy further says, "The preserve ranges widely in climate and terrain. It stretches from almost dry lowland forest at 1,600 feet in Honokowai Valley, to the west forests and montane bogs at 5,400 feet near the Puu Kukui summit."

The conservancy leads periodic hikes to the Preserve. *Call 572-7849.*

Trip 40

Kapalua—Arms Embracing the Sea

In the Hawaiian language, *Kapalua* means "arms embracing the sea." That name seems appropriate given the resort's dramatic lava peninsulas that shelter its five bays.

In the mid 1800s, 2,675 acres were granted to missionary Dwight Baldwin (his home is the one in Lahaina - see Daytrip 38) for his faithful service. It became Honolua Ranch where the principal activities were fishing, raising cattle and farming crops of mango, aloe and coffee bean. Ranch manager David Fleming was the first to experiment with a new fruit called hala-kahiki or pineapple. The ranch later became Baldwin Packers when most of the ranch's acres were converted to pineapple fields. Eventually Baldwin Packers became the largest producer of private-label pineapple and pineapple juice in the nation and today, this pineapple plantation is owned by the Maui Land and Pineapple Company.

Situated on Maui's scenic northwest coast at the foot of the verdant West Maui mountains, Kapalua is a 1,500-acre destination resort set amidst 23,000 acres of this privately-owned pineapple plantation. With a single landowner, the resort has the advantage of careful planning.

Kapalua Resort and the planned community within it offer such features as a rare native rainforest, a protected marine life conservation district, an ancient Hawaiian burial ground and golf courses that double as wildlife sanctuaries. There's also the historic Honolua Store, churches and plantation homes.

GETTING THERE:

By car, take either Highway 30 directly into the resort, or turn left off the highway at the sign to Honokowai. This will take you to the Lower Honoapiilani Highway.

PRACTICALITIES:

Your toolkit should include the usual: sunscreen, sunglasses, a hat and comfortable walking shoes. One of the best beaches in the world is here, so take a swimsuit.

FOOD AND DRINK:

Erik's Seafood Grotto (4242 Lower Honoapiilani Hwy. in the Kahana Villa condos) Up to nine different selections of fresh island fish are prepared daily. All-time view of the ocean, Molokai and Lanai. Lunch & dinner daily. ☎ 669-4806. $ to $$

Jameson's Grill (on the 18th hole of the Bay Course) Try the baked artichoke for a taste treat. Steaks and seafood are plentiful. Open for lunch and dinner daily. Reservations, ☎ 669-5653. $$

Honolua Store (on Office Rd. in the resort) Original plantation store, with light breakfast and lunches. You can buy everything from fresh pineapple ($18.95 for a 6-pack to take home) to logo T-shirts. Breakfast and lunch daily. ☎ 669-6128 $ to $$

Koho Grill & Bar (located in Napili Plaza Shopping Center) Casual family dining with an emphasis on burgers and salads. Lunch and dinner daily. ☎ 669-5299. $ to $$

SUGGESTED TOUR:

Numbers in parentheses correspond to numbers on the map.

We suggest you get on the lower highway and travel through the little villages of Honokowai, Kahana and Napili. There is a small park on the *makai* side about two miles down the road called S Turns. That pretty well sums up the shoreline along this road.

Just beyond mile marker 30, turn left and go down a short road to a small parking lot. Follow a path under a walkway and soon you will be at **Kapalua Bay Beach** (1) saluted as the best beach in America by the University of Maryland's prestigious Laboratory of Coastal Research. They surveyed 650 beaches nationwide to come up with this winner. It is the perfect white sand crescent with gorgeous turquoise water for swimming and snorkeling. Up the sweeping lawn is the **Kapalua Bay Hotel** (2). The stand at the edge of the beach rents everything from chaise lounges ($7) to snorkel sets ($15), boogie boards ($15), kayaks ($60) and even Aqua Eye ($18), which is a board with a built-in snorkel so you don't have to get wet while viewing the tremendous sea life.

Turn left when you get back on the highway. Note the huge homes along the road owned by tycoons and wealthy lawyers from the mainland. Just a bit up the road is a left turn that will take you to the **Kapalua Shops** (3). It is worth a stop to go to the Kapalua Logo Shop, where you can buy all manner of items with the well-recognized Kapalua butterfly with a tiny pineapple in the center. The **Maui Pineapple Plantation Tour** leaves from the Logo

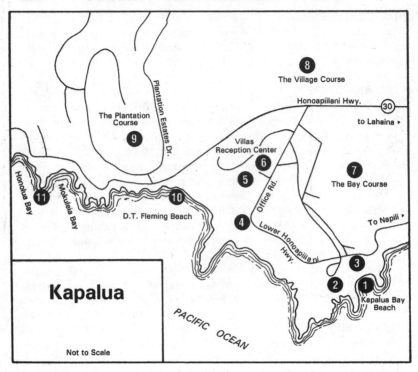

Shop twice a day in the morning and afternoon, Mondays through Fridays. Take advantage of the unique opportunity to tour a working pineapple plantation and cannery on the slopes of the West Maui mountains. Pick your own pineapple to take home. *Cost is $19. For reservations call 669-8088.*

Continue on the highway, and go straight to the dead end at the **Kumulani Chapel** (4). This tiny old sanctuary served the plantation for many years, but now is used for weddings. Note the single-wall redwood construction and mahogany ceiling.

Turn left and go up Office Road, turning left into the **Ritz-Carlton Hotel** (5). Every month this elegant hotel presents an Artist-in-Residence program with The Village Galleries. During the monthly weekend event they host a prominent artist, who sets up a studio at the hotel and invites guests to create their own art treasures. *Call 669-1800 for more information.* The hotel also offers a series of Eco-Tours on private land. After a hotel continental breakfast, you are taken by van to higher elevations where an experienced guide leads you out into the lush West Maui mountains through streams, waterfalls and native vegetation. *There is a six-hour excursion on Tuesdays through Fridays, costing $100 for hotel guests and $10 more for non-guests.*

On Saturdays and Sundays there is a four-hour excursion that costs $60 for guests and $65 for non-guests. Call 669-6200 for more information.

Once you come out of the Ritz, turn left again and almost immediately you will see the **Kapalua Resort Activities Desk** (6) in the Villas Reception Center. All kinds of wonderful things to do are available here. Sign up for tennis times on either **The Tennis Garden** or **The Village Tennis Center.** These courts have been recognized as among the best in the nation. *Court fees are $10 per person per day for guests and $12 for non-guests. Call 669-5677 or 665-0112.* **Ironwood Ranch** offers some spectacular adventures on horseback in these hills and valleys above the pineapple plantation. An example is the Sunset Ride to view the brilliance and tranquillity of a West Maui sunset from astride a horse. *Cost for the three-hour trip (2 hours on the horse) is $100.* The Picnic in Paradise Ride takes to you to one of Maui's most remote and picturesque settings. *The four-and-a-half-hour trip (2 hours on the horse) includes lunch and a short hike through a bamboo forest. The cost is $135. They offer many other rides starting from $75. Call 669-4991 or 669-4702 for reservations.*

The Kapalua Nature Society was created to manage the resort's many environmental programs such as yearly certification of Kapalua's three golf courses as Audubon Cooperative Sanctuaries. They also reach out into the community by leading visitors on spectacular hikes to the 70-year-old **Maunalei Arboretum** and **Puu Kaeo.** This half-day trip includes about a two-mile easy-to-moderate walking pace hike. It starts from 1,200 feet above sea level to the summit of Puu Kaeo at 1,635 feet. The **Manienie Ridge Hike** is approximately four miles and takes you to the ridge, with breathtaking views of Honokohau Valley below. Commentary by expert guides on both hikes provides a good understanding of the surroundings and culture of the area. *Both hikes are on private land and cost $80 each for adults and $50 for kids 12–18 including lunch. Call 669-8088 for reservations.*

As you re-enter Office Road turn left, and then right following signs that direct you to the Kapalua Bay Hotel. On your left are the red-colored remains of old pineapple sheds. The spectacular stand of huge Cook Island pines on both sides of the road frame a sweeping view over the golf course to the ocean below. Make another left and this will take you to Pineapple Hill, which in the beginning was the gracious old plantation home of D.T. Fleming. Take Simpson Way, turn right to the upper Honoapiilani Highway, and then turn left. This will provide you with an overview of Kapalua's golf acreage.

Arnold Palmer designed both the par-72 **Bay Course** (7) and the par-71 *mauka* spread called **The Village Course** (8). A third course called **The Plantation Course** (9) on the *makai* and *mauka* sides of the highway was designed by Ben Crenshaw and Bill Coore. A staff of 30 professionals, the largest in the state, share their expertise around 54 holes of the finest golf in the world. Kapalua's Touring Pro Hale Irwin says of golf at the resort, "There is something distinctively different about playing at Kapalua. Some days I think it is the setting. Other days, it is the way I play. No matter what, it is an experience I always remember as only happening here. It is an experience that makes me feel this is a special place." *Guests pay $85 greens fees at the Bay and Village Courses and $90 at the Plantation Course. Non-guests are $130 for the former and $140 for the latter. Call 669-8044 for tee times.*

As you continue on the highway, look for a sign that directs you to Lower Honoapiilani Road and turn left. A short distance down this narrow road will bring you to **D.T. Fleming Beach** (10), which is one of the best known on Maui. A great sunning and sitting beach, it is usually hazardous for swimming. The lifeguards post signs—it is advisable to follow them. Wonderful picnic spot.

As you retrace your steps, turn left on the highway, which will take you to **Mokuleia** and **Honolua Bays** (11). These two bays have been set aside by the state as a Marine Life Conservation District. You can't touch or take any of the marine life in these stunning underwater parks. But they are accessible to snorkelers and divers to examine remnants of old lava tubes, beautiful coral formations and abundant fish such as manini, uhu, octopus, damsel fish and Hawaii's official state fish, which is the humuhumunukunukuapuaa.

Ferry to the
Private Island

There are many fun ways to reach Lanai, only 10 miles off the coast of Maui. You can fly into the new Lanai Airport from Maui, but that seems so conventional. How about taking a powered raft, or a sleek 50' sailing ketch? There's a smooth catamaran, and last but not least, a working ferry. That will be our choice for this daytrip simply because it provides lots of flexibility to explore Lanai.

The lifestyle on Lanai is family-oriented. Lanaians have grown up enjoying the same gifts of the land as visitors—fishing, hunting, riding, hiking, swimming, beachcombing and exploring. Some Lanai City houses display antler racks alongside marlin tails, attesting to the bounty of the sea and the land. The next Daytrip, which is number 42, will complete the myriad activities that keep visitors coming back.

At 141 square miles, Lanai is the smallest of the inhabited Hawaiian Islands. It is only 18 miles long and 13 miles wide. Along its 47 miles of shoreline are several beautiful beaches, but in truth only a couple are good for swimming.

The island has a rich history. According to legend, Lanai was inhabited by *ka polo* or evil ghosts. The son of a Maui chief, Kaululaau, supposedly redeemed himself of his troublesome childhood by chasing the ghosts away. In the 19th century, Lanai was inhabited by ranchers and church people. In 1904, entrepreneur Charles Gay began buying land on Lanai and within four years, he owned it all. Jim Dole, bought the whole place from Gay in 1922 and began his fantastic run of producing the world's best-known pineapple for next 60 years. Dole's 19,000 acres of pineapple have been reduced today to about 200 acres—mostly grown for show for visitors and for use by residents.

David Murdock, through Castle & Cooke which he controls, is the present owner of all but two percent of Lanai. Because of that, Mr. Murdock started out by calling this the Private Island.

GETTING THERE:

By ferry, Expeditions leaves Lahaina Harbor with five daily departures, and the same numbers of return trips. The 50-minute (each way) trip costs $50 round-trip. *Call 661-3756.*

By catamaran, the 64' **Trilogy** leaves daily from Lahaina and includes snorkeling along the way, a van tour of Lanai City, BBQ lunch at a private picnic spot, and return. Cost is $149 for adults, $74.50 for kids 3–12. *Call 661-4743 for reservations.*

By inflatable raft, a full day on **Ocean Rafting Lanai** from Lahaina includes morning snorkeling (including equipment), a BBQ lunch and then the afternoon on the beach for $109 for adults. *Call 667-0680.*

By sailboat from Lahaina, the **Pacific Whale Foundation** offers six-hour snorkeling trips aboard the 50' ketch Whale II, with a marine mammal naturalist on board. Lunch and equipment are included. $73 for adults, $39 for kids 4–12. *Call 879-8811 for reservations.*

PRACTICALITIES:

Swimwear is a must as are sunscreen and sunglasses. A hat and comfortable walking shoes are also a good idea.

FOOD AND DRINK:

Tanigawa's (on 7th Ave. between Jacaranda and Ilima in Lanai City) Old-style eatery with local foods like Loco Moco Bento and Lup Chong Omelet. Open daily except Wed. for breakfast and lunch. ☎ 565-6537. $

Blue Ginger Café (on 7th Ave. between Jacaranda and Ilima in Lanai City) Terrific bakery serving fresh malasadas for 75¢, cinnamon rolls for 85¢ and bean donuts for $1.50. Breakfast, lunch and dinner daily. ☎ 565-6363. $

Henry Clay's Rotisserie (in the Hotel Lanai in Lanai City) Unusual dinner dishes like venison, rabbit, and duckling plus fresh Lanai catch-of-the-day. Gourmet pizzas as well. Dinner daily in casual atmosphere. ☎ 565-4700. $ to $$.

LOCAL ATTRACTIONS:

Numbers in parentheses correspond to numbers on the map.

The first thing you notice as you wait on the Lahaina Pier to board the ferry Expeditions for Lanai are the mounds of goods—from food to paper goods, to tires to appliances—stacked along the pier. It looks like a bunch of people are moving. Then it dawns on you that these are Lanai residents who have taken the ferry to Maui for the day to shop for merchandise priced way below what they can buy on their island. (Maui now has multiple discounters, and Lanai has no malls or "big box" retailers.) We're going to their

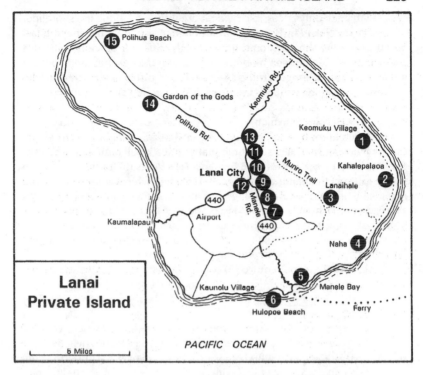

island to play and they've come to our island to stock up. That's what Hawaii's only scheduled ferry is all about.

Lots of hugs and kisses later between Maui and Lanai families—and we're off. As the 50' ferry plows through the relatively smooth waters of what is called the Lahaina Roadstead (that portion of water between Lahaina and Lanai where the whales love to frolic in winter), Lanai comes closer and closer. You note that the island slopes gently upward on the east side until it reaches a peak and then drops precipitously on its western edge—almost like the shape of a whale. Look carefully along the east shore because an old church in abandoned **Keomoku Village** (1) can be seen on clear days. This village in the 1890s was the center of an effort to grow sugar cane that eventually failed. The closest eastern point of the island is **Kahalepalaoa** (2), which was the site of an old wharf used for shipping sugar cane to Maui.

Deep gulches spread down from 3,370-foot **Lanaihale** (3), the highest mountain on the island. The stately stand of Norfolk pines that march along the mountain ridges were planted long ago to catch the moisture of the clouds constantly moving over the island. Long strands of white sand beaches that are only accessible by boat are visible all along the shoreline. One of them, **Naha** (4), is the site of an ancient fishpond and it is the last beach before the shore becomes *pali* or high cliffs. Periodically sail boats and other craft can be seen moored off these remote beaches, and you can just imagine the passengers and crew enjoying themselves in a paradise lost.

Very soon the ferry rounds the black *pali* shoreline and motors into tiny

Manele Bay Harbor (5), which has about a dozen boat slips—and no beach. It was once part of an ancient Hawaiian village and today is a Marine Life Conservation District. It is suggested that you walk half a mile on a road to the left of the harbor to **Hulopoe Bay and Tide Pools** (6) for the morning to swim, explore, sunbathe and snorkel. This bay, which is separated from Manele by black rock outcroppings, has an excellent swimming beach. It is an extension of the Marine Life Conservation District at Manele and is a preferred habitat of Hawaiian spinner dolphins. The tide pools are a wonderful place to discover fascinating inhabitants of these "natural aquariums." This shoreline can also be explored in a sea-kayak where no experience is necessary. **Lanai Eco-Adventure Co.** will show you the vast wealth of marine life surrounding Lanai, led by an informative guide paddling a kayak that leaves the delicate ecosystem undisturbed. *The trip costs $69. Call 565-7737.*

Before noon, you may want to walk back to the harbor where you can catch a taxi up the hill to town. After a steep climb past the **Manele Bay Hotel** the road straightens out and passes through **Palawai Basin** (7) in south central Lanai that was once filled with pineapple, but today is used primarily for grazing cattle.

After about eight miles on one of only three paved roads on the island, you reach restful **Lanai City** (8). This is a company town of 2,800 residents, and the only town on Lanai. Except for some very rich people who have upscale second homes near the two new golf courses, everyone lives here. It is very low-key. Some of the hulking old buildings from the pineapple days still stand. Most of the trim houses have lovely gardens. At 1,700 feet, it is noticeably cooler than the shore.

On Lanai Avenue in the center of town is the island's only conglomerate, called **Lanai City Service/Dollar Rent-a-car/Nani's Corner/Napa Auto Parts** (9). Remember, this a very small town with no stops lights and no golden arches, so these guys provide quite a service. If you want to explore the sights, Lanai City Service will rent you a Jeep for $119 or a good bicycle for $20. *Call 565-7227.*

Whichever means of transportation you choose, stop by the **Hotel Lanai** (10), a vintage 11-room plantation-style inn that was built in 1923 as a guest lodge primarily for visiting Dole Company executives. You can rent a room for $95. *Call 565-4700.* A road to the left of the hotel is called Nani, and that will take you to the **Cavendish Golf Course** (11), a public nine-hole course in the pines that is free for residents. Visitors are asked to leave a donation for maintaining the course. If you turn left on 5th from Nani and follow to Gay, it will take you to the Hawaiian church with the longest name, **Kalanakila Oka Malamalama Hoomana Iroedane Hou Church** (12).

Get back on Lanai Avenue and follow it to the end, which will deliver you to **The Lodge at Koele** (13). This luxurious 102-room hotel is part of the new Lanai. Just compare it with the Hotel Lanai. It is meant to represent the relaxed yet refined atmosphere of a plantation manager's house. The sweeping lobby has gigantic stone fireplaces as bookends. The grounds alone are worth the visit. Out the rear door is a reflecting pond and above that an authentic English conservatory filled with orchids. Pathways wander among flowering gardens with benches to view the sweeping lawns. Cool breezes come though the towering pines and paperbark trees at your back. Rooms start at $315. *Call 565-7300.*

As you leave the Lodge, turn right and then left by the stables. About six miles away over a dirt road is **Kanepuu** or **Garden of the Gods** (14). Before you get to the distinctive formation of red rocks in the garden, you will pass through dryland forests that have been fenced by the Nature Conservancy. Some 48 native species can be found here, including endangered Lanai sandalwood, rare Hawaiian gardenia and local cousins of olive and persimmon.

Another five miles over a very bumpy road passable only by four-wheel is **Polihua Beach** (15). Famous for turtles that nest there, the translation of *Polihua* means *Poli* (cove of bay) and *hua* (eggs). Due to strong currents, swimming is very dangerous and should not be attempted. Under no circumstances should you drive on the beach, or in any way disturb the marine life, including the turtles.

Lanai Contrasts

Lanai holds some amazing contrasts. In many ways it is a throwback to old Hawaii, with a small village built by the sizable pineapple plantation that long dominated the island. Lanai has no high-rise hotels, no stop lights, no shopping malls, no golden arches and no crowds. Within that laid-back, rural atmosphere, however, are two world-class hotels—one built on the beach and the other in the hills.

This transition took place when David Murdock gained control of Castle & Cooke several years ago. That company owned Dole Pineapple, which owned the island of Lanai, which came as part of the whole package. Technically, Murdock only owns 98 percent of the 141-square-mile Lanai.

Mr. Murdock reduced thousands of gray-green acres of spiky pineapple plants to 200 acres when he made the decision in the late 1980s that visitors held more promise than pineapple. Lanai is also about second or third homes for those who can afford them.

GETTING THERE:

By air, this tiny island is served by more than 100 flights a week via Island Air and Hawaiian Air. Island Air's toll-free number is (800) 367-5250.

By water, there are numerous choices from Lahaina. See Daytrip 41.

PRACTICALITIES:

Obviously you will spend time in the sun, so bring strong sunscreen. Swimwear is essential along with sunglasses. Golf is big time on Lanai, so bring your clubs.

FOOD AND DRINK:

Besides these hotel restaurants, see Daytrip 41 for other eateries in town.

Terrace Restaurant (off the main lobby of the Lodge at Koele) You must start the day with fresh pineapple from down the road. Excellent menu selections for lunch and dinner daily. Fresh seafood for dinner is suggested. Reservations, ☎ 565-7300. $, $$, $$$+

The Formal Dining Room (on the main floor of the Lodge at Koele) As the name suggests, a jacket is required for dinner, which is unusual for Hawaii. Award winning dining including such features as Roasted Lanai Venison Loin. Dinner only daily. Reservations, ☎ 565-7300. $$$+

The Pool Grille (next to the pool at the Manele Bay Hotel) Four classic salads including a Island Fresh Fish Caesar. Sandwiches and Saimin of Chinese noodles. Lunch only. $$

Hulopoe Court (to the left down from the lobby of the Manele Bay Hotel) For breakfast have the Manele Bay Juice, which is Haleakala guava nectar, strawberry and Lanai pineapple juices. For dinner try the Seared Mahi Mahi. Breakfast, lunch and dinner daily. Reservations, ☎ 565-7700. $$ to $$$+

Ihilani Restaurant (to the right down from the lobby of the Manele Bay Hotel) Contemporary regional cuisine of the islands includes Grilled Mahi Mahi with Fiddle Head Ferns and Hawaiian Seaweed Seafood Sauce. Dinner only. Reservations, ☎ 565-7700. $$ to $$$+

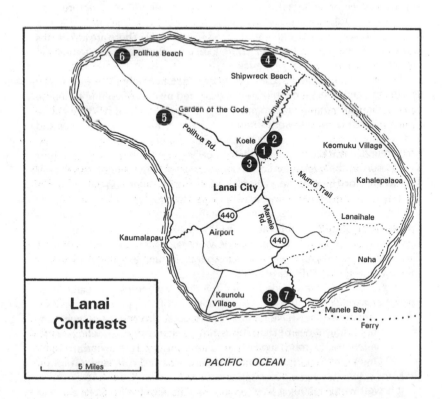

Lanai
Contrasts

5 Miles

PACIFIC OCEAN

LOCAL ATTRACTIONS:

Numbers in parentheses correspond to numbers on the map.

The **Lodge at Koele** (1) is upcountry, located amidst huge Cook Island pines, which are symbolic of Lanai. The cool weather and the setting definitely create the feel of a upland country inn. The architects set out to create the atmosphere of a traditional English country manor, and frankly, they achieved that goal.

It is a rather small hotel at only 100-plus rooms, but that is part of its charm. Some of the rooms and suites have fireplaces. The furnishings do not seem like your normal hotel room: there are hand-carved four poster beds, ceiling fans and oil paintings by local artists.

While there are lots of things to do on Lanai, the hotel's three-story lobby tugs at you to stay and read or play backgammon or just sit and relax. Framed by two huge, stone fireplaces, the elegant lobby is furnished with artwork from the South Pacific, Europe, Asia and Lanai itself. What pulls you outside, however, are the acres of manicured lawns framed by beds of bright-colored flowers. A small path invites you to take a tour of the grounds that includes ponds, reflecting pools, a croquet court, decorative sculptures and a hothouse filled with unusual orchids.

You can stay at the Lodge starting at $315 per night. There are also suites that go for $600 and up. Croquet Court, Executive Putting Green, tennis and the Spa are complimentary for guests.

If you have the urge for golf, **The Experience at Koele** (2) is just that. It is a magnificent championship course designed by one of golfing's all-time greats, Greg Norman. The course's signature hole drops 250 feet to a wooded gorge below. It winds through stands of Cook Island pine trees and indigenous plants. To say it has become internationally acclaimed can be backed up by that fact that recently the Lodge at Koele was named the Best Golf Resort in the World by *Condé Nast Traveler* Magazine's readers poll. Greens fees for 18 holes are $100 for guests and $150 for non-guests. If you are staying at the Manele Bay Hotel, you pay the guest rate here.

If horseback riding along wooded upland trails and through hidden valleys interests you, **The Stables at Koele** (3) will take you on a one-hour Koele Ride that ends up with a spectacular view of Maui, Molokai and Lanai City. Cost is $65 per person. They also offer other rides such as a three-hour Paniolo Lunch Ride for $90 per person.

In a 200-acre pine-wooded valley overlooking Molokai is **Lanai Pine Sporting Clays.** This facility offers different levels of play for both the skilled and new shooters. They have certified instructors who teach safe gun handling. Among four types of shooting is the 14-Stand Course, which introduces challenges of terrain, surprise and target variety. 100 targets are $125 and 50 targets are $65, both of which include gun and cartridge. *Call 565-3800 for reservations.*

It is well worth renting a Jeep from **Lanai City Service** for $119 a day to explore the surrounding countryside. ☎ *565-7227*. There's a paved road that goes north from the Lodge about 8.5 miles down to **Kaiolohia Bay**, better known as **Shipwreck Beach**, (4) so-named because of the rusting hulks that rammed into the offshore reef. This beach on the northeast shore can be reached by walking a short distance from the end of the road. Swimming is not advisable. Also consider a trip to **Garden of the Gods** (5) and then on to **Polihua Beach** (6). The first are unusual rock formations about six miles from the hotel, and the beach is another five miles beyond that. Periodically, turtles nest here. Do not disturb. No swimming either, or driving on the beach.

To shift gears to the best swimming beach on the island, turn in your Jeep and hop on the hotel shuttle, which will take you a few miles to the **Manele Bay Hotel** (7). To quote from the hotel's own work, "This grand seaside villa encompasses intimate courtyards filled with lush tropical gardens, abounding waterfalls, tranquil pools and aromatic flowers. Just steps from the hotel is Hulopoe Beach, the island's finest sugar-white sand beach, which borders a deep-blue bay."

The hyperbole is pretty accurate. The lobby is a masterpiece filled with Oriental artifacts and exceptional paintings. There are massive murals by the well-known mural artist John Wullbrandt. While inspiring in size and scope, it doesn't have the intimacy of the Lodge's lobby. But then again, at 250 rooms this hotel is more than twice the size of the Lodge. Rooms at the hotel start at $250. Butler Floor Suites go for up to $2,000 per night.

The beach and bay are the real draw here. The snorkeling and diving are among the best in Hawaii. The hotel offers a complimentary introduction to snorkeling and scuba diving. If you want to get more serious, the 51' **Trilogy** catamaran offers a morning snorkel, sail and scuba trip right off the protected shores of Lanai. Included for $130 is a continental breakfast and deli lunch. *Call 565-7700 for reservations.*

If the sea lures you for fishing, **Spinning Dolphin Charters of Lanai** will take you out from Manele Harbor on their 28' Omega sport fishing boat. You can fish for marlin, ahi, mahi mahi and ono in the teeming waters off Lanai. A half-day of four hours is $400 and a full day is $600. *Call 565-7700 for reservations.*

Just like its sister hotel in the hills, The Manele Bay Hotel has a superb golf course nearby. Jack Nicklaus stepped up to the plate to put this one together, which is called the **Challenge at Manele** (8). It is built on natural lava outcroppings overlooking the hotel and bay. The course's dramatic 12th hole plays from a cliff 150 feet above the crashing surf below and requires a demanding 200 yard tee shot across the ocean. It's a challenge all right. Greens fees for 18 holes are $100 for guests and $150 for non-guests. Guests of the Lodge pay the guest rate.

It's possible to get into the wondrous natural world of Lanai with the **Lanai Eco-Adventure Company.** They offer kayak trips to explore the island's unique marine eco system first hand. No experience in handling one of these stable sea kayaks is necessary as you paddle in clear, tropical waters. You may see sea turtles or spinner dolphins. They conclude the trip on a secluded beach with fresh tropical fruit, juice and stories of the adventure. Cost is $69. This same company will get you into the hills too, for what they call the Hiking Explorer. You'll be able to experience the untouched beauty of the rolling valleys and brisk uplands. Learn about island history and how the early Hawaiians lived. The hike costs $69. *Call 565-7737.*

Molokai—Most Hawaiian Island

Molokai is an island where the past and present mingle, where the traditions of the Hawaiian culture have been preserved and are yours to share. Today approximately 50 percent of the island's population of 6,700 are of native Hawaiian ancestry, with the result that is has often been called the most Hawaiian island. It is the birthplace of the hula. Here, tradition holds, the goddess Laka first danced the hula, then traveled throughout the islands teaching others the graceful movements and chants that have been passed down through generations to today's *kumu hula* or hula teachers. On the third Saturday in May, the annual hula festival Molokai Ka Hula Piko draws 4,000.

Peaceful and uncommercialized, Molokai rewards visitors with such scenic wonders as the world's highest sea cliffs, waterfalls cascading from nearly 2,000 feet to the sea and rainforests with plants and birds found nowhere else on Earth. From the golf course on the west end, you can see the diversity of the island's landscape, which changes from upcountry ranchlands in one sweep to a three-mile white sand beach and the blue ocean.

Without the normal distractions of shopping malls, many movie theaters and fast-food restaurants, you are free to explore the ocean by snorkeling, kayaking, skin-diving, fishing, surfing, whale watching (in season) and sailing. Equally fascinating is adventuring over the 10-mile-wide by 30-mile-long island's mountains and valleys by hiking, mountain biking, four-wheeling or horseback riding.

Of great interest is Kalaupapa, the peninsula off the north coast of Molokai where lepers were first sent to fend for themselves in 1886. The settlement can be visited today, and that will be covered in Daytrip 44.

GETTING THERE:
   By air, Island Air has a dozen flights a day into the Molokai Airport. **Hawaiian Air** also has frequent flights to Molokai.
   By car, from the airport turn left and head out Highway 480. Turn left on Highway 470 for Kualapuu.

PRACTICALITIES:

Keep on using strong sunscreen to protect your skin, good sunglasses to protect you eyes, and even a good hat for your topside. Friendly as Molokai is, don't leave anything in you car, locked or unlocked.

FOOD AND DRINK:

Banyan Tree Terrace Restaurant (in Pau Hana Inn in Kaunakakai) Old style, long-time casual dining on American and Hawaiian food. Specialties are fresh fish from Molokai waters and prime rib. Breakfast, lunch and dinner daily. ☎ 553-5342. $ to $$

Kanemitsu Bakery (in Kaunakakai since 1935) World-famous baked goods, especially the breads. Try the pastries too. Breakfast and lunch daily except Tues. ☎ 553-5855. $

Molokai Pizza Café (in Kaunakakai) An interesting combination of pizza, sandwiches, salads, pasta and fresh fish. Big take-out business too. Lunch and dinner daily. ☎ 553-3288. $ to $$

Molokai Drive Inn (in Kaunakakai since 1960) Burgers, salads and local foods like plate lunches in very casual atmosphere. Breakfast, lunch and dinner daily. ☎ 553-5655. $

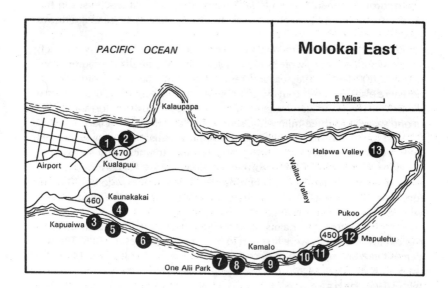

LOCAL ATTRACTIONS:

Numbers in parentheses correspond to numbers on the map.

To get started right on this full daytrip, go to Kualapuu town for a great cup of coffee at the **Coffees of Hawaii Plantation** (1). Here you can sip one of the heavenly, freshly roasted coffees grown on their 500-acre plantation right at your feet. Try the Original Molokai Muleskinner Coffee. There are tours of the coffee plantation on a mule-drawn wagon to discover how coffee is prepared, from planting through harvest to milling and roasting. *The Plantation Store and Espresso Bar are open daily from 10–3. The tour is twice a day, Mondays through Fridays, and once on Saturdays. Cost is $14. Kids 4–12 are $7. Call 567-9241.*

Next is the **Molokai Museum and Cultural Center** (2) at the R.W. Meyer Sugar Mill, built in 1878. On the National Register of Historic Places, this small museum features completely restored sugar processing machinery from the last century, including the mule-driven cane crusher. *Open Mon.–Sat. 10–2. Gift shop. Admission is $2.50. Call 567-6436.* For the first time in more than a century, the private 1,300-acre R.W. Meyer farm has been opened selectively for hiking and four-wheel drive expeditions. The Meyer program takes you back 300 years to re-discover ancient Hawaiians and their culture, and shows you one of the most dramatically beautiful and historic properties in all of the islands. *Guided hikes are 8:30 to 1:30 Mon.–Sat. and cost $35. Take your own lunch. Four-wheel drive tours are available 8:30 to noon Mon.–Sat. and the cost is $50. Call 567-6624 for more information and reservations.*

As you head east on Highway 460, as soon as the highway levels out, you will see the **Kapuaiwa Coconut Grove** (3) on your right. One of the few remaining royal groves, 1,000 trees were planted here by King Kamehameha V in the 1800s. Located across the highway from "Church Row," the grove borders a beach where fresh-water springs bubble up in the shallows. This is more a "looking" beach than a swimming beach, as you will find with most of the beach parks along Molokai's south shore.

They sing a well-known song about the little town that serves as the island's capital, the town called **Kaunakakai** (4). The song is called "The Cock-eyed Mayor of Kaunakakai"—and apparently the town had only one mayor a long time ago. The town has an Old West feel with a single street lined with old-fashioned shops selling everything from local produce to island crafts.

At the water's edge is the **Kaunakakai Wharf** (5). See if you can find the rocks that are the remains of Kamehameha's summer home where he came to vacation and relax at this very spot. Here you will find all manner of water activities. **Molokai Charters** offers a half day of sailing and whale watching (in season) on their 42' sloop *Satan's Doll*. Cost is $40. There's also a full day of sailing to Lanai for swimming, snorkeling and whale watching with lunch included. *Cost is $75 per person. Call 553-5852 for reservations.*

Lani's Kayak Tour and Rental has snorkeling and fishing adventures on Mondays through Saturdays. They also offer a tour-guide service. *Call 558-8563 for rates and reservations.* The **Alyce C** offers sport fishing on their 31' boat that takes you right to the game fish off the coast of Molokai. *Half-day charters are $300. Call 558-8377.*

Next on this southside jaunt of the island are the **Ancient Hawaiian Fishponds** (6). Approximately 50 of these unique structures, originally built in the 13th century, fringe the south shore of Molokai. The idea behind a fishpond was to make harvesting the sea a sure thing for the ancient Hawaiians. Small fish could swim in through controlled gates called *makahas*. They would fatten up in the fishpond and be available for catch anytime. What is amazing is that so many of these Molokai fishponds have survived to this day. A few have been restored and are still in use. Some of those with names are the **Kalokoeli Fishpond,** which is two miles from Kaunakakai, the **Keawanui Fishpond** about 12 miles from town and the **Ualapue Fishpond** just a bit farther.

One Alii Park II (7) is a grassy and peaceful beach park with limited facilities. No swimming, but you may want to stop for a rest or picnic lunch. Farther along on what has now become Highway 450 (Kamehameha V Highway) is the **Kakahaia National Wildlife Refuge** (8). It is another key piece in the attempt to protect the Hawaiian stilt, the endangered bird with pink legs. These birds are shy, so you may not see any. They are protected, which means humans are to stay clear. On the *makai* side of the road opposite the refuge is a nice strip park with the same name.

The Belgian missionary priest, Father Damien deVeuster, left his mark in many ways on Molokai—the best known of which is his work within the leper colony at Kalaupapa. It is said he will soon be sainted by the Catholic Church for his work among the disfigured lepers, from whom he himself caught the awful disease. Two architectural gems were designed and built by Father Damien. One of these is **St. Joseph's Church** (9), built in 1876 and located at Kamalo on the *makai* side of the road. Damien built **Our Lady of Sorrows** (10) in 1874, and it is located at about five miles farther on the *mauka* side. Both are beautiful in their simplicity.

Follow the highway to just beyond St. Joseph's, and there you will find a simple monument on the *makai* side of the highway that marks the spot where two pioneer aviators made an emergency landing on the first trans-Pacific commercial flight in 1927. The **Smith and Bronte Landing** (11) signifies the end of a treacherous trip where the pilots survived intact, but their plane was a total loss.

A real treat is the **Molokai Horse and Wagon Ride** (12) in Mapulehu beyond mile marker 15. You start this fascinating trip on the *makai* side of the road in a 50-acre mango grove. This grove contains 2,000 trees with 32 varieties of mangoes that were planted by Hawaii Sugar Planters about 70 years ago in an attempt to find other crops to grow on Molokai. The wagon ride takes you down a deserted lane surrounded by flowering trees and lush tropical vegetation to the ancient Hawaiian *heiau* named Iliiliopae. Your guide will tell you the history and legends of this ancient place of worship, which is 33' long and 90' wide. *The wagon ride cost is $35 for adults and $17.50 for kids 2–11. There's also a horseback ride over the same territory that costs $40.*

At the end of the road is the **Halawa Valley and Beach Park** (13). Getting there is half the fun since as you drive the 18 or so miles the road gets narrower and narrower. At times it hugs the coastline and other times it climbs through dense forest and then suddenly pops up in rolling pastureland. The views of the ocean and Maui are stunning. From the overlook, you can see the waterfall on your left. You can also savor the big view of the amphitheater-like valleys below. Once down in the valley, you will find scenic picnic areas. The beach and swimming are marginal. The remoteness of it all is what makes the trip worthwhile.

Molokai Mules and More

It's pretty exciting to descend 1,600 feet down a steep cliff while swaying back and forth on a mule. That will be the better part of today's excursion. The goal for this descent—and return the same way—is to visit an isolated peninsula of land on the island of Molokai where lepers were shunned for many years in what was called a "living tomb." In the early days, once sent to Kalaupapa, you never left. The disease was stopped in its tracks many years before the State of Hawaii would allow the lepers to leave Kalaupapa in 1969. Some left at that time, but others stayed behind to continue the simple, easy-going lifestyle prevalent in the leper colony of old.

Now the windswept sprawl of land that is about two and a half miles long and two miles wide is a very pleasant place to visit. As the matter of fact, Kalaupapa is a National Historical Park administered by the Hawaii State Department of Health and the National Park Service.

The mules will bring us back up the steep *pali* about mid-afternoon. That will give us enough time to cover the west end of the island, which claims to have the longest white sand beach in the Hawaiian Islands. From there we will try to catch the famous Molokai sunset.

GETTING THERE:

By air, Island Air has a dozen flights a day into the Molokai Airport. **Hawaiian Air** also flies into Molokai frequently.

By car, if you are already on the island, go to 25 Mule Barn Parkway on Highway 470. It's on the left in Kalae.

PRACTICALITIES:

Long pants are recommended for this mule ride, as are covered shoes. By all means take sunscreen, sunglasses and a hat. You might even want to slip a small bottle of water and a snack into your fannypack, since no food can be purchased down below.

FOOD AND DRINK:

Kualapuu Cookhouse (Kualapuu on Hwy. 480) Home-style cooking in a casual atmosphere. Famous for freshly made pies and cakes.

Open for breakfast, lunch and dinner daily, closed Sundays. ☎ 567-6185. $

Outpost Natural Foods (in Kaunakakai) Fresh produce, juices, vegetarian lunch bar with low-fat specials. Open Sun.–Thurs. for lunch and dinner, Fri. lunch. Sat. ☎ 553-3377. $

Maunaloa Village Grill & Bar (in Maunaloa town) Clearly a ranch and cowboy atmosphere. Burgers, salads and steaks aplenty. Paniolo entertainment on weekends. Open daily for breakfast, lunch & dinner. ☎ 552-2734. $ to $$

Ohia Lodge (in the Kaluakoi Hotel) At the edge of Kepuhi Beach, enjoy hearty breakfasts and satisfying dinners daily, all with ocean views and spectacular sunsets. ☎ 552-2555. $ to $$

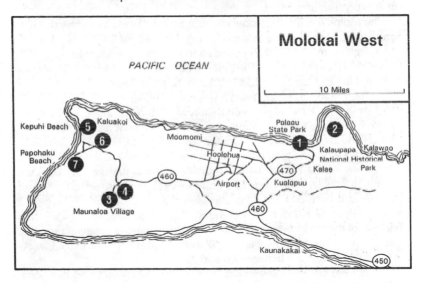

SUGGESTED TOUR:

Numbers in parentheses correspond to numbers on the map.

We suggest you start your day early by going up Highway 470 to the end for a visit to **Palaau State Park** (1), which is right at the edge of the *pali* overlooking Kalaupapa peninsula. The park provides an excellent look at where this trip will be taking you. Exhibits at the overlook provide important facts about Kalaupapa and its history.

There are actually three ways to get to Kalaupapa, and none are by car since there is no road. You can go by air from the Molokai Airport (at $52, this way provides breathtaking aerial views and is easier on your rump than by mule). You can also hike a narrow trail down and up the 1,600-foot *pali*. The most popular is the mule ride down the same trail.

It's obvious the **Molokai Mule Ride** (2) offers great fun. The three-mile-plus trail has 26 switch-backs and features wonderful views of the peninsula below at every turn. The trail was originally built in 1886 by an immigrant from Madeira who, it is believed, followed the course of an ancient Hawaiian footpath. The trail was recently restored by the National Park Service—all 1,630 steps.

The mule ride begins at the Molokai Mule barn in Kalae in central Molokai at 8:30 and concludes at about 3:30 in the afternoon. Riders are matched up with their mule (choose Valentine, or Pale Face or Friendly, or how about Small Fry or Disney) at the barn. These veterans of the Kalaupapa trail, as the muleskinners will explain, are on "automatic pilot." Riders can just settle into their saddle and enjoy the spectacular views that open up at every turn of the trail.

The Molokai Mule Ride operates one tour a day on Mondays through Saturdays. Check-in is at 8 in the morning. Riders must be at least 16 years old, weigh no more than 250 pounds and be able to "relax and keep your center balance at all times." *The cost is $120, which includes the trip down and up, tour and lunch. Call 567-7550 for reservations.*

Richard Marks' **Damien Tours** has the only blanket permit to admit the general public to Kalaupapa, so ultimately all who visit connect up with him for the half-day, narrated ground tour of the settlement and National Historical Park. The mule ride includes the cost of the tour, but hikers and plane riders pay $30 for the tour. A rusty old school bus serves as the tour vehicle. Jimmy, one of the Kalaupapa tour guides, explains that he's lived in the colony for 55 years. He came as a child in 1942 as a suspected leper, and even though he didn't have the disease on arrival, he had contracted it within a short period of time. Cured for a long time now, he says he stays because of the very comfortable lifestyle. This tiny community at one time had 600 residents, but now it is only 57 former patients (plus about 45 workers), and their ages are between 68 and 78.

Things are very low-key in Kalaupapa. The colony still includes some trim, small houses occupied by the remaining residents, churches, a hospital, store and library. The speed limit for the few cars is 5 mph. At the pier, Jimmy tells you there is great excitement over the once-a-year barge service, when all residents gather to see if anyone got a new car.

One of the highlights of the tour is the visit to **St. Philomena Church**, known as Father Damien's Church, where the history of Kalaupapa is told in the recently restored structure. The tour also includes a picnic lunch at Judd Park overlooking the famous Molokai north coast, and the world's highest sea cliffs, soaring some 3,000 feet almost straight up.

Once you have un-kinked your legs from the ride up, get in your car and head out Highway 460 toward Maunaloa, which for many years was a company town for Dole and Del Monte pineapple when that crop flourished on Molokai. The pineapple is all gone now, but the town is being restored and added to with such features as Molokai's first movie theaters. One of the striking new activities to replace agriculture is the **Molokai Ranch** (3). The Ranch is an exciting new lodging and recreation program where visitors design their own travel adventure, choosing from a variety of different campsites and a long list of activities—such as guided kayaking, ocean adventures, beach activities, mountain biking and cultural hikes.

Located just south of Ranch headquarters in Maunaloa, the **Paniolo Camp** is a collection of 40 comfortable one- and two-unit tents mounted on wooden platforms. Each tent features a queen bed, self-composting toilet, solar-powered lights and hot water showers. Within Paniolo Camp is an open-air dining pavilion, swimming pool, fire circle and volleyball and horseshoe areas for guests. Among the major activities to choose from are **The Paniolo Trail Adventure,** in which guests go from the world's highest sea cliffs to the cool *mauka* lands of the 54,000-acre ranch to explore the beautiful pristine island while learning about its rich cultural heritage. *Offered Mondays through Saturdays. Cost is $60.* **The Paniolo Roundup** is a chance for visitors to learn horsemanship and experience the thrills of traditional cowboy competition, from barrel racing to pole bending. *Offered Mondays through Saturdays. Cost is $90.* There's also mountain biking, hiking and whale watching in season.

The Ranch also has a major rodeo arena with four major events each year. A stay in the camp is $185 per person which includes three cowboy-sized meals a day and your choice of activities, cold drinks and snacks, and courtesy airport transportation. **Kolo Camp,** set on a bluff overlooking the ocean, offers yurt camping. These circular tents on a raised platform also have queen beds and the amenities of Paniolo Camp. *The rate is $215 per person. Call 552-2791 or (800) 254-8871 for reservations.*

Worth a visit in Maunaloa is the **Big Wind Kite Factory** (4). This well-known manufacturer of kites and windsocks will teach you how to control two-string aerobatic stunt kites at their special aeronautical testing facility. *Located at 120 Maunaloa Highway, it is open daily 8:30–5 and Sunday 10–2.* ☎ *552-2364.*

As you leave Maunaloa, turn left for the **Kaluakoi Hotel & Golf Resort** (5), the only true hotel on the island. It offers cottages and suites some with spectacular views of the beach and ocean on the east end. Ocean-view rooms are $115. The **Kaluakoi Golf Course** (6) connected to the hotel claims to have an ocean view from every hole. *Greens fees are $40 for guests and $60 for non-guests. Call 552-2739 for tee times.*

After you leave the hotel, turn right and head for **Papohaku Beach Park** (7), just down the road. This lovely 10-acre park fronts the three-mile Papohaku Beach. The swimming can be tricky, so pay attention to posted signs telling of water conditions. There are terrific picnic areas and camping is permitted. The reason for coming out here—besides the claimed longest beach in Hawaii—is to take a stroll to see one of the grandest sunsets in the

Hawaiian Islands. Wait patiently for it. Just as the sun slips below the horizon, look carefully and see if you can spot the tiny "green flash."

This park is best known for hosting the Molokai Ka Hula Piko, an annual celebration of the birth of hula that took place on Molokai hundreds of years ago. The last festival was so popular it drew 4,000 people. The festival is held the third Saturday in May.

Section V

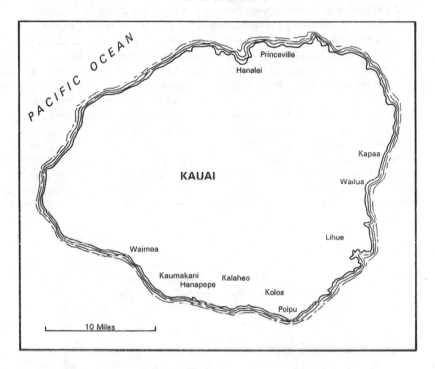

PACIFIC OCEAN

Princeville
Hanalei

Kapaa

KAUAI

Wailua

Lihue

Waimea

Kaumakani   Kalaheo
Hanapepe

Koloa

Poipu

10 Miles

DAYTRIPS ON
KAUAI

Kauai is the oldest of the six main islands in the Hawaiian chain. It lies 70 miles northwest of Oahu across one of the most rugged stretches of ocean in the Pacific. That may explain why it was never conquered by Kamehameha I, the king who eventually unified all the other Hawaiian islands. Kauai is almost a circle, 33 miles wide and 25 miles long. It is remarkable for its spectacular and widely varied landscape—from Waimea Canyon, the Grand Canyon of the Pacific, to the Na Pali Coast with cliffs rising 2,700 feet straight out of the ocean.

Within Kauai's 550 square miles, there are distinct micro-climates including coastal sand dunes, desert-like plateaus, verdant river valleys, foothills and mist-shrouded mountain tops. Mount Waialeale in the center of the island is reportedly the wettest spot on Earth, receiving 451 inches of rain a year. There is a benefit to all that moisture. The name "The Garden Island" signifies much more than a casual nickname as we will discover in the many gardens all across the island.

Vast changes to the island occurred when strangers came ashore. The first was the explorer Captain James Cook and his crew, who landed on Kauai at Waimea in 1778. The native Hawaiians were shocked by their large ships, unusual attire and strange language. The second was a brief stand by Russian traders who erected a fort at the mouth of the Waimea River. Then came the missionaries in the early 1800s. Missionary descendants became successful sugar planters. Like most other islands where sugar became an industry, it brought an influx of immigrants from Asia and Europe, who have shaped much of Kauai's history and contributed mightily to its cultural diversity.

GETTING TO KAUAI:

Kauai is the only major Hawaiian Island without direct service from the mainland. Frequent inter-island flights make it easy, however, to fly into Honolulu and then on to Kauai. **Aloha Airlines** serves Kauai with 12 flights a day. They even have First Class service as well. **Hawaiian Airlines** also offers service to Lihue Airport on Kauai.

ACCOMMODATIONS ON KAUAI:

A full range of accommodations cover the island—all the way from five-star luxury to tiny bed-and-breakfast spots in the cool upcountry. **Aston Hotels & Resorts** has five condominiums and one hotel offering a full price range. One that provides a true Hawaii experience is the Waimea Plantation Cottages. These individual bungalows along the beach were restored by the family that has owned them from the very start in the early 1900s. Don't expect room service, but do expect to feel like you are staying in the Old Hawaii. *Aston's toll-free number is (800) 922-7866.*

GETTING AROUND:

There is a public transportation system on Kauai, but it isn't well suited for visitors. To find out about routes and times, call 241-6410. There are many tour buses as well, but you are usually held to their itinerary instead of the daytrips as outlined here. There are expensive taxis. Rental cars from **Budget** are available at the airport and selected hotels. *Budget's toll-free reservation number is (800) 527-0700.* Just about all the other major car rental companies are represented at the airport.

PRACTICALITIES:

Time is perhaps the most precious commodity when visiting Kauai. There is so much to see and do that you probably will not have enough time to do everything. But that's okay, because you can always come back.

Protection in the form of sunglasses and sunscreen is a must. Protect your possessions, too, by not leaving anything in your rental car whether locked or unlocked.

VISITOR INFORMATION:

For a Visitor Packet and activities:

Kauai Visitors Bureau, 3016 Umi Street, Lihue, HI 96766, ☎ (800) 262-1400.

Camping permits for state parks:

Hawaii State Department of Land & Natural Resources, Lihue, HI 96766, ☎ (808) 241-3446.

Camping permits for county parks:

County of Kauai, ☎ (808) 271-6660.

Kauai weather: ☎ (808) 245-6001.

Trip 45

West to Waimea

Two features dominate this part of Kauai—one natural and one man made. Over the years, nature created a huge gash often called the "Grand Canyon of the Pacific," or Waimea Canyon. It took millions of years to form. Over a much shorter time span, starting in the early 1880s, man set about plowing thousands and thousands of acres into sugar cane plantations. You can't miss either phenomena as you make your way around the dry side of this island.

The only military installation on Kauai—the Navy's Pacific Missile Range Facility—is stretched out along one of the westside beaches known as Barking Sands. And oh, how good the beaches are on this side! Long, and in some cases very broad, they contrast with some of the pocket beaches on the north shore of this island.

Foreigners didn't just land on this part of the island to have a look around. The Russians actually schemed to take over the whole place. Here's what happened: One of their trading vessels was shipwrecked off the coast of Waimea in 1815; its crew was rescued by natives; they set up a trading post; and then in a bit of typical treachery, they tried to wrest control of all the islands from the king. Luckily it didn't work.

GETTING THERE:

By car, there's only one route. It's Route 50, called the Kaumualii Highway after Kauai's last king.

PRACTICALITIES:

Any time is a good time to visit this part of Kauai. There are lots of active things to do—like hiking and mountain bike riding—so bring appropriate shoes if these interest you. And mosquito repellent. For just stretching out on the wide sand beaches, bring a mat, sunglasses, sunscreen and reading material. Leave nothing in your car, locked or unlocked.

FOOD AND DRINK:

Mike's Place (9875 Waimea Rd. in town) Casual breakfast, lunch and dinner daily. Fish and chips, smoothies (try the Kona Ironman), deli sandwiches, soups and salads. ☎ 338-0330. $

Wrangler Steak House (9852 Kaumualli Hwy.) From delicious tempura to prime rib. Lunch is served in a kaukau tin, which is layers of food like the old plantation workers ate. Lunch and dinner weekdays. Dinner Sat., brunch on Sunday. Gift shop. ☎ 338-1218. $$

Kokee Lodge (in Kokee State Park) Lunch counter with simple foods for picnicking in the park or to eat in. Daily service. Gift shop. ☎ 335-6061. $

Menehune Food Mart (8171 Kekaha Rd. at the start of the road up Waimea Canyon) Plenty of good quality sandwiches, snacks and cold drinks in case you want to picnic in the park or at the beach. ☎ 337-1335. $

LOCAL ATTRACTIONS:

Numbers in parentheses correspond to numbers on the map.

To get started, you should consider checking out some of the attractions near Waimea town and the town itself. The first is **Fort Elisabeth** (1), a State Historical Park often called Russian Fort. It is on the water side of the highway just before you get to town. Little remains of the fort except the foundation, but a footpath takes you around the 300-foot diameter and an excellent state brochure tells you about the buildings that were there originally. It was built in 1815, but taken over by the Hawaiians in 1817 after the Russians were expelled from Hawaii.

As you head into town you will see that the Russians were not the first foreigners to step ashore here, because a statue of the famous Captain James Cook says he arrived at the mouth of the Waimea River in January, 1778. The Hawaiians believed Cook to be their god Lono, and were overwhelmed by the white man and his huge ships. Waimea town seems sleepy now, but it has had several transformations during its bustling past. King Kaumualii lived here, and he initiated the exotic sandalwood trade with China. Taro was a major crop, as was rice at one time. The New England missionaries came in the early 1800s. And then in 1844, the Waimea Sugar Company set up the first mill in the area. If you stop by the Waimea Public Library any weekday, a three-page guide to a self-directed walking tour of the town is available free. The tour takes about an hour.

Just up Menehune Road that runs along the Waimea River is the **Menehune Ditch** (2). Legend has it that these little people constructed the water course in one night by the light of a full moon. Perhaps they were Tahitians who came to Hawaii about AD 1000. In any case, a newspaper article says that when the first Kauai census was taken in the 1850s, 65 people claimed to be *menehune*.

Just outside of town, on the left, are the **Waimea Plantation Cottages** (3). This is a chance to turn back the clock to old Hawaii as you stroll through the dozen or so cottages toward the beach. The Faye family's two-story

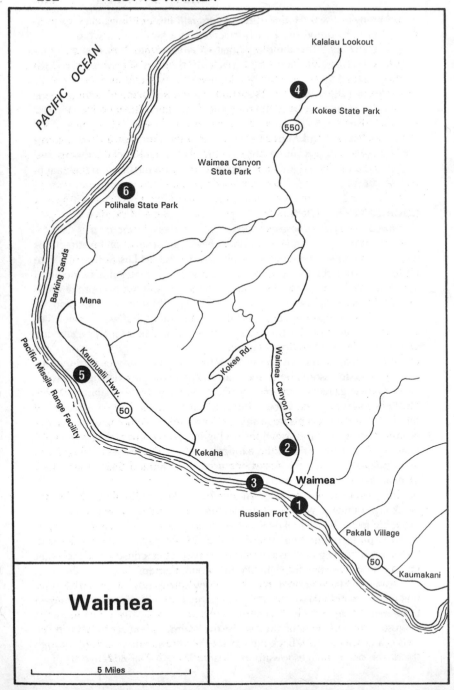

PACIFIC OCEAN

Kalalau Lookout

4

Kokee State Park

550

Waimea Canyon
State Park

6
Polihale State Park

Barking Sands

Mana

Kaumualii Hwy.

Pacific Missile Range Facility

5

50

Kokee Rd.

Waimea Canyon Dr.

Kekaha

2

3   **Waimea**

1

Russian Fort

Pakala Village

50

Kaumakani

Waimea

5 Miles

house, built in 1900, is among the wonderful old buildings now open to guests.

Now it's time to head up to **Waimea Canyon State Park** and the adjacent **Kokee State Park** (4) on either routes 550 or 50. After you go through the lower cane fields, the road quickly starts to twist and turn for about 12 miles through the 1,900-acre Waimea Park. A good piece of advice, if you are driving, is to only stop at the designated lookouts. The tendency to want to take it all in can be dangerous. But when you do stop, what you will see is a dramatic 3,000-foot-deep canyon with hues of orange and red against tropical green. A suggestion is to go all the way to the Kalalau Lookout first, and then the topmost Puu O Kila Lookout. The views truly are staggering—of jagged mountain ridgelines and heaving ocean below—that can only be seen from above or from the water since no roads circle the island. An early arrival may help avoid possible mist that gathers later in the day.

Kokee is almost 4,000 feet above Kauai's tropical beaches. This cool region (a couple of times a year in winter there may be frost on the big grassy meadow by the Lodge) was born from six million years of fiery fury. There is plenty to do. If you are interested in hunting pigs, deer or goats, required permits may be obtained by calling the State Division of Forestry and Wildlife at 245-4433.

Hiking is probably among the finest in the state throughout the 4,345 acres that make up the park at Kokee. There are 20-plus trails for the Na Pali Overlook, Waimea Vista, Forest and **Alakai Swamp**. The latter is a preserve that runs 10 miles long and two miles wide. Periodically, there is a boardwalk over some of the boggy terrain where you can view some of Hawaii's rarest flora and fauna. Because of the moisture, most of the vegetation is dwarfed. *You can write Hawaii Nature Guides at P.O. Box 70, Kealia, HI 96751 for a complete guide to all the Kokee trails.* Camping is also available at four idyllic sites. *Write for permits to Division of State Parks, 3060 Eiwa St., P.O. Box 1671, Lihue, HI 96766.* If you'd rather stay in a cabin, Kokee Lodge offers a half dozen rustic ones for around $45 a night. *Call them at 335-6061.*

The **Kokee Natural History Museum** is a small facility that asks for donations. It basically tells the story of the area including Mount Waialeale, the wettest spot on Earth and the true center of Kauai. The latest measurements show an average rainfall of 451" at the summit, but there is a sense that it is much more because the strong winds at the top may blow some of the moisture sideways causing it to miss being counted.

There are two ways to come down from Kokee—by car, or by bicycle. If you want to ride down the spectacular road on a bicycle with guides in front and back, **Bicycle Downhill** offers morning cruises on Tuesdays through Saturdays and afternoon cruises on Mondays, Wednesdays, and Fridays. They stop along the way to take in the views and serve light refreshments. *Cost is $65. Reservations can be made at ☎ 742-7421.*

Either way you come down, make sure you stop and take in **Niihau** in the distance. This is the "Forbidden Island," although some have described it as the "Intriguing Island." Imagine a place where Hawaiian is the first language and there is no electricity—and therefore no television and telephone. It's hard to think of anywhere else in the United States where those conditions exist.

Once you are down, get back on the Kaumualii Highway. A beach that runs right along the road is called **Davidsons' Beach.** There are no facilities, and frankly, better beaches ahead. For the next 5.5 miles, you will be on Hawaii's longest straight-away. About the only thing to see along the way are some seed corn facilities. There will be sign on the left for the **Pacific Missile Range Facility** (5). Lots of chain link fence and gates. However, the beach at Major's Bay is often open to the public, depending on what rockets the Navy is tracking or shooting off. Show your license and auto insurance card at the gate. There are super waves coming into an almost empty beach and terrific sunsets.

After the paved state road ends (clearly declared with a sign), be sure to go .8 of a mile to the entrance to **Polihale State Park** (6), which is a fairly wide dirt cane haul road—usually without a sign. If you turn sooner, you will be on a private can haul road and can get in all kinds of trouble. Once on the dirt road, be prepared to go another 4.5 miles to reach a wide expanse of white sand beach that stretches 10 miles back to Kekaha. It is without doubt the biggest beach in Hawaii, but beyond that are the majestic Na Pali cliffs that thrust up behind you. During the winter months, the water level rises to form Queen's Pond, a perfect place to view the sunset. Good facilities.

Where did **Barking Sands** get its name? The claim is that as you slide down the sand dunes—some of which are 60' high—the sand will make a barking sound. Good luck.

Kalaheo/Makaweli

Those familiar with Kauai may scratch their heads over Makaweli as a spot to visit. Their puzzlement is understandable since it's only a Post Office along the highway. But, it is the start of a wonderfully authentic sugar plantation tour. Not only is that noteworthy, but it's the sugar plantation owned by the Robinson family who also owns Niihau, that mysterious island off Kauai's west coast where you and I can't visit. Maybe as they take us on the tour of their working sugar plantation, they will let us in on some secrets about Niihau.

During the span of this daytrip—from close to Waimea town (Makaweli) to the Lawai Valley—several of the old sugar family names will turn up: Alexander; McBryde; Robinson. How Kauai got its name as the Garden Island will be even clearer after touring the Allerton Gardens.

GETTING THERE:

By car, find the main road in this part of the island, which is Route 50 (Kaumualii Highway). Make your way on Route 520 or 530 to Poipu and go right toward Spouting Horn.

PRACTICALITIES:

This area requires the usual: sunglasses, sunscreen, comfortable shoes and a hat. Bottled water is another consideration. Whether you lock your car or not, don't leave anything in it. Why tempt people?

FOOD AND DRINK:

Green Garden (1-3749 Kaumualii Hwy., Hanapepe) Nearing 50 years, this wonderfully comfortable eating spot offers a true cosmopolitan menu with Japanese, Chinese, Hawaiian and American dishes. Heavy foliage, thus the name. Breakfast, lunch and dinner daily. Closed Tues. ☎ 335-5422. $ to $$

Sinaloa Mexican Restaurant (1-3959 Kaumualii Hwy. in Hanapepe) Their claim to using fresh ingredients this far from Mexico accounts for their widespread reputation. The fresh-daily tortillas are so ex-

cellent they are distributed island-wide. Open daily for lunch and
dinner. ☎ 335-0006. $ to $$

Brick Oven Pizza (2-2555 Kaumualii Hwy. in Kalaheo) If you really
want to know how good the pizza is here, just read the guest register. It's filled with praise. This is a must. Fun paintings on the walls.
☎ 332-8561. $ to $$

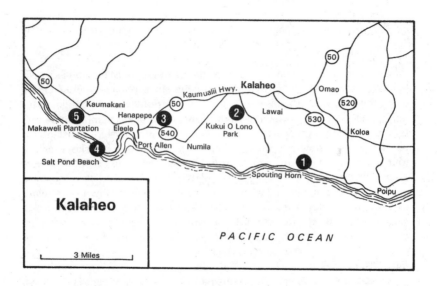

SUGGESTED TOUR:

Numbers in parentheses correspond to numbers on the map.

*NATIONAL TROPICAL BOTANICAL GARDEN (1), P.O. Box 340, Lawai,
HI 96765. Reservations ☎ 332-7324. *Four tours daily Tues.–Sat. Admission
$25.*

You know you're in for a treat when they pick you up in an antique "Hilo
Sampan" from the parking lot at Spouting Horn. The old bessie struggles to
take you high above the mouth of the Lawai River to an old sugar cane railroad trestle. Here the tour guide stops to point out the Allerton Estate mansion way below near the beach. You also learn that the estate was originally
another summer home for Queen Emma, wife of Kamehameha IV. It became
a part of a large sugar plantation in the early 1880s. McBryde Sugar damned
the river and used the water for irrigation.

Eventually the tour winds its way down to the floor of the valley where
the formal part begins. Science is a big part of NTBG, but the fun part is the

one-and-a-half-to-two-hour tour of the Allerton Estate. Allerton's father was one of the founders of the First National Bank of Chicago. His son bought 100 acres of the valley in 1937, and set about building a big home near the beach and making the valley into a showplace of tropical landscaping. Yes, there are plenty of unusual and interesting plants and trees, but the fascinating part is the sculpture set in what he called "rooms," which are really heavily planted areas. For instance, there's statuary at both entrances to the Thanksgiving Room where Allerton once threw a huge holiday bash for family and friends.

Allerton used water features and sculpture in unusual and interesting ways throughout the gardens. It is a restful, beautiful place.

Once you make your way back to Koloa, turn left on Route 530 through the Lawai Valley. After a few miles, it meets up again with Route 50 (Kaumualii Highway). Turn left and once in Kalaheo, look for Papalina Road. Turn left and follow the signs to **Kukui O Lono Park and Golf Course** (2), open 6:30 to 6:30. Now you're way up high with dramatic views in all directions. The park, a gift of Walter McBryde, is great for picnics among the Japanese Gardens and ancient Hawaiian Rocks. At the very top, the public golf course is open every day of the week and is lots of fun. Nine or 18 holes is $7. You can rent clubs and a pull cart. The Snack Bar serves breakfast and lunch every day.

Turn left on Highway 50. As you start down a long hill, the dark green crop on your left is coffee grown by Alexander & Baldwin. They have about 3,500 acres planted in coffee in an attempt to find a replacement for sugar cane. It is sold under the name Kauai Coffee.

Start to look for the **Hanapepe Lookout** (3) on your right. This will give you a view of the steep valley and river below that leads into Hanapepe town. Once down at sea level, take the time to go into a town that feels like a step back in time with its vintage cars, plantation buildings and slow pace. During WWII, Hanapepe was one of Kauai's busiest towns with thousands of GIs and sailors who were sent from the mainland and the rest of Hawaii to train for Pacific Theater duty. Check out the art galleries in some of the restored buildings.

Just outside of town you will see signs to the left for **Salt Pond Beach Park** (4). The beach itself is a lovely crescent with reef protection on the left side. Camping is available by permit and there are good facilities. The ancient salt ponds as you approach the beach park are authentic "pans" in which salt water is evaporated. The pans are handed down from generation to generation.

Turn left on the highway and head for Kaumakani.

*MAKAWELI SUGAR PLANTATION TOUR (5), P.O. Box 156, Kaumakani, HI 96747. After the 18–mile marker on Kaumualii Highway, look for the Kaumakani Shopping Village on the left. The Plantation Tour Visitor Center is next door to Thrifty Mart. ☎ 335–3133. *Four tours daily. Admission $15. Gift shop and snacks.*

Because sugar has played such a huge part in Hawaii's recent history, this tour of an authentic sugar plantation is a must. And a similar experience can't be had anywhere else in Hawaii.

At the Visitor Center, you start out with a brief video of how it all began. Remember back to the Waikiki daytrip where it was pointed out that a widow and her grown children came from New Zealand to Hawaii on their way to Oregon. King Kalakaua befriended Mrs. Sinclair and offered her all the land from downtown Honolulu to Diamond Head for $10,000, but she didn't want it because it wasn't good for cattle ranching. Before you feel sorry for Mrs. Sinclair, however, you should know that her offspring and their offspring have assembled 50,000 acres of cattle ranch and sugar plantation on Kauai — and they still own Niihau.

This is the plantation you will tour. It is called Gay & Robinson (located in Makaweli) after her two sons-in-law. And your tour guide may very well be a Robinson since they still run the place. How Gay & Robinson performs every step is important since this may very well be the last sugar plantation in Hawaii in a few years.

You start by driving through one of the "camps" where plantation workers live. Housing costs about $100 per month since it is owned by the plantation. Next you shoot down a dirt road to the ocean to observe seed cane being cut by hand. That increases yield. Over pretty bumpy plantation roads, you make your way next to seed cane being planted by machine, but covered by hand. That increases yield, too. Harvesting is next and chances are good that you will see a huge, planned cane fire. After the cane is burned, it is piled high in the fields to be hauled to the sugar mill. All this is pretty dusty and dirty, and you are thankful for the air-conditioned van you are touring in.

At the sugar mill, your tour guide will drive you around the perimeter and explain how they take all that gangly black cane and turn it into pure white sugar. Then it's back to the Visitor Center to find out about cleaning, crushing and boiling the cane. And finally, you get a piece of sugar cane to gnaw on for its refreshing sweet taste.

Lihue/Koloa/Poipu

This daytrip will keep you pretty busy. You'll need to get up early, but for encouragement we have a special treat for you. Your day will include some very interesting history, many wonderful beaches to sit on and ocean to splash around in, activities that are varied and exciting, and then some good food and drink.

GETTING THERE:

By car, start in Lihue and get on Route 51. Look for the entrance to the Kauai Marriott and the sign that says Beach Access.

PRACTICALITIES:

Sunscreen, sunglasses, hat and beachwear. You may want a simple picnic container. The best is a plastic bag that can be used to carry stuff to the beach, and not left in your rental car. Leave nothing in your car, locked or unlocked.

FOOD AND DRINK:

Tip Top Café (3173 Akahi St. in Lihue). Open for breakfast and lunch daily, X: Mon. Pick up your morning picnic goodies here. Delicious Tip Top cookies. ☎ 245-2333. $

Tomcats Grill (5402 Koloa Rd. in old Koloa Town) Nice selection of salads, sandwiches and burgers. Appetizers are called "Kat Nips," and kid's menu "For the Kittens." Big beer selection too. Lunch and dinner daily. ☎ 742-8887. $ to $$

Gaylord's (3-2087 Kaumualii Hwy. at Kilohana in Lihue) This is gracious dining in a gracious setting. The view is out over the lawns of the Wilcox Estate toward the mountains. The food is world class, featuring fresh seafood, duck, and island specials. Lunch and dinner daily and Sunday brunch. ☎ 245-9593. $$ to $$$

Brennecke's Beach Broiler (2100 Hoone Rd. in Poipu) This is a real gathering spot right on the beach. Dine upstairs on fresh seafood and prime rib. Very casual. Downstairs is a fun gift shop, activities center and deli. Open daily for lunch and dinner. ☎ 742-7588. $ to $$

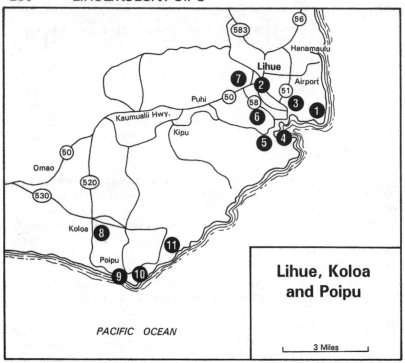

Lihue, Koloa and Poipu

PACIFIC OCEAN

3 Miles

SUGGESTED TOUR:

Numbers in parentheses correspond to numbers on the map.

We promise that if you're willing to get up early to watch the sunrise from a special place, you won't be disappointed. Call the weather number at 245-6001 to find out the time for the sunrise. That will tell you when to ask for your hotel wake-up call.

Get on Route 51 and look for the entrance to the Kauai Marriott. The sign will say Beach Access. Take this partially dirt road about 2.5 miles as it runs between the airport and the golf course to **Ninini Point** (1). You will be right next to a small lighthouse. There are picnic benches from which you can enjoy your morning coffee and the spectacular sunrise.

After that excitement, there's even more in store. **Safari Helicopters** at 3225 Akahi Street in Lihue offers a 45-minute flight that is a total thrill. If you haven't done it, you're missing out on sweeping airborne views of cascading waterfalls, deep gorges, vast sugar cane fields and much more. Sometimes they run a circle island flight for under $100. *Call for reservations 246-0136.*

Now head over to the:

*KAUAI MUSEUM (2), 4428 Rice St., Lihue, Kauai. HI 96766, ☎ 245-6931. *Open Mon.–Fri. 9–4, Sat. 9–1, closed Sun. Admission is $5 for adults; $4 for seniors, $1 for children 6–17 and under 6 free. Museum shop and courtyard café.*

This is a neat way to learn about all kinds of island stuff like: volcanic eruptions that formed the islands; the Polynesians who first arrived in the islands by canoe; the missionaries who introduced their way of life to the islanders; the sugar planters and the different ethnic cultures who contributed much to Kauai's history. Kauai is the only outer island that has a museum just about Kauai.

If you want to see lots and lots of artwork and sculpture for free, head for the **Kauai Marriott** (3) off Route 51. This is a pretty amazing sight. There are over 400 art objects scattered throughout the hotel and its grounds. They were collected by Chris Hemmeter and his family in their heyday. Not much of Hawaiiana feeling in the hotel, but **Kalapaki Beach and Bay** are a perfect blending of the Hawaii of yesterday and today. The bay is a favorite surfing, swimming and fishing spot. You often see huge cruise ships slipping out of the harbor.

Back on Route 51, you will pass the main shipping pier for Kauai. Tugs, barges, sugar transport ships and cruise liners are all crowded together in **Nawiliwili Harbor** (4). Turn left on Niumalu Road, which will take you up behind a giant concrete building that holds tons and tons or raw sugar for shipment to California. Continue on that road and then right on Hulemalu until it rises to a lookout. On the left is **Alekoko Fishpond** (5) better known as Menehune Fishpond. The legend is that the little people built it in a night for a young chief. What makes this fishpond different than most is that it was built inland on a river instead of along the coast. There is an explanation of how a fishpond works: they had three *makaha* (fenced openings) that provided good water flow into and drainage out of the pond; large fish could not pass through the *makaha*, while young fish could pass freely in and out.

Retrace your route and turn left on what is now Route 58. About a mile on your left is the **Grove Farm Homestead** (6). A visit provides you with a fascinating look into the island's past. Grove Farm, one of the earliest sugar plantations, was founded in 1864. The two-hour tour takes visitors to the more fascinating parts of the 82-acre homestead, including the gracious old Wilcox home and the cottage of the plantation housekeeper amidst tropical gardens, orchards and rolling lawns. *Adult admission is $5 for tours given twice a day on Monday, Wednesday and Thursday. Kids under 12 are $2. Reservations are a must. Call 245-3202.*

Another Wilcox estate is next on the tour. Turn left when you come to Route 50 and very soon on the right you will see **Kilohana** (7) at 3-2087 Kaumualii Highway. This 16,000-square-foot handsome Tudor mansion was built in 1935 by Gaylord Wilcox. He wanted the best and he got rich wood paneling, fine custom furniture and art from the Orient. There is no admission because shops have been tucked away in many of the mansion's rooms. Horse-drawn carriages take you throughout the 35 acres of beautifully landscaped grounds.

From Route 50 turn left on 520. Immediately you will be in the stately Tree Tunnel that runs for about half a mile. It's quite a sight. The 19th-century plantation town of **Koloa** (8) is a few miles farther down the road. It was the site of Hawaii's first successful sugar mill. Today you can still see remains of the mill, along with many restored buildings housing various shops and restaurants. Koloa Landing, on the edge of town, was the state's third-largest whaling port in the 1800s, and also was used for the export of raw sugar and sweet potatoes. There's a small History Center back behind some shops.

As you leave town for Poipu, you will pass an old church built by the missionaries in 1835. Then Poipu Road bends left as you approach the water. Look for any right turn that will take you to the beach. **Poipu Beach Park** (9) is a gem. Before you get to the sand, there is a nice strip of green lawn. On the left is a little protected bay with calm water and white sand ideal for kids. Separating that bay from more open water and sand is a small rocky point. You will see snorkelers, boogie boarders, divers and surfers all frolicking in the smallish waves. This beach park has just about everything for the family, including good facilities.

Back on the main road, turn right and just beyond the Hyatt there are signs to **Shipwreck Beach** (10) off Ainako Street. Before Poipu became popular and the condos and hotels encroached, this wide beach stood out by itself. At Shipwreck, there's much more wave action—for those serious surfers —than at the previous beach park. Good facilities provided by the hotel.

Turn right on the road to head for what has been called the best unspoiled beach in Hawaii. Continue on past where the pavement ends and turn right on what looks like a cane haul road. You will come to a gate that is open from 7:30–7 in spite of a kind of threatening sign that says no trespassing. Continue on to **Mahaulepu Beach** (11). Sand dunes greet you before you make your way to a lovely curve of white sand and water protected by a reef. You will find truly secluded swimming and sunning. This is the site where George C. Scott portrayed Ernest Hemingway in the movie "Islands in the Stream." Farther along the coast are several pocket beaches with kiawe trees almost at water's edge.

On the way back, you will see **CJM Country Stables.** Their rides are ideally suited to the beginner as well as the more experienced rider. CJM offers three tours daily except Sunday. At 2 in the afternoon during the summer, and a half-hour earlier in winter, they offer the Hidden Beach Ride. It's two hours of thrilling scenery and fun exploration. *Cost is $56. Call 742-6096 for reservations.*

East Side Wailua/Kapaa

The east side, which stretches from outside Lihue to Kapaa through Wailua, is the most populated area of the island. Wailua was once the home of the island's royalty. The banks of the Wailua River, the only navigable river in Hawaii, were a sacred area in ancient Hawaii and a favored dwelling place reserved for the kings and high chiefs of Kauai.

Proceeding a bit farther, you come to the Royal Coconut Coast, so named for its acres of ancient coconut groves. This is where the *alii* or chiefs once lived, and there are still reminders of their lives to observe today.

This part of the island has a greater relationship with the mountains since they are less precipitous here. Upland pastures and small farms are mixed with housing. Higher up, there are excellent recreational spots as well. And the Wailua River offers just about any water sport you can think of except surfing. But that's available too, just outside the mouth of the river.

GETTING THERE:

Whether you're coming from the south or the north, Wailua and Kapaa—and spots in between—are each along Highway 56 (Kuhio Highway).

PRACTICALITIES:

The weather is almost always perfect on the east side of Kauai. It can be breezy along the shoreline, but that helps to keep the temperature pleasant all year round. Sunglasses, sunscreen, a hat and comfortable shoes will all pay off big time on this part of Kauai. Take everything out of your car whether you lock it or not.

FOOD AND DRINK:

   Kapaa Rib, Fish & Chowder House (4-1639 Kuhio Hwy. in Kapaa) Good dining atmosphere with seafood and steaks as specialties. Try the Coconut Curry Fish. This is also the home of the popular Garden Room. Open for dinner daily. Reservations suggested, ☎ 822-7488. $ to $$

   A Pacific Café (4-138 Kuhio Hwy. in Kauai Village) Fine dining where they grow their own salads, veggies and herbs. Try the Wok-Charred

Hawaiian Mahi Mahi with Garlic Sesame Seed Crust and a Lime Ginger Sauce. Open daily for dinner. Reservations, ☎ 822-0013. $$ to $$$

Aloha Diner (971 F Kuhio Hwy. in Waipouli Complex) Not a fancy setting, but a good array of authentic Hawaiian food. Mostly local people eat here because of its quality. Lunch and dinner Tues.–Sat. Lunch only Mon., Sun. ☎ 822-3851. $

Wailua Marina Restaurant (on the waterfront in Wailua State Park) For almost 30 years, this big, comfortable spot has been serving up popular family fare. Generous portions are its trademark. Open daily for lunch and dinner. ☎ 822-4311. $ to $$.

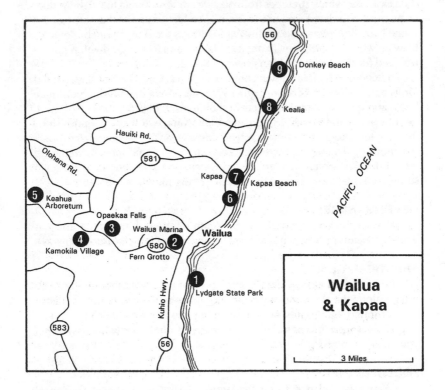

LOCAL ATTRACTIONS:

Numbers in parentheses correspond to numbers on the map.

As you leave Lihue on the Kuhio Highway, after about four miles look on the right for signs to **Lydgate State Park** (1). What makes this well maintained park a family haven are the two lava rock enclosed pools that are perfect for kids—and for adult snorkelers. Lydgate offers complete facilities including picnic areas, pavilions, showers and the imaginative Kamalani Playground.

Just a short distance on the highway again, turn left for **Wailua Marina State Park** (2). Up the road on the right, you will note a series of covered, open-sided barge-like boats. These are the ever-popular **Smith's Motorboats** that have been plying the Wailua River for about 25 years. While cruising the river, boat operators share the fascinating legends of the area, and family members entertain with Hawaiian songs. The destination of these voyages is the famous **Fern Grotto.** In this beautiful, tropical jungle setting, nature has formed a natural amphitheater with remarkable acoustics. The ceiling of the grotto is heavily festooned with ferns. The chances of your seeing a wedding at the Grotto are about 100 percent. *Boats leave daily every half-hour from 9–11:30 and 12:30–3 p.m. No reservations needed. Just show up 15 minutes before departure. Adults are $15 and kids 2–12 are $7.50. Call 821-6892 for further information.*

Freckles Smith, the boat owner, knew a good thing when he saw it. So in addition to the Wailua River motorboats, he started **Smith's Tropical Paradise,** also in the Wailua River State Park at 174 Wailua Road. This 30-acre park can be walked during the day for an adult admission of $5 (kids 3–12 are $2.50). The meandering path will take you by a bamboo rainforest, a Polynesian village, a heliconia/ginger garden, a Filipino village, a Japanese island and more. *Open daily from 8:30–3.*

The park re-opens at 5 in the afternoon Monday, Wednesday and Friday for the Garden Luau and International Pageant. You can make your way around the park either on foot or by taking a tram. At 6 o'clock, the Imu Ceremony begins, which is the unearthing of the traditional pig cooked in an underground oven. Musical groups entertain until the luau begins at 6:30. The rather showy International Pageant features ethnic dances from around the Pacific Rim. *Adults are $52, kids 7–13 $27 and 3–6 $18. Call 821-6895 for reservations.*

On the north side of the river is Highway 580 (Kuamoo Road). At the base of the river are several kayak rental companies—if you want to explore the river that way. Water-ski companies are also located here.

About two miles up on 580, there is a turn-out for **Opaekaa Falls** (3). At first you see a deep gash, and then as your eyes follow the stream, you see the falls cascading down as runoff from the 5,148-foot Mount Waialeale. Across the road is a series of interpretive signs telling the story of the *heiau* along the Wailua River. Holoholoku, near the mouth of the river, is the first of these sacred temples.

Just up the road on the left is a Hawaiian Warrior sign for **Kamokila Village** (4). Down this very steep and winding road is a re-created folk village illustrating ancient Hawaiian lifestyles. It is right on the bank of the Wailua River. The low-key, but informative tour is well worth every dime of the $5 donation (for adults). If you want to experience an authentic, yet re-created,

Hawaiian village and its lifestyle, this is the one. This was the site of some of the opening shots for Dustin Hoffman's movie "Outbreak." They also offer kayak tours for $25 that are an easier haul to the fern grotto than those farther down the river. If you want, they lead you to a little-known bridal veil waterfall, and then a short hike that opens out onto a pool at the base of Wailua Falls. There's no phone since this a truly re-created village, so you just have to go there for the experience.

Back on the highway turn left and keep going all the way to the end. This will take you to **Keahua Arboretum** (5). It is a very pleasant picnic area among fairly dense tropical foliage. A stream runs through it where you can cool off in a man-made swimming hole. Across the road is the Kuilau trail, which is moderately strenuous for a total distance of about 4 miles.

As you head down Highway 580, look for a left turn for Highway 581 after about three miles. Meandering along what becomes Kamalu Road, you will see small farms raising food crops and horses. About two miles from where you turned off you will find a Bed-and-Breakfast that could be anywhere in New England. It's called **Rosewood** and features a white picket fence, red geraniums, Victorian gingerbread and yellow paint. Besides the Main House, there's also The Victorian Cottage, but the real clue that you're in Hawaii and not New Hampshire is the Thatched Cottage that really looks like a grass shack. The latter is one bedroom and one bath and can be rented for $85. *872 Kamalu Road. Call 822-5216 for reservations.*

Highway 581 bends to the right and heads back down to Kapaa. Once you get to the main highway, you might consider turning right and backtracking just a couple of miles to the **Coconut Marketplace** (6). Besides a rich variety of shops and restaurants (and one of the only movie theaters on the island), the shopping center offers free hula shows Mondays, Wednesdays, Fridays and Saturdays at 5. This is the real stuff, with performers from the world famous *hula halua* (school) Na Hula O Kaohikukapulani. They are lead by *kumu* hula teacher *kapu* Kinimaka-Alquiza who features *auana* (modern) and *kahiko* (ancient) hula dances by adults and *keikis*.

If you head north on Kuhio Highway, there are several beaches well worth exploring. **Kapaa Beach Park** (7) is just past Niu Street. It has full facilities and is a good picnic spot since supplies are close at hand in Kapaa town. A bit farther up the road on the north side of Kapaa Stream is **Kealia Beach** (8), one of the east side's most popular beaches even though it lacks facilities. If you're a surfer or just like to watch, try this beach. The north end is generally calmer—and thus better for swimming with caution—and you can walk along an old cane road and get a terrific view back toward Kappa.

Even more off the beaten path is Kumukumu or **Donkey Beach** (9). Look first for the 11-mile marker, and just before the 12-mile marker is a dirt road on the right. It is usually chained, so be prepared to walk. It is one of the wider beaches on Kauai, surrounded on the land side by grass and ironwood trees. There are no facilities, including lifeguards, so watch your swimming.

Near North Shore

There are lots of fascinating stories about the north shore of Kauai—and many legends as well. There is so much to see and do on this part of the island that we felt compelled to divide up the fun into the near north shore and the far north shore.

In this daytrip we start at the lovely white-sand beach at Anahola, then gradually climb to the 1,600-foot-elevation plateau that is Princeville. This resort was once a 10,000-acre cattle ranch. Today, about 1,500 acres have been developed into a lovely spread of golf courses, shops, homes, a five-star hotel and numerous activities.

GETTING THERE:

By car, stay on the Kuhio Highway (Route 56). You can't miss it.

PRACTICALITIES:

There are stories about the large amount of moisture at Princeville, but don't let that deter you. Yes, in the winter months there is more rain, but that's what makes the mountain waterfalls so gorgeous and the foliage so lush. The rain usually only lasts a short time, and then it's back on the golf course or back to the beach.

Beachwear including sunscreen, sunglasses and snorkel equipment are suggested. Strip your car of your possessions and take them with you, whether you lock or not.

FOOD AND DRINK:

Duane's Ono Char Burger (At the bottom of the hill in Anahola) Wide variety of burger combos including such specialties as avocado. Very casual. Outdoor seating under umbrellas. Open Mon.–Sat. 10–6 and Sun. 11–6. ☎ 822-9181. $

Casa di Amici (2484 Keneke St., next to Kong Lung in Kilauea) Tasty, (mostly) Italian food served in light or regular portions. They serve ahi as a southern Italian classic. Open for lunch and dinner daily. Reservations for dinner, ☎ 828-1555. $$

Bali Hai Restaurant (5380 Honiki Rd. in Hanalei Bay Resort in Princeville) Truly a stunning view of Bali Hai in the distance. Innovative menu. Try the baked mahimahi with crabmeat crust. All three meals daily. Reservations, ☎ 826-6522. $$ to $$$

Princeville Restaurant & Bar (at the Prince Golf Course Clubhouse) The Clubhouse is worth a visit. It is quite grandiose for the north shore, but definitely makes a statement. Good, simple food with a huge view. Breakfast and lunch daily. ☎ 826-5050. $

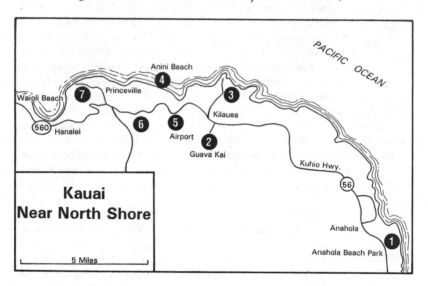

Kauai
Near North Shore

5 Miles

LOCAL ATTRACTIONS:

Numbers in parentheses correspond to numbers on the map.

There are really two main parts to Anahola Beach. If you turn right off the main highway on Anahola Road, you will travel down just short of a mile to **Anahola Beach Park** (1) with facilities in a small park. The sandy beach is great for walking. The swimming is pretty good inside the reef, but should be done with caution. Snorkeling here can be very good. You will see surfers out a ways. If you go back onto the highway and go right about half a mile, there is a right turn at Aliomanu Street. This will lead you down to the north side of the beach, which is separated from the beach park by a lagoon. If you follow along the road, there are many nifty beach houses.

Back on the highway, turn right and enjoy the drive through what used to be sugar plantations for about the next seven to ten miles. Soon you will see signs that you are approaching Kilauea town. Watch for **Guava Kai Plantation** (2) on the left. Turn at Kuawa Road and about half a mile up you will come to a Visitor Center set among some 480 acres of guava trees. The Center offers free guava juice, and you'll learn how guava is grown and processed into a wide variety of luscious treats. Take a free tour through their Nature Walk and Picnic Area, and see the processing plant. *Free admission. Open daily 9–5.* ☎ *828-1925.*

As you leave, if you go straight across the highway, make a right and then a left turn on Keneke Street, you will be headed for the former plantation town of Kilauea and the **Kilauea National Wildlife Refuge** (3). The bumpy road will take you to a narrow point where the Kilauea Lighthouse has stood since the turn of the century. As you walk along the path to the interpretive center, the peninsula drops away to the ocean and you face a dramatic cliff on the opposite side. Here thousands of boobies, tropic birds, frigate birds, shearwaters and albatross swoop and dive in this well-protected refuge. The view of the coastline in either direction is breathtaking. On the right you can see the secret beach at the bottom of Crater Hill. *The refuge is open 10–4 Mon.–Fri., except major holidays. You can register for a hike up Crater Hill by calling 828-1413. Admission to the Refuge is $2 for adults, children under 16 are free.*

As you come back on Keneke Street, be sure to stop at **Kong Lung Store** at number 2490. It is an eclectic mix of gifts, jewelry, home furnishings, clothing with some Hawaiiana and Oriental pieces. Next door is a bakery that although it keeps short and irregular hours, has wonderful breakfast goodies.

At the end of Keneke Street is the beautiful, but tiny, **Christ Memorial Episcopal Church** with about 14 pews. The church's motto is, "Visitors Welcomes, Strangers Expected." The church isn't especially old. In 1939 the Kilauea Sugar Company, ever mindful of the religious needs of its workers and community members, deeded the church yard to Christ Memorial Church and gave the native stone for its building. Services are 7:30 and 8:30.

Continue north on Highway 56. As you start down through dense trees headed toward a river, there is a turn-out on the right. If you park there, you can walk back a few yards and see a small, but intense waterfall. At the overlook, you have a view of the Kalihiwai River and Valley.

After going over a sweeping concrete bridge and starting up the hill again, look for Kalihiwai Road on the right. Follow this road down to **Anini Beach Park** (4), where you will find the ultimate in Hawaii beaches. You can do just about every beach activity you can think of here. There are full facilities. Windsurfing lessons are available from Anini Beach Windsurfing. ☎ *826-9463.* Great for a picnic since the winds tend to be lighter here. Across the road is the **Kauai Polo Club Field** where, on Sunday afternoons at 3, exciting matches are held from April through September. There are few places in the world where you can watch the sport of kings being played at the edge of a white sand beach. Small admission charge to the polo grounds. *Call 826-6177 for information.*

If you continue along the road next to the beach, it goes for another mile or so past lovely beach homes, including one built by Sylvester Stallone.

As you climb back up to the highway, turn right and head toward **Princeville Airport** (5) on the left. The only aircraft that fly out of the airport are Astar Helicopters operated by Hawaii Helicopters. They offer three tours daily from 7 until the last flight which is usually late afternoon. The 30-minute tour of the Napali Coast is a jaw-dropping experience as you fly along sheer cliffs, into valleys with sideways waterfalls and along the ocean churning below. It's a winner at $99. *Call 826-6591 for reservations.*

The north shore is filled with activities as we said, not the least of which is horseback riding. The family-operated **Princeville Ranch Stables** (6), located just outside of Princeville off Highway 56, has been offering superb rides for all abilities since 1978. They have four distinctive rides, starting with the three-hour Anini Bluff and Beach Ride that winds along the bluff above before descending a trail to the beach. The cost is $95. For the adventurous, there is the four-hour Waterfall Picnic Ride that includes riding across ranch land, a short, steep hike and a relaxing swim and picnic lunch at Kalihiwai Falls. This tour is offered three times a day on Mondays through Saturdays. Cost is $105. *Call 826-6777 for reservations and information.*

Princeville Resort (7) is really all about golf. Sure, there are gorgeous homes and condominiums, a classy hotel that cascades down the bluff to the beach below, and a small, fun-filled shopping center. But back to golf. There are two courses: the 27-hole **Makai Course;** and the 18-hole **Prince Course**. Robert Trent Jones designed them both, so you know they are challenging. Some golfers say the toughest part of the course is concentrating on their game since the temptation to sneak a peek at the spectacular mountains on one side and the deep blue ocean on the other can ruin a game. The Makai Course is really three courses in one—the Ocean Nine ventures closest to the water; the Lakes Nine winds its way around serene lakes; and the Woods Nine is a pleasant diversion through native woodlands. Golf Digest lists the Makai Course in its Top 50 Resort Courses and has included it in "America's 100 Greatest Golf Courses" for 16 consecutive years.

The Prince Course is considered one of Trent Jones' masterpieces. Looking as if it emerged full-blown from nature, it chugs uphill, jumps ravines, and careens downhill like a roller coaster. Again, Golf Digest honored the relatively new course as number one in Hawaii and also placed it on its prestigious list of "America's 100 Greatest Golf Courses."

Standard rates for 18 holes on the Makai Course are $115 and on the Prince Course $150. That includes cart, range balls and use of the Spa for a day. *For reservations and information call 826-2727.*

Whether you golf, horseback ride or take a helicopter tour, take your time to drive through the resort enjoying the views and the ambiance. At the end of the road, you will come to the Princeville Sheraton. If you are inclined to make it down to the beach at the base of the hotel, be prepared for quite a climb up. It is pretty steep, with steps in some places. Public access to the beach is available to the left of the hotel guard shack. Parking is on the right in a specially marked lot. It is worth the effort.

Far North Shore

In the previous trip, we were mostly high on the bluffs along the north shore, including the Princeville plateau. In this section, we will go down to the ocean to play and to make discoveries along one of the most fascinating coastlines in Hawaii. We start in the Hanalei Valley, move into fabled Hanalei town and then work our way along a string of crescent beaches that you expect to find in movies. (In fact, Lumahai starred in the classic "South Pacific"). All the while, the fluted mountains, deep valleys and spouting waterfalls are on your left all the way to Haena.

During this day, you can be very active, or kick back on any one of the beaches along the way—or do some of both. The overriding activity, however, is turning your neck to take in the scenery.

GETTING THERE:
   By car, follow the Kuhio Highway (Route 56) all the way to the end.

PRACTICALITIES:
   Beachwear, sunscreen, sunglasses, a hat and comfortable shoes, as always, will help you be well prepared. Hiking boots or shoes are a necessity if you decide to tackle the Kalalau Trail. Snorkeling, fins and equipment like that can be rented along the way, as we will point out. Whether you lock your car or not, take everything with you.

FOOD AND DRINK:
   Postcards (5-5075B Kuhio Hwy. in Hanalei town) Small seating area in the re-built Hanalei Museum Building. Lots of fresh island fruits, seafood and natural foods. Very Hanalei. Breakfast and dinner daily. ☎ 826-1191. $ to $$
   Tahiti Nui (5-5134 Kuhio Hwy. in Hanalei town) Great South Seas atmosphere. Known for fresh fish and authentic luau Wed. and Fri. Live Hawaiian music Fri. and Sat. Lunch and dinner daily. Reservations, ☎ 826-6277. $ to $$
   Hanalei Dolphin (5-5016 Kuhio Hwy. in Hanalei town) Sits next to the

river and serves lunch outside. Try the Haole Chicken served with sweet/sour sauce. Fish is the specialty and they even have a fish market next door. Lunch and dinner daily. Reservations, ☎ 826-6113. $ to $$

Bubba's (5-5130 Kuhio Hwy. in Hanalei town) You gotta try the Hubba Bubba that starts with rice, then a hamburger, then a hot dog topped with chili and onions. World famous, old-fashioned hamburgers. Lunch & dinner daily. ☎ 826-7839. $

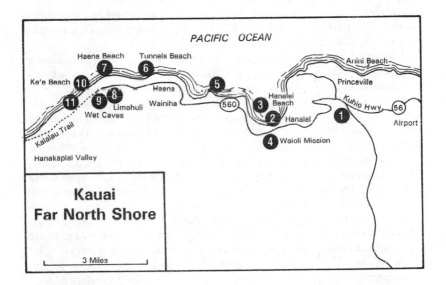

Kauai
Far North Shore

3 Miles

LOCAL ATTRACTIONS:

Numbers in parentheses correspond to numbers on the map.

The one-lane bridge across the Hanalei River is a good clue to the pace and lifestyle you will find from here to the end of the road. This rickety, narrow bridge has been fiercely protected by residents. That means you will see no tour buses, large vans or other bulky people-movers like you do elsewhere in the islands. And perish the thought that a large construction truck could make it across this tiny bridge to assist in building a high-rise. This is the famous low-key, low-rise, kick-back Hanalei.

As you drive over the bridge, turn left and the road will take you into the verdant Hanalei Valley, also called the **Hanalei National Wildlife Refuge** (1). This prime agricultural area provides waterbird habitat as well as producing about a third of the taro grown in Hawaii for poi. As you drive back in the valley, you will see along the river a patchwork of ponds growing taro with its the distinctive triangular shaped leaves. Years ago, the valley also had a large rice mill. Neither the rice nor the mill is still around, and today there are considerably less wetlands.

Back at the bridge, go straight, which will take you to Hanalei Town. We suggest a stop at the **Ching Young Center** (2) where you will find—among other interesting merchants—**Pedal 'N Paddle.** This outfit will rent you just about anything you need for having fun along the north shore. They have snorkels, masks and fins, Boogie boards, bikes, tents and kayaks. With the latter, they cleverly provide you not only the boat, but also a rack for your car, ice chest, padded back rests, life vests, a dry bag and, of course, paddles. They'll also help you with which rivers or bays to paddle. Now, that's a complete package. Two-person kayaks start at $45 a day. *They're open daily 9–5. Call 826-9069.*

You can't come to this part of Hawaii without experiencing the splendor of the Na Pali Coast. The Hawaiian Islands have their share of extraordinary scenery, but even in all that glory, this is a standout. Part of the intrigue of the Na Pali Coast is it's inaccessibility, which means you can only see it in one of three ways: by hiking it, which we will discuss later on; by helicopter, which we mentioned in the previous daytrip; or by boat. **Hanalei Sea Tours** at 5-5075A Kuhio Highway offers tours on two types of seacraft—either the popular inflatable "Zodiac" rafts with a rigid hull or a powered, double-hulled catamaran. We suggest the Nualolo Kai Day Tour which takes about five hours. This tour is fully narrated and includes a beach landing at Nualolo Kai, where the licensed crew guides passengers on a short hike through the ruins of an ancient Hawaiian fishing village. They serve a gourmet style picnic. Weather permitting, you can also explore giant sea caves and cruise through cascading waterfalls. Chances are very good that you will see spinning dolphins, sea turtles, and in winter, humpback whales. This is a must. This tour leaves daily from Hanalei. *Cost for adults is $110 and for kids 3–12 is $90. They also offer mini-tours and half-day tours from $60. Call 826-7254 for reservations.* **Captain Zodiac** in Hanalei also offers a variety of Na Pali trips. There are two-, three-, four- and five-hour tours to explore this exciting coastline. *Costs range from $50-$120. Beach landings, lunch and snorkeling are included in all but the short tour.* ☎ *826-9371.*

If you turn right off the highway you will run into Weke Avenue, which for most of its distance runs along the shore of **Hanalei Bay** (3). This is the bay made famous in songs and tales of the Hippie generation. Look for Hanalei Pavilion, which has facilities and access to the beach. The crescent of white sand runs for about two miles encircling a usually peaceful body of water. Sail boats from around the world are always anchored in the summer months. This is a top spot to enjoy the beach for sunning and the calm waters for swimming. Toward the end of the beach nearest the river is the Hanalei Pier that around the turn of the century served to shuttle cattle from the Princeville Ranch out to waiting boats for shipment to Honolulu.

Back on the highway you will see a Victorian-style green church on the left. The **Waioli Hui'ia Church** was built in 1834 by missionaries who came from New England to bring religion to the natives. If you walk straight back from the church across a wide, grassy field, you will come to a building that surprises many visitors. Here, in a heavily wooded area of palms and other tropical plants, sits a white clapboard house. The **Waioli Mission House** (4) could be found in any of hundreds of small towns in New England. It frankly looks totally out of place; its only nod to its Hawaii setting is an upstairs lanai. Built in 1836 by the enterprising Wilcox family, the furnishings that came with them from Connecticut are still in place, as though they just stepped out to pray at the nearby church. *The Mission House is open to the public for half-hour guided tours Tuesdays, Thursdays and Saturdays. Donations are requested. Reservations are not needed, but if you need more information call 245-3202.*

As you head out to the end of the road, be prepared for seven one-lane bridges. Unlike the one across the Hanalei River, these are smaller versions that cross numerous streams on the way out to Haena. They have the same affect as the river bridge though, in slowing down the pace and keeping out heavy traffic.

The road curves and climbs up and down as it makes its way along the coastline. About three miles out of town, on a rather sharp curve and below a precipitous bluff, is **Lumahia Beach** (5). This is a "picture" beach that was used in the movie "South Pacific." Use your imagination to see Mitzi Gaynor singing that memorable song, "Gonna Wash That Man Right Outta My Hair" at this exact spot.

After another three miles or so, look for a YMCA sign and turn right. A dirt road leads through ironwood trees to **Tunnels Beach** (6). This white sand gem curves for about three-quarters of a mile. If the tide is right, you can swim its full length in wonderfully calm water. Sitting right along the highway not far from Tunnels is **Haena Beach Park** (7), a grassy area very popular with local people on weekends. It has full facilities including a barbecue pavilion.

Another mile down the road on the left is **Limahuli Garden and Preserve** (8), voted in 1997 the top natural botanical garden in the entire United States. It got its start in 1976 when Juliet Rice Wichman (a member of one of Hawaii's most prominent families) deeded the first 13 acres to the garden. In 1994, her grandson and director of the garden, Charles "Chipper" Rice Wichman, Jr., gifted his inheritance from his grandmother to the garden bringing its total size to 1,002 acres. Presently, the Preserve exemplifies harmony between the more intensively managed parts of the site, where the various collections of exotic tropical plants are grown, with the other vast areas that are managed as a preserve. *Admission is $25 for guided tours with advance reservations required, or $10 for self-guided tours with no reservations required. The Gardens are open Tues.–Fri. & Sun. from 9:30 to 4. Call 826-1053.*

After you drive down a slight dip in the road that takes you through a shallow stream, you will find two large wet caves created by the heaving and thrusting of molten lava on this part of the island. Be sure to stop and inspect **Waikanaloa and Waikapalae Wet Caves** (9).

At the very end of the road is **Ke'e Beach** (10), again the location for parts of the movie "The Thorn Birds." No wonder the movie moguls seized on this scene—it's about perfect. This sand is sugar white; the reef pushes back any annoying waves, making snorkeling and swimming prime; and as you look in the distance, there is beautiful Bali Hai jutting out from the coastline.

For those who aren't inclined to enjoy the beach here, there is always the ancient Hawaiian pathway called the **Kalalau Trail** (11). It leaves from the end of the road and winds up and down along the Na Pali Coast for about 11 miles. To go that distance, however, it is recommended that you be in good shape and have the proper equipment. Perhaps of interest to the non-serious hiker—but nonetheless those who can handle a strenuous hike—is Hanakapiai Valley, about two miles from the start. From there you can hike inland as an option to Hanakapiai Falls. If you keep going all the way to Kalalau, the scenery is stupendous. You will see soaring spires carved over millions of years from the sheer cliffs, dramatic waterfalls with sea birds swooping and diving their full length, and of course, the swirling ocean below. This is the Na Pali Coast up close and personal. Go this far, however, only if you have notified others of your route and are prepared to hike back out.

Hawaii Timeline

700 A.D. Estimated date when Polynesians first came to Hawaii.
1527   Probable arrival of shipwrecked Spaniards on the Big Island.
1736   Birth of Kamehameha I in Kohala on the Big Island.
1778   Discovery of Kauai by Capt. James Cook, first white man in Hawaii.
1792   Arrival of Capt. Vancouver on the Big Island.
1794   Cessation of Hawaii to Great Britain.
1795   Five islands come under Kamehameha I's control.
1797   Birth of Liholiho or Kamehameha II in Hilo.
1810   Cessation of Kauai by Kaumalii to Kamehameha I.
1813   Birth of Kauikeaouli or Kamehameha III.
1819   Death of Kamehameha I at Kailua-Kona on the Big Island.
1819   Accession of Kamehameha II.
1820   Arrival of first American missionaries on Maui.
1820   Arrival of first whale ship at Honolulu.
1824   Death of Kamehameha II.
1825   Accession of Kamehameha III.
1827   First laws published.
1830   Birth of Prince Lot or Kamehameha V.
1832   Birth of Lunalilo.
1832   First commercial sugar production.
1836   Birth of David Kalakaua.
1834   Birth of Alexander Liholiho or Kamehameha IV.
1838   Birth of Queen Lydia Liliuokalani.
1840   First Constitution proclaimed.
1848   Great Mahele, the first private ownership of land.
1849   Treaty concluded with the United States.
1851   Protectorate offered to the United States.
1852   First Chinese contract laborers arrive.
1854   Death of Kamehameha III.
1855   Accession of King Kamehameha IV.
1856   Marriage of Kamehameha IV to Queen Emma.
1863   Death of Kamehameha IV.
1863   Accession of King Kamehameha V.
1872   Death of Kamehameha V.

1873   Accession of William C. Lunalilo, first elected King.
1874   Death of King Lunalilo.
1874   Election of David Kalakaua as King.
1875   Birth of Princess Kaiulani.
1876   Reciprocity Sugar Treaty signed.
1877   Princess Liliuokalani proclaimed heir-apparent.
1884   Death of Bernice Pauahi Bishop creates massive Bishop Estate.
1885   Death of Queen Emma.
1885   First Japanese immigrants arrive in Hawaii.
1887   New constitution proclaimed.
1891   Death of King Kalakaua.
1891   Accession of Queen Liliuokalani.
1893   Overthrow of the monarchy and start of the provisional government.
1897   Pineapple production starts.
1898   American annexation secured.
1900   Territorial government begun.
1901   Moana Hotel opens as first large commercial hotel in Waikiki.
1917   Death of Queen Liliuokalani.
1936   Pan Am starts first passenger service from California.
1941   Pearl Harbor bombed, start of World War II.
1954   Democratic Party revolution.
1959   Statehood.
1962   Kaanapali on Maui opens as first large-scale resort destination.
1967   Tourism hits one million.
1996   Three sugar plantations close leaving only four.

Index

Special interest attractions are listed under their category headings.

Daytrips

• OTHER AMERICAN TITLES •

DAYTRIPS FLORIDA
By Blair Howard. Fifty one-day adventures from bases in Miami, Orlando, St. Petersburg, Jacksonville, and Pensacola. From little-known discoveries to bustling theme parks, from America's oldest city to isolated getaways— this guide covers it all. 320 pages, 47 maps, 28 B&W photos. ISBN: 0-8038-9380-9.

DAYTRIPS NEW ENGLAND
By Earl Steinbicker. Discover the 50 most delightful excursions within a day's drive of Boston or Central New England, from Maine to Connecticut. Includes Boston walking tours. 336 pages, 60 maps, 48 B&W photos. ISBN: 0-8038-9379-5.

DAYTRIPS WASHINGTON, DC
By Earl Steinbicker. Fifty one-day adventures in the Nation's Capital, and to nearby Virginia, Maryland, Delaware, and Pennsylvania. Both walking and driving tours are featured. 352 pages, 60 maps, 48 B&W photos. ISBN: 0-8038-9373-6.

DAYTRIPS NEW YORK
Edited by Earl Steinbicker. 107 easy excursions by car throughout southern New York State, New Jersey, eastern Pennsylvania, Connecticut, and southern Massachusetts. 7th edition, 336 pages, 44 maps, 46 B&W photos. ISBN: 0-8038-9371-X.

• IN PRODUCTION •

DAYTRIPS PENNSYLVANIA DUTCH COUNTRY & PHILADELPHIA
By Earl Steinbicker. Thoroughly explores the City of Brotherly Love, then goes on to probe southeastern Pennsylvania, southern New Jersey, and Delaware before moving west to Lancaster, the "Dutch" country, and Gettysburg. 320 pages, 54 maps. ISBN: 0-8038-9394-9.

DAYTRIPS SAN FRANCISCO & NORTHERN CALIFORNIA

By David Cheever. Fifty enjoyable one-day adventures from the sea to the mountains; from north of the wine country to south of Monterey. Includes 16 self-guided discovery tours of San Francisco itself. 352 pages, 64 maps. ISBN: 0-8038-9441-4

Daytrips

•EUROPEAN TITLES•

DAYTRIPS SWITZERLAND

By Norman P.T. Renouf. 45 one-day adventures in and from convenient bases including Zurich and Geneva, with forays into nearby German, Austria, and Italy. 320 pages, 38 maps. ISBN: 0-8038-9414-7.

DAYTRIPS SPAIN AND PORTUGAL

By Norman P.T. Renouf. Fifty one-day adventures by rail, bus or car—including many walking tours, as well as side trips to Gibraltar and Morocco. All of the major tourist sites are covered, plus several excursions to little-known, off-the-beaten-path destinations. 368 pages, 18 full-color photos, 28 b&w photos, 51 two-color maps. ISBN: 0-8038-9389-2.

DAYTRIPS IRELAND

By Patricia Tunison Preston. Covers the entire Emerald Isle with 50 one-day self-guided tours both within and from the major tourist areas. 400 pages plus 16 pages of color photos; 58 photos in all, and 55 maps. ISBN: 0-8038-9385-X.

DAYTRIPS LONDON

By Earl Steinbicker. Explores the metropolis on 10 one-day walking tours, then describes 40 daytrips to destinations throughout southern England—all by either rail or car. 5th edition, 336 pages, 57 maps, 94 B&W photos. ISBN: 0-8038-9367-1.

DAYTRIPS FRANCE

By Earl Steinbicker. Describes 45 daytrips—including 5 walking tours of Paris, 23 excursions from the city, 5 in Provence, and 12 along the Riviera. 4th edition, 336 pages, 55 maps, 89 B&W photos. ISBN: 0-8038-9366-3.

DAYTRIPS GERMANY

By Earl Steinbicker. 60 of Germany's most enticing destinations can be savored on daytrips from Munich, Frankfurt, Hamburg, and Berlin. Walking tours of the big cities are included. 5th edition, 352 pages, 67 maps. ISBN: 0-8038-9428-7.

DAYTRIPS HOLLAND, BELGIUM AND LUXEMBOURG

By Earl Steinbicker. Many unusual places are covered on these 40 daytrips, along with all the favorites plus the 3 major cities. 2nd edition, 288 pages, 45 maps, 69 B&W photos. ISBN: 0-8038-9368-X.

DAYTRIPS ITALY

By Earl Steinbicker. Features 40 one-day adventures in and around Rome, Florence, Milan, Venice, and Naples. 3rd edition, 304 pages, 45 maps, 69 B&W photos. ISBN: 0-8038-9372-8.

DAYTRIPS ISRAEL

By Earl Steinbicker. 25 one-day adventures by bus or car to the Holy Land's most interesting sites. Includes Jerusalem walking tours. 2nd edition, 206 pages, 40 maps, 40 B&W photos. ISBN: 0-8038-9374-4.

HASTINGS HOUSE
Book Publishers
Norwalk CT 06850
FAX (203) 838-4084
Phone orders toll free (800) 206-7822
Internet: http://upub.com

About the Author:

David Cheever has resided in the Hawaiian Islands for 30 years. During those decades he has spent most of his time in the fields of advertising and marketing, helping clients grow their businesses. Over the years, David has written dozens of pieces for visitor clients on several islands. His other clients include health care, financial, food and legal firms. His awards include being named Marketing Person of the Year and Advertising Person of the Year.

Cheever is active in running, hiking and biking and has participated in 12 marathons. He has also entered over 100 other bicycle, hiking and running events on every major island. To say that he knows every foot of the islands would be close to the truth. He has walked 112 miles arount the island of Oako.

Cheever resides in Honolulu with his wife Cindy. They have three grown children.